A SEASON IN THE RED

A SEASON IN THE RED

Managing Manchester United in the
Shadow of Sir Alex Ferguson

By Jamie Jackson

Aurum
Press

First published in Great Britain
2015 by Aurum Press Ltd
74–77 White Lion Street
Islington
London N1 9PF
www.aurumpress.co.uk

A catalogue record for this book is
available from the British Library.

ISBN 978 1 78131 512 5
Paperback ISBN 978 1 78131 530 9
Ebook ISBN 978 1 78131 541 5

1 3 5 7 9 10 8 6 4 2
2015 2017 2019 2018 2016

Typeset in Berling LT Std by SX Composing DTP, Rayleigh, Essex
Printed by CPI Group (UK) Ltd, Croydon, CR0 4YY

For Gaynor, my adorable wife, Sonny and Martha,
my other two angels: you have all written this with me.

xxx

CONTENTS

PROLOGUE

'You're Getting Sacked in the Morning'

THE DAY

David Moyes is alone. The morning of 22 April 2014 is beginning to lighten and he contemplates the wreckage of an unfinished season, a career rocked, a dream soured. He is in the manager's office at Carrington, the training ground of the world's most famous football club, Manchester United. On the door, in white capital letters on a black border, the name plate reads: David Moyes. He remembers his first official day, 1 July 2013, and being photographed by the door, next to his name. Then the picture of him sitting where he sits now, new in the job – he is *still* new in the job – the desk bare, before settling into the challenge many other managers of reputation might have baulked at: being the immediate successor to Sir Alex Ferguson.

He had taken a moment when no one else was around to try his predecessor's chair for the first time because 'I thought I would have to see how it feels in case anybody thought I looked stupid'. He looks around the office now and it is bare once more. The room is spacious and there are large windows looking out on to the training pitches of the rebranded Aon Training Complex. He sits in the black leather chair at the long, angled desk and gazes at the computer screen, the HD TV, the SKY+ remote, the Manchester United mouse-mat cut in the shape of the club badge.

David Moyes is thinking, clearing his head. Soon the building will come to life with people arriving to start their daily routine at British football's most successful club. The twenty-times champions. The defending title-holders. Winners by a street last season. With an irresistible swagger. This was the legacy bequeathed by Ferguson, the greatest manager in domestic football history, perhaps anywhere.

Now United stand seventh in the Premier League. They are sinking and everyone is laughing. Not to his face, but he knows they are. A lot of people have waited a long, long time for this. The decline and fall of the great Manchester United Empire after nigh on three decades of Ferguson's rule. Finally it has happened. Not gradually, this is a collapse. A sickening freefall, a public disrobing. It is David Moyes's fault, they say. All his fault. The players don't believe in him anymore, if they ever did. Neither do the fans. And the media, well, they have no loyalty, but who does? This is football in the twenty-first century.

This is where David Moyes wants to be. In this office, where he sits now, having left Everton after eleven years of good, solid, consistent management. This office that was Ferguson's: The Great Ferguson who personally anointed him, drove his candidacy, rubber-stamped him to the owners, the Glazers. This office inherited from a *bona fide* managerial genius. And it is his, David Moyes's, though not for much longer – an hour or so, but not much more.

Then Ed Woodward will come. Eight o'clock, he said. By then the statement will already have been drawn up in a much smaller office elsewhere at Carrington by United's media department. Meet at 8 a.m. at the training ground, Woodward ordered, and nothing else. This was all the executive vice-chairman needed to say. The story had leaked on the websites of the national newspapers the day before. At 3 p.m., Easter Monday, this was how Moyes found out. Not from the club. Not from Woodward, man-to-man, but from journalists. Bloody hacks. The Manchester football correspondents' latest splash. Moyes could not believe it – could not believe he would not be told first. 'This is Manchester United we're talking about,' he will say later. But it was true. He had been utterly humiliated by Manchester United.

In the end, he had been forced to believe it. Forced to go to bed and endure a listless, sleepless night, knowing that when he awoke it would be ended. Now the desk is cleared, it is bare again, and David Moyes is showered after a final run around the training pitches. In the dark, alone, running over the grass that should have been his domain for six years, at least. He is still a fit man, the hands-on tracksuit manager who insisted on taking training sessions. But the photographic evidence of these past ten months is unavoidable. In three days he turns fifty-one, but he looks a decade older, gaunt, the face more lined, the bright blue of his eyes dimmed, and he is pale-skinned and skeletal. He needs a break but he does not want one. Not when it is enforced by what is about to come this morning.

Then David Moyes, ever dignified, will address the players, speak to a group who let him down so badly. From champions by eleven points to seventh position with only four games left, twenty-three points behind the leaders, Liverpool, who are back on their perch again. The players who in this traumatic season – in this difficult, soul-searching year of David Moyes's life – went to the press behind his back to voice their doubts while failing to do what they are paid small fortunes each week to do: perform and win football matches. He will say goodbye and wish them good luck for the future. Then drive away. Drive away from Carrington, for the last time.

THE DAYS AFTER

David Moyes: 'What upset [my wife] was the fact that I was being told by members of the press that day that I was out. I just never expected that to happen. I would never have left a job. The job at Everton was so good. I worked for a great chairman, great people at the club. It was not easy to begin with at Everton, either. We had a couple of tough years before we had the club the way we wanted it. But the reason I went to United was because I thought I was joining a club that would give me time. I saw what I thought were important similarities between United and Everton. Like the focus on developing young players. To have been appointed as manager of Manchester United, one of the biggest football clubs in the world, was, and remains, something of which I will always be incredibly proud.

'I was devastated to lose the job because it was something I felt I could make a real success of. We knew it was going to take time to make the necessary changes. It was going to take time to evolve. But we were in the process of making other important changes. In the end, I don't feel I was given time to succeed or fail. I know it comes with the territory, and I know if you lose matches you risk being sacked. But how it affected my family made it hard.'

THE DAY BEFORE

There is a calm, clear sky over the M60 as I receive confirmation of the story from sources that David Moyes will be sacked as Manchester United manager. The report will go live on the *Guardian* website at 3 p.m. Except Moyes does not know yet. It is 11.30 a.m., 21 April 2014. I, along with the rest of the Manchester football correspondents, am about to break news that will leave Moyes livid at finding out first from journalists rather than his employers. The story will reverberate around the football world and shake Manchester United. Tremors that will be felt all summer as Louis van Gaal replaces the Scot. Tremors that will continue to be felt when the Dutchman, one-time mentor to another managerial Colossus, Jose Mourinho, has an awful beginning to the following season as new manager, overseeing the poorest start since 1986–87 when Ron Atkinson was sacked. But that is all in the future. Moyes has been a dead man walking since the insipid 2–0 Champions League reverse to Olympiakos in Athens in February. The consecutive 3–0 home league defeats in March to Liverpool and Manchester City, United's two fiercest and for many fans most detested rivals, confirmed the culling of Moyes as inevitable. The timing was a mere, final detail.

The executioner's song finally started up after the 2–0 loss at Everton on Easter Day. My match report ended: 'Moyes may spend now until the end of the season peering over his shoulder. He cannot afford to have many more performances like this.' Yet again United were sluggish, unconvincing and rudderless. The rabble put out at Goodison Park by the Scot were close to comatose, and not for the first time under him.

Moyes's mantra throughout a moribund championship defence has been that, in the wake of Sir Alex Ferguson's departure following a glittering twenty-six-season reign, the United executive always recognised his first term in charge would be tough. So in the media room at Goodison towards the end of an awkward post-match press conference, I asked Moyes: 'Does the board still recognise it was going to be a difficult campaign?' He refused to answer and walked off and out of the room. Away from Goodison Park for the last time as manager of Manchester United on a match-day.

Twenty-four hours later I arrive at Stanley Park and park the car. It is a short walk to Anfield. I am here to conduct an interview ahead of next Sunday's pivotal Premier League clash between Liverpool and Chelsea. Then Steven Gerrard will suffer *that* slip to allow Chelsea victory and hand Manchester City the championship. But before any of this the *Guardian* sports desk is called to let them know what is about to happen, that the story is embargoed until 3 p.m. I ring off and begin writing.

David Moyes will be sacked as Manchester United's manager with the owners, the Glazer family, and Ed Woodward, the vice-president, in discussions over when to end the Scot's reign.

United's 2–0 defeat at Everton on Sunday was the latest evidence to the executive that Moyes is the wrong man to lead the club and it is now only a matter of time before the decision is taken. Should he go before the end of the season, which appears likely, United may put Ryan Giggs in temporary charge. The 40-year-old, who is player-coach, would command the instant respect of the squad and would consider taking up the role, even if only temporary.

The Holland coach, Louis van Gaal, Borussia Dortmund's Jürgen Klopp, Diego Simeone of Atlético Madrid and Paris Saint-Germain's Laurent Blanc will all be discussed as the next potential permanent United manager. Everton's Roberto Martínez, who has excelled in Moyes's old job, would be an outside choice. As reported by the Guardian, Moyes has been under scrutiny since last month following the 3–0 loss to Liverpool. The chief concern for the board is how badly the side have played throughout the season, with little sign of improvement. Questions were asked at the highest level about whether he could be trusted to carry out a £150 million rebuild.

By 7 p.m. that evening I have appeared on Channel 4 News to discuss the story. Louis van Gaal is already lined up. It is a few days until May. The season is nearly over. Summer is about to begin.

BOOK ONE
Sir Alex Ferguson

It was important to me to leave an organisation in the strongest possible shape and I believe I have done so.

– Sir Alex Ferguson

Chapter 1

Shadows Falling

The moment had to arrive. Yet it was the moment the fans, players, owners, and the rest of football could not quite accept would happen. The Sir Alex Ferguson ploy was to laugh off any question about when he would finally end his epic tenure as Manchester United manager. As if this was a tomorrow that would never come. Then, the day before, Wednesday, 8 May, around 10.15 p.m., the reports broke about Ferguson's retirement. Now comes the announcement from the club along with the knight's words to confirm it. Whoever replaces Ferguson should simply be able to enjoy what the great man has bequeathed: Legacy, legacy, legacy. The next man cannot fail, correct? He dare not fail, right? He cannot succeed, right? Let's be frank, how can he? This is The Impossible Job made possible by a genius. Brighter than a Cambridge University metaphysics graduates parade. More cunning than Winston Churchill. Better at it all than everyone. This is Sir Alex Ferguson.

And despite his anointment of David Moyes, his backing, his respect and due deference, he will not go away because he cannot go away. As David Gill, Manchester United chief executive, said: 'The one thing we can say about Sir Alex Ferguson – he'll know when he should be involving himself and when he should not be involving himself. I think everyone can rest assured that the new manager will get space. I think any person, the new manager coming in, will inherit a great squad, a great infrastructure off the pitch and great staff around him, so the new person will be walking into – yes, a difficult situation with those number of trophies – but he will also know he will have the support of the Manchester United family and the squad to take that forward, so it's a dream job, I think.'

Matt Busby
Wilf McGuinness
Matt Busby (after McGuinness failed)
Frank O'Farrell

Sir Alex Ferguson
David Moyes
Shadows falling

Shadows
falling

The Dream Job. The Dream Job is a dream. And it is David Moyes's.

On the day Ferguson steps away from the arena that has been his Palladium for nearly twenty-seven years, across town news comes through that Roberto Mancini is to be sacked at Manchester City. He becomes the fourteenth City managerial departure during Ferguson's gilded tenure. The front page of Monday's *Guardian Sport* section is a humdinger:

It's goodbye from me . . .
And it's goodbye from him

Underneath this headline, in the middle of the splash, a picture of Ferguson looking emotional on the occasion of his last match at Old Trafford – when he gets the best send-off possible, being presented with the Premier League trophy. Starkly juxtaposed is a picture of Mancini looking emotionally drained. On Saturday City had lost the FA Cup final to a last-minute Ben Watson goal that gave the trophy to the soon-to-be relegated Wigan Athletic.

City's championship defence crumpled weeks ago and they will limp home eleven yawning points behind United. Leading the page, to the left of the Ferguson–Mancini photographs, is the report of Ferguson's farewell, which comes after United's dying-moments 2–1 win over Swansea: Fergie-time for one last glorious time. To the right of the Ferguson–Mancini montage is the story of the Italian's imminent sacking and the expected appointment of Manuel Pellegrini, the Malaga coach, as his replacement. The headline on the Ferguson story is the killer quote from his farewell speech: 'You stood by me. Now stand by Moyes'. The Mancini headline is more sober: 'City to dismiss manager and target Pellegrini'. So on the day United are officially crowned champions and say the fondest goodbye to British football's greatest manager, the manager of the mob from across the divide is to be sacked. 'Tis Champagne and whisky chasers all-round for the red congregation.

Ferguson's last words are no long goodbye but are strategically thought out and to the point. They are aimed directly at the fans and show that even as he steps away the Godfather is trying to protect the future. 'I'd also like to remind you that when we had bad times here, the club stood by me, all my staff stood by me, the players stood by me. Your job now is to stand by our new manager. That is important.' United supporters are loyal but even Ferguson knows how they can turn as they did during the dark years when the club went three successive seasons without the Premier League title, in 2003–04, 2004–05 and 2005–06. The era of Eric Djemba-Djemba and Kleberson when, during the last of those seasons, Old Trafford actually demanded Ferguson's removal. Yet the knight had been granted two fallow terms before the rebellion really began. David Moyes will be granted no such grace.

Somewhere the new manager is watching this. Somewhere he is thanking Ferguson for his words and his support. But there have been other words. Said by Ferguson in his official retirement statement. 'The quality of this league-winning squad, and the balance of ages within it, bodes well for continued success at the highest level whilst the structure of the youth set-up will ensure that the long-term future of the club remains a bright one.'

The long-term future of the club remains a bright one.

*

The epicentre is gone. The epicentre reforms. The moment the lights fade on Ferguson, and he tiptoes off into an endless sunset, is the moment Manchester United can finally unleash the Hydra-headed beast they have been nurturing in a darkened recess of Old Trafford. This beast is commercial and, my, how it needs to be sated. And it will never be sated. Now Ferguson is no more, Ed Woodward, as the Glazers' representative on earth, can go to town to make the product perspire like never before. Sweat it, baby! This is New-Age Manchester United 2.0, a digital-savvy, socially-hip reboot for these post-Ferguson times. Now the media are to have a starring role. The Great Man had no time for the lights, camera and action unless he could turn it to his advantage. The iron-grip that came from stuffing the Old Trafford trophy room with thirteen Premier League titles, two UEFA Champions Leagues, five FA Cups, four League Cups, a Cup-Winners' Cup and two FIFA World Club titles accrued enough collateral for the Glazers to allow Ferguson to run media policy along with everything else. The modus operandi consisted of Ferguson and all at United continually being on-message, wary of anyone with a notebook, microphone, television camera, Facebook, Twitter or Instagram account, despite football being in an era of 24/7, second-by-second rolling news.

With Ferguson's departure, the club's media policy is relaxed, too. Fergie's Rule is consigned to the Ice Age of the United tale. The thaw is instant. The curtain goes up on The Ed Woodward Show at 8.40 a.m. on 24 July. This is the precise moment a missive is fired out from the club's Twitter account revealing:

Injury update: @WayneRooney on course to make a return against AIK in Stockholm. #mutour

Chapter 2

The Art of Being Ed Woodward

All we're doing is selling diamonds. We don't make the diamonds.
The diamonds have been made by the 135-year history of the club
and the players.

— Ed Woodward

The existence of Ed Woodward is a cause for curiosity and celebration in the joyless, lacking-piss-and-vinegar world of elite football. Here is the highest-ranking executive at the world's biggest club. He has a perpetual spring in his step, a man who enjoys every minute of being the Manchester United executive vice-chairman. This is how it should be. Fun. To find a comparable figure anywhere else in the sport is to embark on a fruitless search. Lord Lucan will be located quicker. Across town at Manchester City, Ferran Soriano is a distant figure. At Chelsea Ron Gourlay was rarely heard from and his replacement Marina Granovskaia is unknown. Arsenal's Ivan

Gazidis hardly teems with joy and that is the quality that marks Woodward out.

The Essex-boy-made-rather-good manages to marry having a smile for everyone with a shrewd business sense that has the club on a perpetual gold rush while making it a happier place to be. Because this is what the Woodward persona has brought: those who work at United are at ease again now the Ferguson–David Gill axis of dourness is no more. The paranoia among the workforce of doing the wrong thing at the wrong moment has evaporated. From the moment Ferguson retired the focus moved to Woodward. The question centred on how he might perform in finding the manager's replacement while filling the Gulliver-sized shoes left by Gill, who had announced his retirement in spring 2013.

Woodward's ascendancy to the very top at Manchester United says much about the insight of the Glazer family. To appoint Woodward as the distant owners' man-across-the-Atlantic seems to suggest they know a shrewd money-man *and* a good guy when they see one, and are not afraid of this combination. Woodward's backstory offers a glimpse into the persona that drives Manchester United. Born in 1971, he was a sports junky but, aged eleven, developed juvenile arthritis, a disorder which is still a factor in his life. He took a physics degree at Bristol University and became an accountant and a banker. As a sample of the ebullience that emanates from him, listen to this: 'You don't whinge at losing your job at an investment bank when you've been given a chance to work for one.' Woodward came up with that *bon mot* about working at Flemings when it was taken over by J.P. Morgan. It was there that he advised on the

Glazers' takeover of Manchester United and got his big break into the club. For Woodward opportunity always knocks. And when it stops knocking? Time to make it knock again. And again. And again.

Watch MUTV for a few hours and you can see the job Woodward has done. The in-house station is now HD and the programmes, adverts and trailers, the match-day coverage and post- and pre-game packages, the soundtrack and the overall ambience carry the top-end production values of an uber-slick commodity. It also confirms the sense of Manchester United as its own sovereign entity, a principality that has the full element-set possessed by developed societies – a (football) religion, mores, a thriving media with its own state broadcaster and its own particular micro-culture. It is as if a Vatican or Monaco has been situated in the borough of Stretford.

This independent state of Manchester United also has history. The club is as steeped in the stuff as any old-world principality, and this is perhaps the most valuable asset United hold. It is the treasure Woodward continues to mine. Occasionally the executive vice-chairman will reference Liverpool. They may be the clan from along the M62, but Woodward recognises that the other red-clad Leviathan club of the British game also have the rich heritage which cannot quite be replicated at Arsenal, Chelsea or Manchester City. Not at this moment in time. Of course, if the trophies and the power and the glory dry up for the next half a century, then maybe Arsenal, Chelsea or City can catch and overhaul them and leave them relics from a bygone age. But this is the time that Woodward, the Glazers, Manchester United have to play with. A cool fifty years.

Since taking over in 2005 via a highly controversial leveraged deal that loaded a mountain of debt on the club, the Glazers have ridden out wave upon wave of revulsion from United fans. Yet despite the buyout now costing the club around £800 million, the ire towards the Americans is at an historic low, due primarily to the trophies Ferguson continued to claim and the astronomical monies now available to invest in players. The dream of expanding New-Age United 2.0 even further, into America, cements the Woodward–Glazer relationship. That is the final frontier the post-Ferguson, twenty-first century Manchester United has to conquer. The club may be established in Asia, and enjoying purchase in Africa and Australia and the Middle and Far Easts, but forget any continent, there is a *universe* out there to be claimed.

America. The importance of the fifty states to Manchester United under the Glazers is illustrated by a simple, single sentence from Ed Woodard: 'The US is now a priority for the owners after it had previously not been.'

And the strategy is clear. Tour the country as much as possible in the off-season – particularly the East and West Coasts – and be super-slick in monetising the brand. United gaze across town at Manchester City's strategy of setting up New York City FC, who play in the Major League Soccer, as an MCFC stateside proxy who wear the same blue colours, and view it as 'weakening the brand'. Instead, United's method is to allow myriad local operators to 'buy the rights to Manchester United in America', effectively franchising the club's famous name for advertising and other commercial opportunities. The ballpark sums are that Manchester United will be paid around '£1 million' for these rights by a commercial partner who are then able to turn this into a '£2 million' yield and earn a profit of £1 million. The club is currently valued at around £2.1 billion and the US is a major part of the strategy to make Manchester United the first £10 billion-plus sporting entity.

The beauty of America is that it is *the* developing football market. Populated by more than three hundred million potential consumers. And with Woodward, the whizzkid genius in this arena, opening up a new front in glitz and glamour in these post-Ferguson times, there is a feeling of an unstoppable force at work here. Despite his inexperience at being the most powerful man at Old Trafford, part of Woodward's talent involves an instinctive feel for all parts of the business. That could be leaving football matters to the manager, the ability to engage both privately and publicly with a natural common touch, or the lightness with which he wears the focus on him and the responsibilities he holds. If this sounds like the description of a high-flying politician from central casting that is because Woodward's is a similar trapeze-wire act that he manages to portray like a Sunday morning stroll for coffee.

On the Louis van Gaal tour of the United States in summer 2014, in the apt setting of Beverly Hills, Woodward said: 'The Premier League has been very clear in saying America is the number one developing market. It may be strange to describe the US as a developing market, but if you look at the stats from the World Cup, the NBC numbers were two and a half times the previous year's Fox and ESPN numbers and despite finishing seventh we were the number one most-watched team [on US TV]. This is a very good country [for us] from a potential sponsorship perspective, a potential media perspective. We've got more fans here than we have in the UK.' Let's hear that again: 'More fans in the United States of America than at home.' The dream scenario is that United become US soccer's New York Yankees – despite not being American. Ferguson's timing is proving impeccable. He leaves the stage at the Theatre of Dreams precisely as Manchester United want to become Club Hollywood and light up the Sunset Boulevard of America's sporting fantasies. Who would bet against them doing it? Even from an ocean away.

Ed Woodward is a novice in the trench warfare of the transfer market and quickly discovers how hazardous, murky and two-faced it is dealing in the often grotesque world of agents, clubs and players. By 1 September 2013 the sole recruit to strengthen David Moyes's squad is Marouane Fellaini. As an emblem of the wariness of United fans (and players) of Moyes's managerial smarts and Woodward's inexperience, the Belgian is the perfect caricature for both men as lumbering, off-the-pace operators. When Woodward cancels a scheduled meeting with daily news-paper reporters in Sydney during the pre-season tour to fly away and attend urgent transfer business, the fevered arena of Twitter hosts a joke-fest about how the executive vice-chairman must still be travelling back when weeks later not one fresh face has been brought in.

Woodward knows all about the flak he is taking and is more than happy to do so if this protects Moyes. What also becomes apparent is how almost chronic indecision on the part of Moyes has seriously hobbled Woodward's ability to act fast. These are the frustrations of being the top-ranked executive at the club. Realities and truths that cannot be explained to fans. And Woodward has to accept it. An illustration is Thiago Alcantara, the Barcelona midfielder who has been tracked by Manchester United for two or three years. All due diligence is done and Moyes merely has to sign off on the deal. But the new manager wants more time to assess the twenty-two-year-old player and time is always the most precious commodity in transfer dealings. The endgame is that Alcantara signs for Bayern Munich, and Moyes, United *and* Woodward lose a young midfield magician who would have led the pageant in the post-Ferguson era.

Woodward might have been smarter elsewhere. Leighton Baines is missed because Moyes, having just left Everton, knows the fine detail of the club's finances and believes that a joint bid for the left-back and Fellaini will drive the price down. It is also supposedly the strategy designed to acquire the one he really desires: Baines. When this does not work the saga drags on until transfer deadline day when United finally separate their offer for Baines and Fellaini. The result of all this? Everton refuse to sell Baines, forcing United to pay £4 million above Fellaini's buyout clause, thus strengthening the sense that Woodward and Moyes are naïve operatives in the transfer market. Suddenly, United have become a laughing stock for those inclined to guffaw at the land's grandest club.

As the season progresses and the team falters, the fun at United's expense intensifies. The executive vice-chairman's mantra might be 'Business is business and why not *enjoy* the business of business?', but for the playing squad and fans alike this is an anxious time. Everyone is watching to see precisely how

BOOK TWO
David Moyes

I think about Matt Busby's history and then Alex Ferguson's history — they could do a film about it. I have to make sure now that my history and my time is something which the fans and people in the future talk about.

— David Moyes

him, put their faith in David Moyes, instead of the easier choice of Jose Mourinho, the supremely successful Portuguese whose guarantee is trophies, trophies, trophies, well, that goes to show what kind of club he is joining. He is the man who beat the Special One to the Special Job and that gives David Moyes all the authority he could need to manage this club. The drive into Carrington on the first day may be daunting but this is what it is all about. And David Moyes would not have it any other way as he attempts to continue the dynasty built by Sir Alex Ferguson over twenty-seven platinum-plated years.

So to work. Now, right now. The world is watching. The players are watching. Sir Alex Ferguson is watching. After the accession, David Moyes *has* to succeed. It is time to get down to business. There is Wayne Rooney's future to decide, and there is a perpetually increasing, always-morphing list of issues he is expected to control. Since being handed the job on 9 May it has been a crash course, a helter-skelter, pell-mell, fog of serene chaos, trying to get some kind of grip on this football club. And now David Moyes finds himself sitting in the office at Carrington of the recently-departed Sir Alex Ferguson. He is having his picture taken. He is the number one around here, *numero uno*, the gaffer, *Le Grand Fromage*. It should feel official, now. But he is in The Great Man's chair at The Great Man's desk and the desk is bare apart from a couple of remote controls for the television. The expression David Moyes wears is as if at any moment he will quickly rise to his feet because the real manager is about to come back and resume his place on the throne; this is all a hoax and Ryan Giggs and Ed Woodward and Wayne Rooney and Sir Bobby Charlton are all going to burst out from behind the curtains and start cackling at the very thought of David William Moyes taking over from Sir Alex 'Football, Bloody Hell' Ferguson.

Six weeks later he will publicly confirm this awkwardness, this unease, saying ahead of the trip to Swansea City for the league opener: 'Sitting in the chair for the first time felt odd. I did it myself with nobody looking. I thought I would have to see how it feels in case anybody thought I looked stupid.' Why? Why does he say that? For a man who speaks of *gallus* – Glaswegian slang for being streetwise and possessing large cojones – this is odd and naïve. *'I thought I would have to see how it feels in case anybody thought I looked stupid.'*

Like Ferguson's retirement, Moyes's succession has been splashed across the front and back pages of the newspapers, and is all over Twitter, Facebook, television and radio news bulletins. And here at Carrington, on the first day, David Moyes is being followed by a crew from the club's in-house station, MUTV, as he bumps into one of his new players, Ashley Young, and takes a first look at the place that will be his territory for the next six years, courtesy of that unequivocally supportive contract handed him by the Glazers and Ed Woodward.

Any great leader has to be decisive. A truism as old as the dinosaurs, the hills and the Waterloo-myth. So when it emerges on 27 May, nearly five weeks before David Moyes is officially to take charge of Manchester United, that he will bring Phil Neville, Steve Round, Chris Woods and Robbie Cooke from Everton, this seems a good and fine example of leadership for the Scot. Right? Wrong. Well, not wrong. Not quite yet. If Moyes claims a title-winning run of matches he is The New Don of the Sward, a palpable genius. If not, then the wise-heads can write that it was always the wrong decision. But if Moyes is victorious and triumphant, if United are a rip-roaring success who have all-comers skedaddling on each and every game-day, then this goes down as one – the first –- of a sequence of brilliant decisions and Old Trafford has a new Duke of Wellington leading the charge.

Of course, though, if United turn out to be a wishy-washy, yellow-coloured team who play like a bunch of losers with a capital L stuck to their heads, then the axing of Mike Phelan, Renée Meulensteen and Eric Steele will be written up as David Moyes not wishing to move out of his Everton comfort-zone, not wishing to be challenged by the coaches who were not his yes-men but part of a glorious era under Sir Alex Ferguson.

For the time being, let it be that David Moyes is showing bravery by breaking up the trusted Ferguson gang. This is a clear message that he is to be his own man. Yet in deciding thirty years' combined experience of coaching the Ferguson way, three decades of wisdom and expertise soaked up from working with Britain's greatest manager, is of no use to him, then this is also a clear gamble. It had better work, the team had better win, or the players have an easy excuse for why not. These men have been tried, trusted and successful.

Sir Alex Ferguson may admire David Moyes for doing it his way, but he surely has mixed emotions. Ferguson might even believe David Moyes has dropped a resounding clanger. Not that he can let his protégé know. But he will be watching. As The Wise Old Man of Old Trafford always will – stalking corridors of the club David Moyes does not even know exist.

Also joining is Jimmy Lumsden, Moyes's trusted coach since he took over as manager of Preston in 1998 at the tender age of thirty-four. On match-days the sixty-five-year-old Lumsden will take part in boxes – the small-sided, instant-touch exercises that get the players' minds and feet moving quickly – yet there is something incongruous, particularly at Old Trafford, about this senior citizen trying to match the fleetness of Wayne Rooney, Robin van Persie, Juan Mata and company as they allow the ball to do all the work.

Although Phelan and Steele keep their counsel, Meulensteen's exit becomes messy. The following August the sacked Moyes will claim he wanted the Dutchman to remain. 'I was criticised for getting rid of René Meulensteen, but I asked him to stay,' he says. Meulensteen takes to radio to respond. 'He says he asked me to stay but he didn't say what he then said after that. He said, "Well, I would like you to stay, I know how important you have been for the club and what you have done for the club, but I am going to do it all myself." So it was then, "OK, what is the reason for me to stay?" That has not been documented and that is why you get all these wrong, mixed messages about why I didn't stay. We had two massive meetings. Yes, there was an element he would like me to stay but, on the other hand, he said, "Everything you did, I am going to do myself." So, after being there for five years with Alex Ferguson, being an integral part in training, planning, executing and the whole lot, suddenly you have been sidelined.'

What David Moyes soon learns is that the golden rule of management is to get it right. Somehow. Any which way. Sack the old backroom staff, retain them. Reinstate them. Stand on your head while taking training. It is immaterial as long as success follows.

Chapter 4

The Case for Hope

The glint in David Moyes's eye on this 5 July afternoon is to last until he turns up at a restaurant in Sydney thirteen days later, where he will calmly, yet angrily question some interpretations of his quotes on Wayne Rooney apparently only being a back-up to Robin van Persie. Moyes will have a list of those newspapers he is particularly unhappy with and the *Guardian* is towards the top. That is the future. A future that will start hurtling at the Scot faster than he can possibly have imagined when he took the initial briefings from Sir Alex Ferguson on what the job can mean for The Chosen One. What a name. A moniker to die for. The media love it. *Adore* it. Yet this title will soon haunt Moyes, the club, the fans and Ferguson. So will the soon-to-be present that threatens to take United back to the past of the barren, pre-Ferguson days when no league title was claimed between 1967 and 1993. A scene no one imagined when Moyes was handed a gleaming, fecund six-year contract designed to ooze permanence and security. For all parties.

But, for the time being, the present and the future are no paradises lost. It is 4 p.m., and the scene is the Europa Suite at Old Trafford for David Moyes's unveiling as Manchester United manager. The captain, Nemanja Vidić, is alongside but he will not have to field too many questions. Moyes does not seem completely relaxed but this is understandable. Eleven years at Everton do not prepare you for this. Merseyside is Merseyside. Welcome to Manchester. Prepare for this somehow, if you can. Becoming The Big Man at The Big Club and being expected to show movie-star charisma and managerial genius whether sipping a glass of water, answering journalists' questions, or putting football teams out on the grass to win games like a mud-and-boots Mozart whose players conduct mini-symphonies every outing. If it seems an overblown job description that is because it is. Just like United, just like English football, just like the sport. Hype is no pejorative in the lands of the world's game. This is an HD-3D-DD existence where everyone is ready and oh-so-desperate for their close-up.

The first hint of what will become of Moyes is there in his opening words. Hacks live on hints as much as anything else. They are rich food. As succulent as body language and denials and non-denials and no comments and no no-comments, not answering telephone calls and not calling back. This is the stuff of football news reporting, which is the toughest beat in sports hackery, and within moments of offering his first unscripted words as Manchester United manager there is an opening clue as to the way David Moyes will go.

It is his repeated use of the H-bomb. HOPE.

This is the world's introduction to the new United supremo, but it is also his unveiling of the word. Hope. A bright, gleaming, betraying-the-game-is-up-already of a word. Moyes says: 'I *hoped* when Sir Alex's days were up, I would be a consideration for the job.' This is fair usage *and* prudent. A track record of winning precisely zero major honours in a fifteen-year managerial career would hardly have him striding the streets around his home declaiming like a frustrated Napoleon.

The second mention of the H-word is as equally innocuous. In fact it is included in a good, breezy, assured answer. Question: 'Are you intimidated by the presence of Sir Alex Ferguson watching on?' Moyes: 'I *hope* he is sitting in the directors' box. I have already called him two or three times for some advice.' Stylish. A good way to brush off having to deal with the silhouette that will always be there. But from here Moyes starts to sound less confident, weak even. Question: 'What style of play do you hope to implement?' Moyes: 'I *hope* we play the same way, with the same traditions and entertaining, exciting football. I've always said the biggest thing in football is to win, the job here is to win. I would always put winning at the top of the list. Sir Alex would as well. If you had a great entertaining team but didn't win the games, it doesn't quite get you anywhere. You have to get the balance right and *hopefully* I can.'

Question: 'United had a great tradition of late goals under Fergie, the fans will expect that to continue. Can you do that?' Moyes: 'The players who can come on and win games have been incredible and *hopefully* that won't change. *Hopefully* I will have that same magic touch Sir Alex used to have at times when he made remarkable decisions that got him results from nowhere at times. I *hope* I am able to do that.'

Question: 'What did you immediately say to the players when you got them together?' Moyes: 'Not everybody's here and it wasn't as if I was able to go in there and say this is what we are doing. That will come in time. I had a word with the players the other day and said I was surprised that Sir Alex had chosen to retire. But I explained that when he had, he had given me the opportunity to take the job and *hope* they respect that and we work together and try to be successful together.'

For the next poser even the hope is gone. Question: 'Can you replicate Sir Alex's success?' Moyes: 'Sir Alex will always be here – his stand and his statue are here – the supporters need to realise that it was Sir Alex Ferguson's time to go and someone needs to come in. To manage at this level for twenty-five years, I don't think another manager will ever do that at a club at this level.'

Earlier in the press conference, Moyes offers a some-might-say negative analysis of United having to play Chelsea, Liverpool and Manchester City in his first five Premier League matches in charge. 'It's a tough start and I'm not convinced that's the way the balls have come out of the hat when that was being done. I look back over the last five years and I've never seen Manchester United get a tougher start in any season.' This is no rallying cry to his new band of players and the millions who follow United around the globe. Why say it at all? This will be The Season of Puzzlement at Manchester United.

Chapter 5

Trouble in Sydney

The plane is on the runway at Manchester Airport but the captain is not on board. A club source confirms Nemanja Vidić has suspected sciatica. David Moyes is about to navigate his first tour as Manchester United manager through the testing lands of Thailand, Australia, Japan and China without his on-pitch lieutenant. But while Vidić will play no part, it is the player who is to join the central defender as a tour absentee almost as soon as United arrive in Bangkok who will exercise minds throughout.

Tour Life. No one really likes it. One senior member of the party confesses that he detests being away with the club for so long. These are to be three long weeks. A blur of time zones and hotels and football fields and sponsorship appearances and never, ever, *ever* straying off-message. The Holy Grail of the Manchester United footballer on tour: do not create needless headlines. They will find you anyway.

Within hours of United landing there is a major story. Wayne Rooney has a hamstring injury and is to return straight home for treatment. The conspiracy junkies are in clover. And who can blame them? There is no secret that the Liverpudlian is unhappy following a seismic fall-out with Sir Alex Ferguson towards the end of last season and is desperate to leave for Chelsea. And with Rooney having only two years left on his contract the question is who will blink first. If the club want to cash in now he will achieve his wish. If United stand firm and are happy to allow Rooney's contract to wind down should he refuse to agree another, then this leverage becomes neutered.

The Cut Bar & Grill in downtown Sydney is a high-end restaurant for the movers and shakers who pass through the city. And for the wannabe movers and shakers who pass through the city. What the difference is, who knows ... It is a quasi-kind of place. No one really has fun in here. They only think they do. All the fun is happening elsewhere. The place has soft lights and soft sounds and seems always to have been at this point now, approaching 8 p.m., the evening about to move from quietude to a rising murmur in anticipation of something that never arrives. It's what this – all these – places are about.

The joint's *pièce de résistance* is Wagyu beef – Japanese Black, Japanese Polled, Japanese Brown and Japanese Shorthorn – the finest of fine steaks real money can buy. The wine list teems with fine Shiraz and Malbec and Pinot Noir. Some of these come in at 1,450 Australian dollars – around £1,000 – so it's nice Manchester United are hosting. There is probably a waiting list to dine here. And a guest list. And a VIP list. And a VVIP list.

On the evening of 18 July 2013 at around, yes, eight o'clock, the correspondents covering Manchester United for the daily newspapers have assembled for dinner with David Moyes, the tour 'sit-down' as it is known. Yet this nearly doesn't happen. Today is a Thursday. Word has come that Moyes is furious with some of his fellow diners and has considered cancelling due to stories splashed on websites on Sunday evening and on the front and back pages of the newspapers the following day. The opening line of the *Guardian's* account reads: 'Wayne Rooney has been left in no doubt regarding his position at Manchester United with David Moyes, the manager, issuing a stark message that the striker is considered vital only if "we had an injury to Robin van Persie". Ed Woodward, United's executive vice-chairman, also underlined the hard-line stance towards Rooney, claiming the club have no fear of a player's deal running down.'

The quotes emerged when Moyes was speaking to Sunday newspaper journalists a couple of days before in Bangkok on the first leg of the tour, this group of reporters flying in and out of Thailand's capital primarily to speak with the Scot. There is now a large dose of doubt in Moyes's mind. He cannot believe how his words have been reported and he is about to say so. Drinks are ordered and Moyes looks at a list of names and he asks, basically, what has happened? What has happened is the straight reporting of what he said and if he was to look at some of the Sunday newspaper reports – *The People*, for example – he would have read this paragraph: 'Moyes insists Rooney still has an important role to play, while leaving him in no doubt that Van Persie is his main man up front. He said: "Overall, my thought on Wayne is that if for any reason we had an injury to Robin van Persie we are going to need him and I want as many options as possible".' *The Sunday Times* similarly quotes him as saying: 'Overall my thought on Wayne is that if for any reason we had an injury to Robin [van Persie] we're going to need him.'

The bigger picture here – the only picture, really – is that whatever the rights and wrongs of this, *He said, We said* dispute, here is another *Bienvenue à Manchester* for Moyes. And the new man in the hottest hot-seat is struggling to compute this. It is a message he continues to struggle to understand. Moyes has still not processed it when, come December, he is ambushed by an Everton fan who claims all kinds of things on social media after they share a drink in a Manchester hotel bar. But this is later. Now, on the first major topic asked of him, Moyes has said the wrong thing and is compounding the mistake by trying to say he has been misrepresented. The consensus is that he has dropped a major bollock. Knows it. But will not admit it. These are the noises coming from within Manchester United. Moyes surely recognises his language was, at best, clumsy. And clumsiness is not brilliant when dealing with journalists whose job it is to scrutinise everything.

There is a certain amount of disbelief at this performance near the bar of the Cut Bar & Grill. But on the credit side (and he deserves a large amount), despite being seriously cheesed off, Moyes is still here and about to sit down and enjoy a good meal and a drink and an honest, expansive chat. Who can argue with that? At the table after this start to the working relationship some feel more awkward than others. The atmosphere might not be great but that's football journalism. The same people have to be dealt with most weeks of the year. The relationship, the world, is an odd one. There are genuine moments of warmth and there are squabbles and disputes. There are forced situations where the manager or press officer or whoever has just been argued with has to be spoken to again on some other matter, sometimes instantly and, of course, courteously.

This is a fine illustration. The atmosphere soon thaws and Moyes is as engaging and as open as he can be. The wine flows. As do the words. Someone asks what advice stands out from the barrage he received on becoming Manchester United manager. '"You'll do it easy",' Moyes says. 'But I'm not saying who it was. I don't take that as a given, because I know it's going to be really hard at Manchester United. I know that.' There is a straight answer about why he brought his own backroom team and Ferguson's were told to leave. 'I needed it to be David Moyes's era now, so that meant me taking some of my own people.' He is also clear that: 'It has to be a new era. Whatever we say, my job now is to make my history. I'm going to be following someone who has made incredible history. I think about Matt Busby's history and then Alex Ferguson's history – they could do a film about it. I have to make sure now that my history and my time is something which the fans and people in the future talk about.'

This sums up the monster Moyes is grappling with. And considering his former unhappiness at how his words on Rooney were reported, he is now relaxed. He talks freely of being the manager for ten or fifteen years, and building his own dynasty and emulating Busby and Ferguson. 'I'd really like that, not just because of the history of Scottish managers, but I think there has been a succession of Scottish managers – Bill Shankly, Jock Stein, Sir Matt, George Graham – you could go on and on. I've probably missed a few out. If I could in some way be tagged on to the end of that list, because I'd been successful at Manchester United, then I'd be delighted. I will need to get the history books on Manchester United, because I wouldn't be the first person to be able to turn around and tell you every cup final or every game we've been involved in or all the players. But I wanted to get myself as knowledgeable as I can. Looking at the history of the club, it's incredible, so I'm really looking forward to getting myself up to speed. Hopefully twenty-five years might give me the chance to get up to speed.' He is joking about lasting a quarter of a century, but it shows Moyes's focus, his determination to succeed. It also shines a light on his honesty. A good virtue to have, but there is a sense that in this job he is maybe too honest.

Moyes probably would not have been annoyed (at all) if particular information had not emerged from sources close to Rooney twenty-four hours before that were in direct response to the daily newspapers reporting of those words spoken to the Sunday newspapers. The future of the striker and the politicking and manoeuvring and chicanery involved here are Moyes's initiation into the having-to-reinvent-the-Rubik's-Cube-while-running-fast-down-the-motorway-as-one-brings-up-a-family-of-five 'challenge' of being the Manchester United number one.

As well as what Moyes said in Bangkok, Ed Woodward's own contribution to the affair did nothing to quieten the sense that Rooney is being told precisely where he stands. Also speaking in the Thai capital, at around the same time as the manager, Woodward states: 'There are no contract renewals that are being discussed. I am not sitting down with any player on an extension and there is no trigger date in the diary. Would we be afraid to run a contract down? Of course not.' The executive vice-chairman is talking in general terms about any Manchester United footballer but this is clearly a message to Rooney that the club will not be pushed about by him, and that having only two seasons left on his current terms is of no concern.

The day before seeing Moyes at the Cut Bar & Grill it emerges from sources close to Wayne Rooney that he is 'confused and angry' by the manager's assessment of him being behind Robin van Persie. He believes he is at the peak point of his career and certainly does not intend to allow his career to go 'backwards' by becoming a mere squad player. The sources also state that Rooney will not countenance having 'anything to prove' due to a track record established over nine seasons at the club. This is dynamite and is already being reported back home and signals Moyes has a seismic battle ahead if Rooney is to be persuaded that, in fact, he is no mere back-up to Van Persie, and has a long-term future at United.

Rooney is an interesting case study. He draws criticism and ire despite all the goals and silverware. He has become an odd figure at United. The highest-paid player, yet a faded totem. The twenty-seven-year-old time-served footballer who became deeply mistrusted by Sir Alex Ferguson. In the Wild West arena of the dressing room his status has crashed. The self-styled 'Big Man' is no more as his team-mates view him as a disappointment, a busted flush. Towards the end of the last campaign Rooney and Ferguson had a meeting – a showdown, in parlance – at the club after the player was either dropped for some of United's more important games or played out of position in midfield. The most significant of these was the Champions League last-16 second leg at Old Trafford against Real Madrid when Ferguson demoted the striker to the substitutes' bench. He did not come on until the seventy-third minute as United were knocked out of Europe. Here was a sensational decision that was a screaming declaration of where the manager's once golden boy now stood.

Rooney was also left out by Ferguson for United's title coronation in May, the win over Swansea. He was not even a replacement that day or in the squad for Ferguson's final match in charge (number 1,500) a week later at West Bromwich Albion. In fact, Rooney's final appearance for Ferguson was as a sixty-ninth-minute replacement in a 1–0 loss at Chelsea at the start of May. Juan Mata played eighty-nine minutes for Chelsea that day. Now, many United fans hope Mata will come to Old Trafford in exchange for Rooney, who is desperate to go the other way. Jose Mourinho, back at Stamford Bridge for a second spell, may be even more brilliant than Sir Alex Ferguson and the Rooney situation is merely strengthening the Chelsea coach's hand.

The way this is being played out, the forward's career at United could be finished – he is basically telling David Moyes he is 'angry and confused' with *David Moyes* and not just the manager's statement that he is now second fiddle to Robin van Persie. And Rooney has contacted the Scot to let him know of his unhappiness. Mourinho is playing Chelsea's hand cleverly, saying: 'If Wayne is second-choice at Man United, then the national team will be affected.'

This has become ping-pong. Rooney's topspin is returned with extra purchase by the club. Manchester United's stance is one of contentment and ease over the player's future, and their position remains that he is not for sale. Later it emerges that Manchester United have rejected a '£20 million Chelsea bid for Wayne Rooney' and the whole episode is becoming comical. A turf war is in danger of breaking out between the two clubs. Chelsea are reportedly not happy with stories that say Juan Mata and/or David Luiz have been offered as make-weights in a deal for Rooney. Information emerges that suggests Mourinho fancies neither of these players. This does not come from United. Yet for whatever reason Chelsea decide to put out a statement that points the finger at United for supposedly briefing the story. 'Chelsea Football Club can confirm that, yesterday, it made a written offer to Manchester United for the transfer of Wayne Rooney. Although the terms of that offer are confidential, for the avoidance of doubt and contrary to what is apparently being briefed to the press in Sydney, the proposed purchase does not include the transfer or loan of any players from Chelsea to Manchester United.' Hilarious.

Next up on a particularly breathless day, just as the hack pack's thoughts are being gathered ahead of their first formal meeting with Ed Woodward, he decides to fly out of Sydney to 'attend urgent transfer business'. An attempt to try and placate Rooney must be on the executive-vice chairman's agenda. The seventh and (thankfully) final story of Wednesday, 17 July concerns how Arsenal have apparently joined Chelsea in the 'battle' for Rooney. It can be exhausting merely thinking about what may occur next:

> As Rooney is injured can anything actually happen? Who puts in writing to the club who is helping with your recovery an official request to leave?;
> Following from that, who bids for a crocked footballer?;
> Erm . . . Chelsea. They have already done so, though this was a paltry £20 million and United did not countenance it;
> Brinkmanship and *blink*-manship: each party – Rooney, United and Chelsea – could use the forty-five days between Wednesday, 17 July 2013 and 2 September as a long-running *mano a mano a mano* duel in the transfer window sun;
> Moyes now perspires behind the scenes – along with Woodward – to convince Rooney he should stay. And while this happens, United and the Rooney camp, who will want to hear what the club is offering, will keep their mouths shut;
> Rooney leaves;
> Rooney stays;
> It all drags on;
> Everyone becomes bored with the whole saga.

The following day there is movement from United. The club are adamant Rooney is not for sale and will not be allowed to depart even if he hands in a transfer request or Chelsea return with a higher bid than the £20 million rejected earlier in the week. What also emerges is that Rooney feels that despite Sir Alex Ferguson's departure, he still remains a key power broker at United. Rooney is concerned that as Ferguson is now a director, he will continue to have an influence over his career despite what David Moyes may tell him.

And then it goes quiet for a few days. Until Japan. By which time United are again buoyant and bullish about the man being billed as the club's prime asset. It seems Woodward's work, when flying out of Australia, 'to attend urgent transfer business' has, indeed, been essential.

Chapter 6

'Wow'

Can a single word be freighted with deep enough significance for this to resonate when considering the moment it was said? 'Wow.' David Moyes utters this at Sydney's Westin Hotel when viewing a montage of Manchester United's gilded history. The issue is not whether the club can or should draw such a reaction. But, more, is it desirable, a healthy sign from the manager? The man charged with leading everyone and everything? The impression for some may be of Moyes appearing as a fan or a football tourist being exposed for the first time to the glory of Manchester United. He is surely aware of the club's rich pedigree and the glamour and pull and power it has. So maybe leave the 'wows' at home.

Four days earlier Ryan Giggs, the man who will replace Moyes for four matches at the end of the upcoming season, says: 'The thing about Manchester United is you have to do it all over again. This is the start of the journey this season and I hope to be lifting a trophy again at the end of the season.' Mr Manchester United is thirty-nine now and still belting out the tunes everyone connected with the club wants to dance to. In contrast, when speaking at the same press conference as Giggs, Moyes hints at the gaucheness that will mark his time at United. 'I managed a very good club at Everton and we had great support out here – we visited Sydney, Melbourne and Brisbane and enjoyed that – but I have to put this into perspective and it's completely different. The amount of support we've had, the amount of interest from the press – we're constantly watched and scrutinised and it's something I'll have to come to terms with.' He never really will.

Two days later Jesse Lingard, a Warrington lad yet to make a senior appearance, becomes the first scorer of the Moyes era as United register their inaugural win under the Scot (the tour opener in Bangkok was a 1–0 defeat to a Thai All-Star XI). Lingard, in fact, scores twice in a 5–1 stroll over the A-League All Stars in Sydney. Danny Welbeck follows suit and Robin van Persie, newly-arrived on tour, slots home United's fifth. There is a spring in Moyes's step and a twinkle in his eye when he is asked afterwards about any mind games Jose Mourinho may try on him in the approaching campaign. 'If you're from Glasgow you quite enjoy those kind of things, so bring it on,' he says with good humour. Of a display against the All Stars which was professional and hinted at how United might steamroller teams under him, Moyes adds: 'It was a good performance. We could maybe have scored a few more goals – we hit the post as well – and had one or two chances. I thought we stepped up and looked a bit more ready, although the temperature suited us a bit more than in Thailand.'

United were in the familiar 4–2–3–1 formation that had Van Persie playing at the tip of the team. Moyes says: 'To get Robin back into the games was important, but it was also impressive that Danny [Welbeck] got a couple of goals. I told him that he could have scored four or five, but you have to keep getting there to score and he did so. I have said to him that if he continues to work as hard for the team as he has been doing he will get his rewards. He made the 'keeper save with his feet, was a bit unlucky at other times, had some great runs and I think he showed a bit of versatility about himself.'

By December Welbeck will be disillusioned under Moyes and forced to challenge the veracity of the manager's claims about him not practising enough. This will not be a great lesson in man-management. Here in Sydney, there are some warm words about Lingard and other young hopefuls. 'Jesse played well and I was hoping he would get a hat-trick,' Moyes says. 'For a young boy [of twenty] to get that for United would be a big thing. Not only did he play well, he worked really hard and showed a lot of maturity. It is good that I could see Jesse, Adnan [Januzaj] and Michael Keane in the second half. [Wilfried] Zaha also started his first game and he was unlucky not to score, and he showed moments that nearly got you out of your seat. That was a promising night for him.'

Moyes's Everton teams were not renowned for liquid football, but here he is saying: 'I hope my systems will be flexible, but the basis is that it forms a basic structure and we can add different types of players when the likes of Nani, Ashley Young come back.' This is one of the crucial questions for fans. Can Moyes continue United's characteristic exhilarating attack-play and change the rigid style for which he is known, or will caution and fear of defeat constrict both manager and team? The answer to this is a large part of what will define Moyes. Because when his United do show themselves to be timid and lacking bravery it causes an almost visceral dislike by supporters who cannot countenance the football he stands for. This is the sacrilege David Moyes commits in the Manchester United religion.

Rio Ferdinand, one of the senior players Moyes has to have onside if he is to succeed, says all the right things in defence of his new manager. In fact, Ferdinand goes as far as to say Moyes was his first choice: 'We've got a manager who's very enthusiastic. He's young and has the desire and appetite to be successful. After the manager we had, that was very much needed and *he's someone I would have chosen.* He's not someone who is looking to come in for three or four years – he'd love to replicate what the last manager has done. There were people who'd have come into the job, who maybe wouldn't have wanted to be here for that amount of time. I'm sure the new manager sees this as a job for the long term.' There is a veiled warning, though. Despite the six-year contract, Moyes has to deliver instantly. 'You can't get away from the fact that the fans, and us as players, expect to win,' says Ferdinand. 'We've been used to it, so to say that the fans won't mind, that we should give the manager a bit of time to bed in, is lying. We want to win. And I am sure he is the same. He doesn't want to come in and say, "Give me a three-year bedding-in time, I can just dilly-dally and be second or third".'

Now it is time to fly to Japan. Tokyo is close and muggy and feels like it will rain elephants and tigers at any moment. But the precipitation never comes. When United move on to Hong Kong for the final leg of their summer odyssey, the anticipated cloudburst finally arrives. In the Japanese capital's riot of neon and noodles, sushi and traffic, and eating joints where orders can be made at a machine and the food is brought to the table, the whole thing feels like a David Mitchell novel. Away from the poetry of the streets, in the stuffy press room at the Nissan Stadium in Yokohama, Moyes is admitting a second bid has been made for Cesc Fabregas and been rebuffed. It seems the Spaniard is waiting to be told he is still loved at Barcelona while playing Manchester United like a fiddle just in case the warm stuff from the Catalan club is not forthcoming. Moyes can throw little light on it, not publicly, anyway. 'Ed's dealing with that rather than me personally here.' How much rejection can one man take? In other words, how long do you risk Manchester United and yourself looking foolish by hanging on just in case Fabregas feels he has to leave his boyhood club? 'A point does come, but I think when you are interested in good players you want to give it every opportunity to materialise,' Moyes offers.

Moyes acknowledges supporters' anxieties at the lack of transfer action. 'I can understand why that might be the feeling. I think everybody had thought this might be the summer – with there being quite a few changes, my new position, other new managers at other clubs – that the transfers are later in the month. That was always the thought I had when I came into the job. And you've got to remember I only started on 1 July as well, so in truth I've only been in this job for three weeks.' Later Moyes and the hierarchy will reflect that he should have been bought out of his Everton contract the instant he accepted the offer to become Ferguson's successor. That way he could have started work immediately. Though this may be the problem with hindsight: it blinds to what actually happened, as surely Moyes *was* working behind the scenes before officially beginning.

United have been joined by Shinji Kagawa, Japan's favourite footballing son, Chris Smalling and Ashley Young, with only Wayne Rooney and Nemanja Vidić, plus a resting Javier Hernández, now still at home. Van Persie continues the sweetness and light offered by Ferdinand in a heartfelt denial that Ferguson's absence means United will be vulnerable next season. They are, of course. This is the fact-of-all-facts for the 2013–14 campaign. But which United player can publicly admit it? None. Of the rivals looking at United as easy prey now Ferguson has gone, Van Persie says: 'They can think what they want to think. It doesn't matter to us. What matters to us is the way that we work. Trust me, we will work very hard. It's a huge challenge to all of us and it is one we are looking forward to. I hope it will be the same this time [as last season] as I want to win more this time. The club wants to win more. Last year we won the league and that was great, but this time we want to win the league and more as well. We have to improve to stay ahead because over the last few years the English league has become better and better. Every single team has got harder to beat. Everyone wants to be successful. Moyes wants to be successful. He has been working very hard and he has spoken to every single player individually.'

Privately, Van Persie is 'gutted' that Ferguson is gone. He signed to work under him, and here comes a hint: 'It's different [without Ferguson]. Of course it was a great year last time. It was my first year with him and the first year at the club I had with him. It was a great year for the club and we all did great things together.' This is a lot of greats. As a Ferguson favourite and the man who shot United to last season's title, Van Persie will need convincing of Moyes's abilities. This is true of all the senior players, though. The lack of honours on the new man's c.v. immediately puts him behind the game. Hire, say, a Mourinho and there is no such credibility gap. When Van Persie conjures up a complimentary adjective for Moyes it is 'nice'. As in: 'He is very nice. He works very well. It's only based on a few sessions but I loved them.'

On match-day the heat is so close in the same arena where United won the 2008 Fifa Club World Cup under Sir Alex Ferguson that every movement is toil. And this is just in the media tribune. David Moyes selects only six A-listers to face Yokohama F-Marinos: David de Gea, Robin van Persie, Patrice Evra, Jonny Evans, Tom Cleverley and Phil Jones. The remainder of the XI comprise a fringe player – Anderson – and the young hopefuls Adnan Januzaj, Fábio da Silva, Wilfried Zaha and Jesse Lingard. There is a calamitous start when the Japanese side score after only twenty-seven seconds through the Brazilian Marquinhos. By the end United lose a second of three games under Moyes, 3–2, despite goals from Lingard and an own goal by Masakazu Tashiro. Does the loss matter? The general rule is that pre-season matches are an iffy guide to how a side is functioning, as fitness and game-rhythm are not yet established. The caveat is that, as everything Moyes does is under forensic examination, a victory would have been welcome.

United fly into Hong Kong. There, the rain hardly stops and in the latest sweaty media room at the Hong Kong Stadium, Moyes is speaking of the upcoming Champions League campaign. It will be only the second of his career, and his first time in the competition proper after Everton were eliminated by Villarreal at the final knockout stage in 2005. Ferguson claimed the competition twice, in 1999 and 2008, and took United to the 2009 and 2011 finals. Sir Matt Busby won the European Cup in 1968. Moyes is a novice. 'For me it will be a thrill and I'm going to have to learn a lot quickly and that's where I'm looking to the likes of Ryan Giggs and a few players around me for the things which I need to be told about. It's not all about the playing side of it – I've been in the Champions League [qualifiers], watched loads of games, managed in the Europa League – everybody has to start somewhere.' How Moyes does with his squad of champions against the continental heavyweights will offer one barometer of his level as a manager.

The end of the tour is nigh. Moyes and United still harbour hope of landing Cesc Fabregas, but the continuing stance is that Wayne Rooney will not be sold even if the Spaniard arrives. Now the day comes – 24 July – for United to go matador and bullring, sending a blunt message to Chelsea or whoever else may want to buy the striker. At 8.40 a.m. BST the tweet about Rooney's impending return to action is sent. In one stroke, this screams he is not for sale and that the post-Sir Alex Ferguson era of the manager's (strangle)hold over all club matters is over and that the £££s, €€€s and $$$s are about to ring into a cacophony on the cash registers.

*

August brings the buzz of a new season as the low-slung summer sun dips and smudges the evenings to throw a golden light on the possibilities of what may occur in the next nine months once the first ball is kicked. Each day of July was like waking up to find the month had just started. Again. But this is August, finally. There has to be feeling for David Moyes. For any Manchester United manager in these post-Ferguson times: every minute is like July. And then comes the sack. But not yet. Not quite yet. Before that occurs, take a few months. Start off fielding fruit in the stocks then take a seat on the gallows and squint out at the crowd as it swells and becomes ever more cocksure. And somehow, under the odd logic of football, it is the manager's own fault merely for deciding to take the job. What else did he expect?

For the moment it is all about that first sight of the ball on the centre-spot of the fresh season. The big kick-off. Boot through sphere. The grass is green, the skies are blue and there is much that can happen. Everything and nothing. The sheer majesty of the imagination. Of dreaming. Of fantasy-land football . . .

And United fans do leave Wembley on Sunday, 11 August in pleasant reverie of what the new season may hold. David Moyes's Manchester United have a first trophy. The Community Shield has been claimed. Wigan Athletic have been beaten 2–0, Robin van Persie scoring both goals. The manager is happy. But not *that* happy. In fact, though calm, Moyes brings to mind the Sydney restaurant scene in deciding to go on the offensive, which is his right, of course. He is denying reports of a rift between himself and the still unhappy Wayne Rooney. The player is still recovering from a shoulder injury. This ruled him out of today's match and last week's England friendly in Sweden, but Rooney will be available for another international friendly, against Scotland, back here at Wembley on Wednesday. This is supposed to have made Moyes unhappy. To stir the pot more, two days before, on Friday, a Rooney post on Facebook which thanked Roy Hodgson, the England manager, while not mentioning David Moyes or the club, is apparently more evidence of problems.

However, here Moyes is, in the room with the theatre-style rowed seats that is the Wembley conference centre, saying: 'Wayne has trained and some of you might not like hearing this but I didn't fall out with Wayne. Some of you wrote untruths. Anybody who wrote anything else is misleading their readers. He trained with the reserves because it was his asking. He couldn't have contact because it was a shoulder injury. It was as a floating player which means he doesn't play for either team, just in case any of you are unclear what I mean about that. He played as a floating player so that he didn't get injured. Anyone who wrote anything else was mistaken. I'm quite enjoying talking about Wayne because I'm hearing so many of you getting it wrong and I know most of you. I think you're a bit cleverer than that but some of you aren't acting that way.' Accusing journalists of penning untruths, misleading readers and not acting clever is an intriguing call from Moyes.

And before the return of the Premier League there is more carping to be done. Who can be sure what tome on psychological warfare David Moyes studied before deciding that the best way to ensure his new Manchester United platoon would swagger through the opening to their campaign was to complain about the first five matches: Swansea City (away), Chelsea (home), Liverpool (away), Crystal Palace (home), and Manchester City (away). Talk about giving his charges a ready-made excuse. But here Moyes is, two days before the trip to Swansea on 15 August, having a moan (not for the first, or last, time) and hinting at a conspiracy and citing Sir Alex Ferguson for corroboration: 'The old manager told me those sort of things happened. It's the hardest start for twenty years that Manchester United have had. I hope it's not because Manchester United won the league quite comfortably last year [that] the fixtures have been made much more difficult. I find it hard to believe that's the way the balls came out of the bag, that's for sure.'

This last sentence is a gem. What, actually, is Moyes saying here? Actually no cryptanalysis is required to decipher it. He is saying that because United won the championship by a canter the Premier League have purposely given them Chelsea, Liverpool and Manchester City in the opening five matches. And 'balls'? When was the last time they were used? A charmingly quaint take on how the fixture list is arranged. For some reason nothing material comes of Moyes's suspicions. The Premier League confirms the matches are decided by itself, the Football Association, police forces, supporters' groups and clubs. A league spokesperson says: 'David has put those concerns to us. We have absolutely assured him the process is random and above board. He has accepted those assurances.'

For a moment let's rewind a week to tune back into the Fabregas affair in which there is some serious movement. Guess what? He never wanted to leave Barcelona. And here the playmaker is placing this on record on 8 August: 'My dream has always been to play at Barça and nothing has changed. I'm very, very happy here and I never thought about leaving. I never had any doubt. Things have been invented. I didn't have to clear up anything, because for me it was clear I wanted to stay. I've always felt valued by the club. Everyone told me they count on me, I never got any sign that made me think otherwise.' Why didn't you say all this in the first place? Baffling. United respond with: 'We appreciate Cesc is a contracted player at Barcelona and completely respect everything Cesc has said today.' (Note the use of the player's forename rather than the usual formal full name.)

Back to Moyes on 15 August and his take on the (lack of) transfers. This is getting embarrassing. 'Yes [we are progressing]. Moving along in the right direction. Everybody wants things done quickly but you have to remember, I got the job on 1 July. I have had five or six weeks now and three of them were on tour. Obviously, we keep working towards getting things [done]. I'm confident we will have players in. We're involved in several players and that will continue. Will we get them before the [2 September] deadline? I hope so. We're working very hard to do so.'

Despite the merry dance Fabregas has led the club now officially ending, Marouane Fellaini, Leighton Baines and Luka Modric remain targets. 'This could be a difficult window for me because obviously the level I have been shopping in in the past is not the level Manchester United have been shopping in,' Moyes admits. 'That has to come into consideration. I want to assess all the players, see them all and give myself the chance to have a look and see what we need.' Like the moan about the fixture list,

Moyes does himself no favours by saying this. However many times this is read, the Scot does not burst from the page as a dynamic force in the business of buying and selling players.

On the Friday before his opening league match at Swansea, Moyes says of his first time in Sir Alex Ferguson's old seat, that immortal line of: 'Sitting in the chair for the first time felt odd. I did it myself with nobody looking. I thought I would have to see how it feels in case anybody thought I looked stupid.' He also says: 'I still go into the office and feel ... Look, Sir Alex is still here and he will be. I went to see him at home the other day. He was great. He is recovering from his hip operation.' There are also some intriguing mental gymnastics. Moyes states he will ask Ferguson for advice, but thus far has not actually done so. 'I will use him for advice. He will be a great mentor for me. I am really looking forward to speaking with him. I have probably had half a dozen conversations with him already.' Then: 'I don't think I have gone there for any advice. I have gone there and said, "This is how things are going. What are you thinking?" He is going to be someone who is around and I want him to be around. On the first day I met him we had discussions about the team within an hour. Within the first ten minutes of talking, and him telling me I was getting the job, we had already had discussions about the team and what would have to be done and what was expected, like sponsors, media, all the things that come from a big club. He would expect me to do the job myself.'

Is this, he-doth-protest-too-much? Or he-can't-take-advice-from-a-priceless-source? Or both? Or neither. With Ferguson still in situ at the club the obvious parallel is with Sir Matt Busby. The latter stepped down in 1969 but continued as general manager when Wilf McGuiness took over. Busby was McGuiness's albatross. And after McGuiness failed, Busby remained at Old Trafford to hover over Frank O'Farrell. 'I have not spoken to Wilf but the point you make is a good one,' Moyes says. 'I have to take over from someone – I will not be better than him. But the club has to keep moving forward and progressing. Yes, there have to be managers at the club, there have to be changes. Yes, I am a rookie at Manchester United, but I am not a rookie overall. I hope I am able to show that as the season progresses.'

The next day there is rain at the Liberty Stadium. There is a slightly surreal feel to the first season opener without Sir Alex Ferguson at the Manchester United helm since August 1986. Swansea are defeated 4–1 by the following first competitive XI chosen by David Moyes: David de Gea, Phil Jones, Rio Ferdinand, Nemanja Vidić, Patrice Evra, Ryan Giggs, Michael Carrick, Tom Cleverley, Antonio Valencia, Danny Welbeck and Robin van Persie. It also features the recovering Wayne Rooney making his first appearance under Moyes as a sixty-second-minute replacement for Giggs. Welbeck and Van Persie score two apiece. There is some surprise at the win, given the ongoing trauma of a still barren transfer window, Moyes's moans about the fixture list and the sense of insecurity that has seeped into the club since Ferguson's departure. Afterwards Ferdinand is probably correct when he says: 'If you believe what's been written in the media and what people have been saying, we would have come away from here with probably zero points. People's expectations of us probably weren't as high as our own. But it's nice to come here – especially in the gaffer's first real competitive game.'

Swansea City, really, should be beaten by the champions of England. Whether they were ever going to be a gauge of United's ability to defend their title is debatable. One reading of Ferdinand's words is that even the players sub-consciously are thinking the same – doubting themselves because they lack true faith in David Moyes. For Ferdinand to even mention the scepticism is a little odd and probably speaks of relief in the ranks.

Transfer deadline day offers no such relief for Ed Woodward and David Moyes. The final twenty-four hours of the window are a slapstick affair that provide a fitting climax to the summer-long, end-of-pier entertainment emanating from Old Trafford. The whole close-season has been like a West End farce in which proceedings have become more and more ridiculous. Except this has been no fiction. Ferdinand mentioned after the Swansea game that the players read the reports and watch Sky Sports News, so what must they think about all the clowning around? They are used to the control and leadership from Sir Alex Ferguson, on and off the field. Despite the transfer machinations having nothing to do with the players, they are as much a focus of all the laughter as the new manager and executive vice-chairman.

After continuing the ploy of going for Leighton Baines and Marouane Fellaini together – a final offer of £36 million was rejected – David Moyes and Ed Woodard admit defeat and make a separate £15 million bid for Baines. This is rejected by Bill Kenwright, Everton's chairman, who branded an earlier joint valuation of £28 million for the two players as 'derisory' and 'insulting'. Kenwright is clearly not enamoured with the antics of his former manager. The endgame of the pursuit of the Everton pair, of Cesc Fabregas, of being in pole position to buy Thiago Alcantara, of considering bids for Luka Modric, of keeping tabs on Cristiano Ronaldo and Gareth Bale, is that Moyes adds only Fellaini for £27.5 million. That is an embarrassing £4 million more than the Everton midfielder's buyout clause, of which Moyes has been conspicuously aware because he was the man who signed him and who awarded him the contract in which this £23.5 million figure was placed. This is all *before* the *coup de grâce* involving Ander Herrera, the Athletic Bilbao midfielder, on the window's final day. A deal for a player who has a buyout clause of around €36 million (£29 million) seems dead until three Spanish lawyers – the never-heard-of before or since, Rodrigo García Lucas, Alvaro Reig Gurrea and Guillermo Gutiérrez – are pictured entering the offices of the Spanish league apparently to close the transfer for United. Yet the club deny the solicitors are working for them (they may have a mandate from Athletic or the Spanish FA, no one seems to know). Besides, United insist any proposed deal for Herrera is already over because they value Herrera at much less than €36 million (though this will be the price paid for him under Louis van Gaal in summer 2014). In Spain, this pursuit of Herrera draws comparison with a Benny Hill sketch.

Still there is one positive: Wayne Rooney. United, apparently, have expended around half the total man hours devoted to the summer window in an effort to convince the striker he can again be happy. On 2 September Rooney is not at Chelsea, or anywhere else for that matter. He remains a Manchester United player.

Chapter 7

Six Games That Kill

The sit-down with Ed Woodward postponed when the executive vice-chairman flew away from the tour in Sydney takes place at the San Carlo restaurant in Manchester towards the end of September. The place is packed and the gathered reporters are seated at a table at the back awaiting Woodward's arrival. Starting to fade in the consciousness is Woodward's Sisyphean summer in the transfer market that ended with only the over-priced Marouane Fellaini being recruited. The fascination now is to see the Glazers' man up close and personal, to try and gain an insight into a guy who has already won friends by taking the very reasonable stance that he wishes to engage and be open.

And here he is for the first time, striding into the restaurant, fizzing good humour and quips and generally commanding the conversation on any topic. If other diners notice Woodward they are discreet enough to leave him alone. The repartee is flowing between Woodward and the *Mirror*'s David McDonnell as both hail from the same part of Essex, know the same haunts, and have similar birthdays. The burgeoning kinship is a wonderful sight to behold. By the end of the evening, Woodward has impressed. He has held court smoothly, answering all questions if he can, and has also shown flashes of a hinterland beyond Manchester United despite the perpetual demands of his position. There is nothing auto-pilot about Woodward: he is curious and interested and has a twinkle and self-depreciation that can surprise for a man so powerful. United would appear to be in safe hands.

The next day there is a less certain feeling at Old Trafford. West Bromwich Albion are the visitors and they stroke the ball around casually as if this famous patch of grass is their fiefdom. On a sunny day United are made to chase the match before a restless crowd. Despite Wayne Rooney – now restored to the starting XI – equalising Morgan Amalfitano's fifty-fourth-minute opener almost immediately, the visitors are not cowed and Saido Berahino scores what proves to be the winner after the hour and their jubilant fans sing: 'We'll sack who we want, we are the Albion, we'll sack who we want'. This is just United's sixth league outing under new management and already the opposition and their support are taking liberties that would not have been allowed by Sir Alex Ferguson. His successor is left ashen-faced, hurt and disbelieving. Afterwards he struggles to find words. Or the apt tone, pitch and register. The last time West Bromwich won here was 1978. The loss leaves United with only seven points out of eighteen. After the win at Swansea, there has been a 0–0 draw with Chelsea at Old Trafford, a 1–0 loss at Liverpool, a 2–0 win over Crystal Palace, again at home, and a 4–1 thumping by Manchester City in the derby at the Etihad Stadium. The football is disjointed, lacks a crucial control in midfield and is the personification of the unconvincing David Moyes.

The best result of this opening sextet of league matches has been the goalless draw with Jose Mourinho's Chelsea towards the end of August. On that day Moyes's United were sharp and Rooney, whose future continued to dangle at that point, had put in as impressive a display as he managed when entering from the bench and creating United's last two goals at Swansea on the opening day. Against Chelsea, the United fans had been emboldened enough to tell the visiting manager to 'sit down, Mourinho', while Moyes emerged with credit and a bounce about him. But the 1–0 defeat at Liverpool that followed meant Moyes continued to have zero league victories at Anfield after eleven years of trying with Everton and now United. Worse was to come. United were four down after only fifty minutes at Manchester City on 22 September. The game ended 4–1 and had prompted Moyes to say his players had not been 'bang at it'.

Now, after the reverse to West Bromwich, Moyes's men are a disheartening twelfth. Already a successful title defence appears beyond them. Moyes looks uncomfortable and swerves the question when asked if he is concerned about how a team who claimed the crown by eleven points are going about trying to retain it. 'I'm concerned after today's [display] but only because we didn't play well. There's a lot of games to go and we can put it right in the games to come. It's not from the lack of trying or lack of forward players. There are plenty of forward players out

SIX GAMES THAT KILL

there, it's just not quite opening teams up the way we would like and we need to try to do that better.' United are lucky not to have suffered a repeat of the Etihad scoreline.

Earlier in the week Liverpool had been knocked out of the League Cup 1–0 at Old Trafford, but now there is this awful reverse. There is near-panic on Moyes's face, and throughout the club, as if the collective nerve is only just being held. But it could go at any moment. If they are not careful, the pretence will be over and the sorry truth revealed that the manager and players have somehow become a hollow shell before October has arrived.

Any slack Moyes's new squad might have allowed him when he first arrived is gone. There are questions being asked among certain cliques about what this guy is about, his training methods and the brand of football he is making them play. There are whispers that Moyes is rubbing some of the dressing room's senior figures up the wrong way with a cack-handed man-management style. Beyond his inner circle, Moyes has already become distant at the training ground.

Chapter 8

Regrets: They've Already Had a Few

Christmas is yet to arrive and the cracks are deepening. After Manchester United lose 1–0 to David Moyes's old club Everton at Old Trafford on 4 December, the manager is having a drink in the Lowry Hotel bar in Salford. Sometime during the evening he poses for a photograph with an Everton fan. Subsequently the fan accuses Moyes on Twitter of calling Everton supporters 'a fucking disgrace' for the way they abused him during the defeat. Moyes denies saying it, and this is the stance the club takes when calls are made to look into the affair. But his clumsy words during the summer transfer window infuriated Everton supporters then, and continue to haunt him now. He had said: 'If I'd been Everton manager and Sir Alex had come asking for Leighton Baines and Marouane Fellaini I'd have found it very difficult to keep them because I always felt the right thing to do was what was right for the players.' There can be sympathy with Moyes for this episode because having a quiet drink and being friendly with a punter should not be a potential minefield. Yet in the fish-tank that is Manchester, the manager has to be careful where he is seen and with whom he engages. Whatever the rights and wrongs of this, it is fact. Sir Alex Ferguson would never have allowed himself to be caught out in such a way.

A couple of days later comes an interesting move from Rio Ferdinand, who decides to go on the record to voice some disquiet over the timing of Moyes's team announcements. The defender questions why his manager names the United side close to kick-off. 'It's hard. It's hard to do that mentally because you spend a lot of nervous energy thinking, "Am I playing?" or "Am I not playing?" and you're just going round in circles in your head and turning into a madman,' Ferdinand says – dares to say. Accusing the manager of sending a player bonkers over as prime a process as the selection and naming of the XI is a very public revelation of how Moyes's policy is going down with this particular member of the squad, and who knows how many others. It causes the slightly ridiculous development – if a step is taken back to comprehend what occurs next – of the Manchester United manager deigning to answer Ferdinand back via the media. 'It would be the same for every player if that was the case because I would think that a lot of the teams do that. But that happened to me and I never felt that way. We do it in different ways. Sometimes we name it, sometimes we name it late on. I think sometimes a lot of managers leave it so the press don't get the teams too early.' This is surely a strategic error. Moyes's best play publicly appears to be to close the issue down rather than offer any explanation of his reasons for naming the side when he chooses. All this justification does is validate Ferdinand as having the right to question his authority. Maybe the manager delivers a private rollicking to the defender, but his comments offer the opposite impression.

Next up is the curious case of Danny Welbeck. At a 1.30 p.m. press conference on Tuesday, 17 December ahead of the following day's Capital Cup game versus Stoke City, Moyes is asked about Welbeck and drops a minor bombshell. 'He's been out with injury but he needs to score more goals. I've got to say we had a word with him about a month ago and we said that he needs to be the last off the training field. Wayne's out there practising his finishing each day, whether it's taking free-kicks, shooting from tight angles or bending them in, whatever it may be, Wayne's practising. I said, "Danny, you need to be out there every day finishing, even if it's fifteen minutes at the end".'

The obvious question comes next when Moyes is asked: 'Did he take heed?' Here, the manager can point to Welbeck's display against Aston Villa two days before in which he was sharp and scored twice in a 3–0 victory. 'He did and to be fair he's out [there]. If you remember when he got through against Villa on the right and just pulled it past the post, it was similar practice to what he's been doing regularly. I thought, "Here you go, put your practice into operation here". I still thought that him getting the goals, he was really sharp and incisive. He's got that. He's a quick boy and all round I think Danny has got an awful lot of attributes and he just has to say, "Hey, come on, I'm going to have to take this on to another level". We're trying to get him to do that.'

On hearing what Moyes has said, the Welbeck camp are not happy. Neither is the player. Twenty-four hours later, and in the mixed zone at Stoke after United have won 2–0, one of the journalists calls him over for a chat. Welbeck obliges. It is his opportunity to have his say back at Moyes. He directly contradicts his manager and denies he needed to be told to do extra training. 'I have been doing that ever since I have been at United. Obviously I have been injured this season so maybe the manager has not seen me on the training pitch as much,' says the puzzled striker, choosing his words carefully. 'Obviously, at Manchester United, I want to be working hard and I have been doing that ever since I was a young kid. I just want to keep on getting better and improving. Those extra hours on the training pitch, whether it be with the boys or individually, I am just looking to improve.'

Despite a fierce hailstorm halting proceedings around the half-hour mark, the game provides a rare evening when all is calm and feels right in Moyes's world: not only do United reach the semi-finals of the League Cup, but the fans can be heard chanting the manager's name. Even so, beyond whatever the truth is about the exchange between Moyes and Welbeck, the overriding impression is that Moyes has missed an opportunity. If Sir Alex Ferguson was the manager informing Welbeck of the need to train more you could imagine him spinning the tale on its head. He would have told journalists that, actually, extra training had all been Welbeck's idea, making no mention of his own need to intervene, as Moyes has. In a classic example of Ferguson man-management, Welbeck would have been placed in the best light publicly and the manager would earn his undying loyalty for doing so. But this does not appear to be Moyes's style.

The Manchester correspondents ask the manager out for a festive dinner and he agrees, and in a private room at the Gaucho Grill, at 5 p.m., a few days before Christmas, seats are taken. The Gaucho is a low-lit place and the room serves the purpose well as there is laughter and jokes and Moyes offers colourful yarns about his days at Everton and Preston. This is a worthwhile occasion, but there remains an awkwardness in the relationship with Moyes that may never ease. On Merseyside, during his eleven years at Everton, Moyes had a relaxed understanding with reporters. Manchester is different and so is Manchester United. In Liverpool Moyes effectively outlived the media corps as he left Everton on his terms, when he wished, to take control of United. Over here in Manchester, Ferguson is an exception. Moyes's hope of lasting longer than the media is close to zilch. The best he can hope for is a good run. The position eats away at the best of men. Forget being England manager, *this* is the impossible job. Roy Hodgson's role in charge of the national team is a part-time affair. The Manchester United manager walks into the place for the first time in the sights of the club's cameras and the wider media's long lenses. This glare and scrutiny, both from within and outside, is there every living, breathing moment until he walks back out again. But forget the media and fans, it is the players who are the real critics in judging how commanding the performance is. Compared to all of this the England job is a stroll. The dinner is over. Time to leave. There will not be another private audience with Moyes.

The sense that the Scot's tenure is in disarray is strengthened by the regular leaks of the Manchester United starting XI before it is officially announced. On the way to Stoke on 18 December for the Capital One Cup tie it emerges that there will be no Wayne Rooney in Moyes's side. At around 6 p.m., less than an hour before it needs to be made public, the United team appears online. It is: De Gea, Rafael, Smalling, Evans, Evra, Valencia, Cleverley, Jones, Anderson, Young, Welbeck but no Rooney. The XI turns out to be one hundred per cent correct (again). The same thing happened ahead of United's 3–0 win at Aston Villa on the previous Sunday, just as it has before. Moyes and the club are aware and are seriously concerned. Indeed, after the victory at Villa, Phil Neville, one of Moyes's coaches, has been heard asking how the team is getting out. This is another fissure in the Moyes's regime. Under Ferguson the club was in virtual lock-down. There were leaks but they were rare. Now whoever is giving the Manchester United side away – and it is an established first-team player – is underlining that Moyes is not held in the same regard as Ferguson. The leaks eventually stop, but the damage has already been done.

By the end of January the notion that Moyes's squad harbour any kind of deep belief in him, or feel any loyalty, is over. For a number of weeks sources inside the dressing room have been offering a glimpse of the feeling towards Moyes, and the message is always the same. 'Moyes is not rated.' 'Training is dull.' 'We're not really sure what he is doing.' Several senior players are rather underwhelmed: they are accustomed to the perennial excellence of Sir Alex Ferguson. There is bemusement within the squad about the direction Moyes is taking the club. It is the same stuff that has been of concern all season: tactics, the messages the players are being given, and the stodgy, uninspiring football he wants them to play. There is also a feeling that Moyes is distant with youth-team coaches and staff and anyone, really, who works in and around Carrington. This was certainly not the Ferguson way. The longer the season goes on, the greater the uncertainty among the players. And Moyes is in trouble because this antipathy is being led by the established members of his squad, which means the junior ones are bound to follow. This is about his credentials to lead the club and team, the poor form all year, and the discarding of René Meulensteen, Mike Phelan and Eric Steele for Steve Round, Phil Neville, Chris Woods and Jimmy Lumsden. There was happiness working with Ferguson's team of coaches, now there is serious disquiet about Moyes and his backroom staff.

This is not a mutiny, but rather a cancerous disillusionment pervading the squad and the whole club. The old truism that once the dressing room goes the gig is up for the manager is unfolding. This is a slow death for Moyes: from not enough wins; his shaky man-management; those uninspiring training sessions; by the ever-increasing mountain of words from reporters documenting the bad football. It is open season on Moyes. Once a manager loses the media it can be as damaging as losing the dressing room. One of the intriguing things at this watershed moment is learning which players do not fancy Moyes and those who do. There are some, of course, in the middle. But midway through January those who do not fancy Moyes, well, really *do not*. And given their pedigree and talent and seniority those are the ones who matter. This disquiet becomes the first story to be published, in the *Guardian* in early January, in which it is revealed the manager is being questioned from within the club, from inside the dressing room, by some of the players who David Moyes is relying on to keep him in employment. A line has been crossed.

The January window comes and goes, and (despite Mourinho's supportive words in the summer) who has just walked in through the Old Trafford gates? Chelsea's Juan Mata. And for a club-record fee of £37.1 million. The playmaker flies into Carrington by helicopter in perhaps the most, arguably only, glamorous moment of the Moyes reign. The Spaniard arrives as a welcome boost to United's flagging season: they are currently seventh, a position around which they hover all term, with thirty-seven points, fourteen behind leaders Arsenal. Mata has a secondary role, too: insurance if Wayne Rooney, who is still considering his future, does leave for Chelsea or anywhere else. Mata says: 'I am thrilled to be joining. United is the perfect place for me.' He tells MUTV: 'Today is a very happy day . . . it's a massive club and I feel very proud to be here.' He could hardly say otherwise.

Chapter 9

The Skies are Wayne Rooney's

The news that Wayne Rooney has finally agreed a bumper contract extension breaks on Friday, 21 February 2014. Rooney's deal appears to be a right royal result for the forward. The understanding is that Ed Woodward and Paul Stretford, Rooney's agent, have got on well during negotiations and that there is a mutual respect on both sides. Stretford had apparently started off the haggling at a cool £380,000-a-week, though this was never confirmed. It seems a staggering sum considering the dudgeon Rooney felt under Ferguson and how he had apparently become of scant value to the club. Yet here is Stretford thrashing out an agreement that ends up £15 million shy of £100 million over the next five-and-a-half years. There is also a promise from David Moyes that he will be the next captain of Manchester United when Nemanja Vidić leaves. Rooney has signed on until

2019, and to earn around £85 million for his travails between now and then is not bad for a footballer viewed as a dud the season before.

This is about as good as the Moyes legacy will get. Hanging on to United's best player since Cristiano Ronaldo left is a fine present to the club. At the press conference at Carrington later a pleased-looking Moyes is asked how he pulled it off. 'I think that all we've done is say to Wayne, "You need to get back to where we think you are". Anyone who watched him when he came back would have said, "Look at him, he's leaner, his style, he got his goals". I think there is more to come as an all-round team player, leader, person. But Wayne takes the credit. He's the one who's done it, he's got on with his work. We always felt if we could get him right it would be great.' Moyes says he drew on the time when he mentored Rooney at Everton, taking him into the first team as a sixteen-year-old, twelve years before. This allowed Moyes to be blunt with Rooney. 'I remember when he came to see me. He came up to my house. I said to him, "If you ask me what's missing ... I think you've gone a bit soft." I thought he hadn't been the hard-working, aggressive player he was. But now in games people are saying, "Look at the effort he's putting in". It's his work-rate, not just for himself but for the team.'

Moyes becomes misty-eyed as the nostalgia surges. 'I did some pictures with Wayne [to mark the new contract] and I felt it was a bit of *déjà vu*, when you think back to how it was.'

Only football can throw up such an unlikely example of the way we were: a pair who were once embroiled in a nasty libel case in 2008, which Moyes won, about comments Rooney made regarding the manager after leaving Everton for United in 2004. Moyes sued Rooney, and the publisher of *My Story So Far*, over allegations from the player that the manager had given the local Liverpool press information about a conversation the pair had following revelations that the teenaged Rooney had visited a brothel. Two years after the case, Moyes revealed Rooney had called to apologise personally. Now Rooney is telling the United website: 'I am made up to be staying at United. In August I will have been at the club for ten years and during that time I have played with some fantastic players and won everything that I hoped I would when I first signed. I now have the chance as one of the club's senior players to help the younger players coming through and to be a part of another great United team.'

Rooney toes the party line at the increasing prospect of United failing to qualify for Champions League football next season. They are eleven points behind fourth-placed Liverpool. But the now even-flusher forward says: 'It's not a massive concern for me. I know the direction that this club is going in, and if we don't make it this season then we will come back stronger and claim a Champions League spot next season. Let's not forget we still have a chance this year. Some of the other teams are playing well but we have a strong squad here. If we have a positive end to the season then who knows what can happen.'

In reality United, under Moyes, have no chance. And this is a major problem for him. For Rooney, after a year of argy-bargy with Ferguson and the subsequent contretemps with Moyes, all's well that ends with a £85 million contract. The skies of English football are Rooney's. The limitations are Moyes's.

Chapter 10

Everybody Wants to Leave United Apart From Somebody

Warning: There now follow three Manchester United displays that may cause trauma in those of a nervous (red) disposition.

anchester United's performance at Olympiakos in Greece on 25 February 2014 is one for the ages. Here is a piece of immortality for David Moyes and the wretched players he sends out on this sultry night at the Karaiskakis Stadium that none of them would have desired. The eleven men Moyes fields in the port town of Pireaus, seven miles south of Athens, are the ones who sign his death warrant. In ninety excruciating minutes, David de Gea, Chris Smalling, Rio Ferdinand, Patrice Evra, Tom Cleverley, Michael Carrick, Antonio Valencia, Wayne Rooney, Ashley Young and Robin van Persie contrive to put in the poorest United display in living memory and construct the gallows upon which Moyes is to meet his fate.

In the media tribune there is serious disbelief. This is difficult to comprehend. Looks are exchanged as the match unfolds. When watching elite footballers this is *never* supposed to occur. The Greeks send a listless, dysfunctional United home with a 2–0 defeat in the opening leg of the Champions League's first knock-out stage. All observers are bemused at what has just been witnessed. Really? Honestly? Oh dear. 'Disjointed' has been a favoured adjective to describe this Moyes team. Tonight try 'discombobulated' and 'desperate' and 'disastrous'. Touch, pass, movement: the base components of the *nonpareil* player's talent, the bare requirements for *any* footballer at any level – they have not been present tonight. The lack of energy and thirst for the cause and, yes, joy in being out there in a red shirt playing for Manchester United on a night like this, is difficult to fathom. This is precisely the type of occasion every player's career has been about. It appears all this has been forgotten.

There has not been an evening like this in a long time for Manchester United. Maybe ever. To lose away to Olympiakos, who are the champions of a league well below Premier League standard, in what was a gift of a last-sixteen tie, should cause the most serious post-mortem yet of David Moyes's United. His team had never looked close to scoring. Towards the end when Chris Smalling put through Robin van Persie, even the usually lethal Dutchman blasted over. Moyes is continuing to grasp for an answer to the searing question of why a side who won the title by eleven points last season is light years off the pace this time. The goals from Alejandro Domínguez and Joel Campbell have not knocked United out yet, but can Moyes really draw the response from his players to overcome the deficit in the second leg at Old Trafford on 19 March? Should he even be given the opportunity to do so after this?

This is the moment when the behind-the-scenes doubts and whispers and low spirits and morale and fading confidence and continually eroding lack of belief in where David Moyes is leading the club becomes a glaring public on-field truth that cannot be ignored: ninety minutes of football filth that is a 'can you believe what Manchester United have just offered' event that is embarrassing for all connected to the reigning champions of England.

The shambles is continuing off the field. Robin van Persie is complaining about team-mates taking up his 'space' during the game. Where is the unity, the closing ranks, the us-and-them battle cry that Sir Alex Ferguson had tattooed on every one of the players he chose for United? Instead, in the heat of the Athens night, Van Persie is questioning the manager's tactics by proxy, through the centre-forward's team-mates. The Dutchman would never *ever* have uttered what he does of Ferguson. 'Our fellow players are sometimes occupying the spaces I want to play in,' Van Persie says. 'And when I see that it makes it difficult for me to come to those spaces as well. So that forces me to adjust my runs, based on the position of my fellow players. And, unfortunately, they're often playing in my zones. I think that's a shame.' Van Persie does find some kind words for Moyes. 'He's working hard at it, and so are we. Sometimes we play well, but not all the time. We don't have luck on our side. It's easy to point the finger at someone, but I'm not like that,' (apart from when team-mates are occupying 'your' space). 'We have to do better ourselves.'

This is close to unprofessional from Van Persie. And it shows the level of respect he has for the manager. When Moyes comes in to face the media he is unaware of the striker's diatribe. Understandably, the Scot is paler than usual. He appears shocked as if the full implications of what he has overseen – what as Manchester United manager he is responsible for – are yet to truly hit him. He admits: 'That's the worst we have played in Europe, that's for sure. It was a really poor performance. We never really got going from the start and we didn't deserve anything because of the way we played. We never really got to grips with things and to a man you could hardly pick anybody out. We just didn't perform.' Fair enough, he shoulders the blame. 'I take responsibility. It is my time and I will always front up. We didn't play well. We have to play better. We can do and the one good thing is that there is still a second game to come. We will do everything we can possibly do to reverse the 2–0 defeat.'

Roy Keane, working as a pundit for ITV, has been on television saying: 'Nobody predicted that. It's been a tough night for the club, the players and the fans. There is a lack of confidence and there are some players who just don't have the quality. They need six or seven players to rebuild the club. Privately, David Moyes will be shocked at the quality he is working with.' Publicly, Moyes is admirably defending his players, though he must be furious. 'There is undoubtedly talent at Manchester United but tonight we didn't show it. Me and the team, we didn't show it together. It is something we will have to do. We will put it right. We are determined to put it right and will have opportunities to do that in the coming weeks. The players are hurting as well. They know how they performed. But it is a team here and it won't change. We will stick together. There is a second game to come. Old Trafford has seen some great nights in the past and I am looking forward to hopefully seeing another one.'

Back on ITV this draws more spleen from Roy Keane. 'That interview was just like the performance: flat,' says the irate Irishman. 'He should say a bit more, have a bit more urgency even in his interview. That just reflected United's performance tonight: flat, with no urgency.' To top off an evening that seems to have become hotter since the match ended, Michael Carrick's wife decides to pile in on Keane. She tweets: 'Roy Keane what a ****, says anything to provoke a reaction . . . That's all . . . Done . . .' Later comes a more emissary-style offering: 'Deleted my tweet . . . Emotions got the better of me . . . Just disappointed.' Lisa Roughead – Mrs Carrick – is not the only one.

The bets are off now. Moyes is surely doomed. On waking the next morning the first and only thing to do is start checking to establish how perilous Moyes's position is. In the car on the way to Athens International Airport it is a hazy morning, the traffic in a nice, easy flow as the messages start to come through. By the time check-in is completed for the flight back to Manchester, there is confirmation that the manager is safe. Moyes retains the full support of the club. Yet the bush telegraph is also saying that the Glazers are not happy. Neither is Ed Woodward. He had not imagined quite how poorly United would fare under Moyes. The Glazers, Woodward and the rest of the club's board have been shaken to the core by the manner of United's performance. For the first time, the six-year contract handed to Moyes seems over-generous and optimistic, perhaps foolhardy. If the club hierarchy were aware when senior players began seriously questioning the manager last month, they did not care. Right up to the Olympiakos embarrassment the Glazers had been impressed with Moyes's attention to detail and the depth with which he had begun to restructure the club. On the morning before the debacle in Piraeus, United may have been seven points from a Champions League position, and thus staring at failure to qualify for world football's blue-riband club competition for the first time in a generation, but so fierce was the faith of the executive in Moyes that they still believed he could turn the corner.

After the defeat to Olympiakos – in fact, *how* the game was lost – this view alters. The Glazers and Woodward began the evening in Athens sure that a once-in-a-lifetime synergy of unfortunate circumstances – an ageing squad, a deficit in central midfield and wide positions, plus the post-Ferguson transition – was contributing to the disappointing first term under Moyes. They end the longest night of United's season with all that certainty gone, to be left *hoping* their analysis is true. Suddenly, the Glazers and Woodward, even Sir Alex Ferguson himself, are squirming.

Feeling discomfort and a lack of confidence in the man appointed to extinguish these two precise predicaments regarding the club's trajectory is not the way to run a billion-pound business that relies on the supremely difficult eventuality of winning football match after football match: the other non-negotiable demanded of Moyes. In all of these counts he is failing.

*

United win their next game – 3–0 at West Bromwich Albion, a positive rout by the manager's standards – but at Carrington two weeks after the show at Olympiakos there is disbelief in some quarters at what the manager says about the next game, which is on Sunday. Liverpool, still United's fiercest rivals, and deadliest enemies, are due to motor into Old Trafford then, and Moyes tells the packed press room that Brendan Rodgers's team will be favourites. At Old Trafford? The manager of Manchester United is billing Liverpool as favourites on their own patch. No opposition side should ever be described this way at the Theatre of Dreams. Moyes may be being honest but really all he has done here is jam both feet in his mouth when saying: 'Their league position suggests they're ahead of us. They possibly do come here favourites.' This also reminds all United and Liverpool fans that the Reds of United are eleven points behind the Reds of Liverpool, much to the glee of the latter and the pain and anger of his own supporters. 'Out of his depth' and 'clueless' are some of the kinder things said about Moyes by those who hear him speak. For a lesson in how to please the supporters and send out a rallying cry the manager might have taken note of the manner in which Ryan Giggs, his player-coach, had fielded a similar question when Arsenal were the visitors in November. 'Are you making us underdogs? Man United versus Arsenal at Old Trafford – underdogs? I wouldn't say we were underdogs,' the Welshman said, making the very question sound foolish, before adding: 'But I take the point that Arsenal are probably the form team and it is going to be a tough game.'

The outing against Liverpool is a disaster. Diego Maradona is here and he witnesses United suffer a 3–0 hiding that features hoof-ball, David Moyes-style. On Friday the Scot had said: 'Overall, we won't change the traditions, the style, what's expected here at Manchester United. We'll try and follow all of them through.' On this evidence the attack-first-and-always blueprint of United has been ditched. Moyes's words are hollow. It is the exciting, fluid football of Rodgers's Liverpool that is taking United apart in their own backyard. The home crowd cannot quite believe how their United – the champion team of England, remember – are being humiliated. Worse of all Steven Gerrard, the ultimate Liverpool emblem, scores two penalties, and eleven minutes into the second half their manager is being regaled by the jubilant Scousers with: 'There's only one Brendan Rodgers.' At this point the Northern Irishman's words in the build-up to the 190th encounter between the clubs seem shrewd. Rodgers had warned that Manchester United would struggle to attract top-line players if they failed to qualify for the Champions League this season, as Liverpool had done since 2009–10. And watching this, well, he may be spot-on.

For Moyes, his own pre-game soundbite feels hollow. 'From what I see every day, positivity is growing around the Aon Training Complex. What goes on there is completely different to what people perceive the situation to be at Manchester United.' Not after this, surely. Luis Suarez, Daniel Sturridge and Raheem Sterling, Liverpool's three amigos, would walk into this mundane Moyes XI, except they would probably offer a polite 'no thank you'.

Marouane Fellaini and Juan Mata – £64.1 million of Moyes transfer investment – are wandering around like two kids in a game played by adults, illustrating how poor the manager's handling of them has been. The sight of Fellaini being replaced in the second half is no shock. At the final whistle Moyes takes the long walk towards the Stretford End and down the tunnel to jeers and invective. United have been thoroughly undressed by Liverpool in their own front room. The three points keep Liverpool on the road – albeit ultimately unsuccessfully – towards a first championship since 1991.

Minutes later Steven Gerrard is piling on the pain. 'We believe that we can win the league. I've come here many times and been played off the park. They are a fantastic team and this is one of the most difficult places to come to, so to come and dominate from start to finish . . . and we are still going away disappointed that we didn't score more goals.'

Wayne Rooney, a Liverpudlian with diehard Everton loyalties, is in agony: 'It's like a nightmare. It's one of the worst days I've ever had in football. It's hard to take. You have to give Liverpool credit – they played well – but it's difficult to take. Nobody wants to lose, especially in this way, in your own stadium. It's not nice. We had a game plan for the second half, which went out the window when they got the second penalty so early on. It made it an uphill battle to come back.' *Nobody wants to lose, especially in this way*. There it is again. The manner of defeat is pointed to by Rooney. Even the man who recently signed on again for the long-term at the club, who Moyes has done so much to persuade will have a bright future at United, cannot help but admit that the team is close to embarrassing.

Rodgers, as all Liverpool managers must, sticks the knife in Moyes. 'I was probably surprised before the game when I heard we were supposedly coming to Old Trafford as favourites,' he declares coolly. 'I would never say that at Liverpool – even if I was bottom of the league. Anfield is Anfield.' Yes, and Old Trafford, home of British football's most successful club, is Old Trafford. Or it used to be. Moyes flounders when pressed for an explanation – never a great look for the leader of United. 'It is difficult to explain it. I just think Liverpool played well. We didn't play as well as we can and we will work to make that better.' There is surely no way back from this. Unless . . .

The return against Olympiakos and the derby with Manchester City are the next home games. If United can beat the Greeks by the three clear goals required to reach the quarter-finals of the Champions League, and the 4–1 defeat by City earlier in the season can be avenged, then maybe, just maybe, Moyes can escape the chop. The day after the day before, Juan Mata sounds an optimistic note for Moyes – and United. 'The storm will pass and the sun will rise again,' the Spaniard says. Yet when the questions start about the manager's job security he is in real trouble. It is very difficult to change that conversation.

The day before the second leg against Olympiakos it begins. Asked about his position and how safe it is Moyes says: 'My future has not changed one bit. I have got a great job, I know exactly the direction I want it to go in. It's not been the season we hoped we would have, but I have ideas of what I want to do and put in place when the time is right. The most important thing now is to get the Olympiakos game played and hopefully get through. If we can it would be a massive lift, but we know we have got ourselves in a poor position being 2–0 down. We have got a lot of belief and we have got to try to make it show in the game.' Yet Moyes concedes he has not been given any guarantees. 'The biggest assurance is that they let me get on with the job. We never discuss it, we talk about the future. We are making big plans for years going forward, this is why it's a six-year contract. This is not a club that works on a short-term vision, it works on a long-term vision.' He hopes. Everyone believes he is a goner. Maybe Moyes does, too. How difficult and nightmarish the job must be when you get up in the morning and go into training and everyone is watching to see your demeanour. And when you drive back home the uncertainty remains. Difficult to imagine.

There is a bigger picture here, though. Something of far more import than David Moyes's difficulties and fate. The real issue is how a clear and potentially season-saving, Champions League qualification-achieving opportunity has already been missed by those whose remit is to ensure they do not. This is about the club and its lifeblood: domestic success and European football. But Ed Woodward, the Glazers, Sir Alex Ferguson, the executive, have failed to act when they still could. The chance was a month ago, on 26 February, the day after the defeat at Olympiakos. Moyes may be culpable for the club's plight but the greater responsibility is with those who took the decision to appoint him in the first place: Ferguson, Woodward and the Glazers. Post-Olympiakos all had a chance, the perfect reason, the clear and damning and *unignorable* evidence to try and right this wrong. Admit the mistake in giving Moyes the job and act swiftly by sacking him. At that point United had eleven matches left of the league season and were in sixth place, eleven points behind Liverpool in the final Champions League berth. This was a sizeable deficit but with the Merseyside club and Manchester City, who were third then, yet to be played there was far more of a fighting chance than where Manchester United are now: twelve points behind City, who are fourth, and with only nine games remaining. Moyes is being allowed to limp along in the hope that somehow all will be fine. The vagaries of football cannot be worked this way.

The Manchester United changing room is now close to despair. The lack of trust is such that even a *bona fide* club legend like Ryan Giggs is being questioned in his role as player-coach by supposed team-mates. What the defeats by Olympiakos and Liverpool have done is strip away all pretence that there is any unity between manager and his staff and the squad. The two camps blame each other. All Moyes can do to try and get back on-message is to beat the Greeks, then City, and hope. And, yes, when a Robin van Persie hat-trick sweeps Olympiakos aside on 19 March, United are still in the Champions League. This is then followed by a 2–0 win at West Ham United. *If* – sport's most capricious word – City can somehow be beaten, Moyes could be out of intensive care. Results are the thing, after all.

Yet this all feels a touch unlikely as a pervasive sense of doom remains. In the 3–0 blitz of Olympiakos, for one night – and it is surely only for one night – Moyes relocates the old Manchester United. The United that comes at opponents in a blur of red and terrorises them with a gunship-attack mode. But a good performance in between a load of, well, garbage is not going to save any Manchester United manager's neck. Olympiakos should be beaten handsomely by United. And there is a cost: Robin van Persie is now missing with a knee injury suffered against the Greeks. He will never play again for Moyes as his club season is over.

Next up are City. At Old Trafford. After the 3–0 humiliation handed the side by Liverpool in the previous home league outing here come the club's other greatest rival. This could all be about to become worse. Far worse. Perhaps these two fixtures were the ones Moyes should have complained about to the Premier League in August.

In the programme notes for City's visit, the manager hints at the peril he is in by talking openly about his prospects. 'Our thoughts are well and truly on the future and our planning is already well underway, not just for next season, but for many seasons to come,' he writes. 'We at the club understand that we are in a period of transition. Football is cyclical and it will not be long before we are on the up.'

It may be some time, actually. A *long* time. United lose 3–0 to Manchester City. This makes the season's score against Manuel Pellegrini's sky blues 1–7. Cue utter despondency and humiliation in the stands. It is a Tuesday evening and Old Trafford is a miserable place to be unless you support the visiting team. Again. The delirious City fans taunt the Chosen One with, 'Moyesie, Moyesie, give us a wave'. Then they turn to the directors' box and demand: 'Fergie, Fergie, give us a wave'. The profile of an agonised Sir Alex Ferguson can be seen in the posh seats as the City support now offer a simple: 'He's the Chosen One'. As the cowed and embarrassed home support begin to leave early, Moyes sits alongside Phil Neville, chin sunk in hand, watching the dying embers of the game, and possibly of his United tenure. Not that he knows this yet, of course. Forty-three seconds are all City require to plant their flag in enemy territory, via an Edin Dzeko goal that immediately crushes any optimism built by the victories over Olympiakos and West Ham. For Moyes's side to hand their opponents such an early present is the worst way to embark upon the challenge of narrowing the points gap to the other Manchester club.

Before Dzeko's opener David Silva, Yaya Touré and Samir Nasri all have an enjoyable wander through the defence, thanks to the sluggishness that has pocked the season. This merely offers the latest evidence that this United squad are just not convinced by their manager and thus are the crucial fraction slower that can be fatal. Forty-three seconds to allow Dzeko to score. The fans turning on you. You look like you have no answers. The full-time whistle goes. Moyes's response to the game is mostly predictable: 'I take responsibility. I have to be the one who plays them, picks them and that is what it is. I think there are a lot of really good players there, some can play better, but there are a lot of really good players in the squad, a lot of international players and players who I think on their day can be a match for most players. We never gave ourselves a great opportunity to get into the game. Manchester City started really fast and conceding a goal after thirty or forty seconds made it difficult.'

So far so predictable. But then comes another collector's item to follow the 'Liverpool are favourites' offering. A United manager decreeing that Manchester City, the detested crew from the east of the town, are the benchmark. 'I think we've played a very good side and it's the sort of standard and level we need to try and aspire to get ourselves to at this moment in time,' says Moyes. This is a comment from the hapless Scot that can only anger supporters further. Some in the press room are beginning to label him 'Agent Moyes' – as in being sent to do an inside demolition job on Manchester United – so who knows what abuse is being thrown his way out there in the real world.

After the media conference it emerges from someone sitting near Ferguson that he was abused by fans for, wait for it . . . appointing Moyes. Yes, this is correct: the greatest manager in Manchester United's history has been receiving brickbats from supporters for his decision to plump for Moyes as his successor. This is open revolt. Moyes has continually cited how the fans have stuck by him. No longer. Even 'The Chosen One' banner, draped over a barrier at the Stretford End, has to be guarded by stewards. If fans are furious enough to turn on Ferguson, this surely is curtains for Moyes. Questioning Ferguson's decision to appoint him will not do Moyes's life expectancy much good. In a nutshell, this ire towards Ferguson is to cause more and graver questions at boardroom level.

This has been quite an evening at the Theatre of Dreams. Unprecedented. But what must the manager be feeling? When he finally drives back to his home near Preston, Moyes surely has a recurring nightmare of this match, this never-ending season. There is no doubt, now, that he has lost his most important constituency: the fans as a mass *inside* Old Trafford. There may have been criticism outside for months, but within the stadium support largely remained. No longer.

Last month Anderson, the perennially overweight midfielder, on being loaned to Fiorentina, said: 'I am sure that lots of players want out.' He may have moved to clarify the comment, but with Nemanja Vidić to leave (the word is he did not even wish to discuss a contract extension), Patrice Evra and Rio Ferdinand seriously considering their futures, and a whole host of others also wondering where the team is heading, the unpalatable truth is that everybody seems to want to leave Manchester United apart from a certain somebody. Even the club grandees are breaking ranks. Before the schooling by City, the solid, reliable Sir Bobby Charlton admits David Moyes's side is playing 'really, really badly'. He adds: 'It doesn't mean we are going to change everything. I'm absolutely certain that we picked the right man.' This just serves as the always-dreaded vote of confidence. From the man who brought Alex Ferguson to the club in 1986 and was fully in the loop about Fergie's opposition to Jose Mourinho being his successor. And to show exactly how the whole cabaret works, the next day the message from those high up at United is that there will be no official vote of confidence, but Moyes does retain the backing of the executive 'for now'. Two words to chill any manager.

The abuse of Sir Alex Ferguson has entered the club into the endgame of Moyes's tenure as manager. Fan power. Heartening really, in a sense. All the money and power, empty public words and posturing, yet when the shark is jumped it is the humble supporter who can ensure the cull. The open revolt against David Moyes at Old Trafford means the question now being asked everywhere can be summed up as: 'How bad does it have to get before Manchester United finally decide to sack David Moyes?'

Or, 'Can he really survive until summer if the hidings continue?' Those at the top of the club are reluctant to be drawn. However, few would deny that the defeat by City is the tipping point for an executive who have been reluctant to pull the trigger on Moyes. In the boardroom it is now, finally, being understood loud and clear – the fans' collective voice is a wail that must be heeded. Publicly, United are continuing to back their manager. Privately, the conversations are advanced about the best strategy out of this mess. The board will be praying there is not yet another dismal showing when Aston Villa visit on Saturday lunchtime, if only to give the bigwigs more time to plot. A defeat to Villa will only cast Moyes further as a man walking towards what could prove the final reckoning – the Champions League quarter-final meeting with Bayern on 1 April.

The statistics reinforce the cast against David Moyes. United are on fifty-one points compared with seventy-four at the same time last year, under Ferguson. They have never previously had fewer than sixty at this stage of a campaign. Old Trafford has mutated from the fortress opponents hope to escape from with only a minor beating to a destination most desirable. They cannot wait to get there. Under Moyes, United have fewer home points (twenty-one) than Norwich City and Hull City, and their count of eighteen goals is the same as Fulham and Cardiff City, who prop up the table. Moyes is discovering just how unfeasible following Ferguson is. It is his fault and it is not his fault. Try being the first to follow Frank Sinatra in Las Vegas. And on Saturday, against Aston Villa, the mess becomes messier as a plane is hired by furious fans to fly-by trailing a banner that says: 'Wrong One – Moyes Out'. The devotion to the club is admirable – spending hard-earned cash to make the protest. Inside the stadium, though, this actually draws applause in support of the beleaguered Scot. Later there are cries of 'Stand up for David Moyes' as Villa are routed 4–1. But it all feels too late; about half a season too late, in fact.

There is one chance remaining, though. A lifeline. A last moment that could save David Moyes. The act that turns his fortunes around. When Manchester United did become *his* club. Whatever happens it will define him. Bayern are in town for the Champions League quarter-final first leg. Be eliminated at this stage and United will have to wait over a year until August 2015, at the earliest, to be back in the competition as all hope is gone as far as qualifying for next season's tournament is concerned. And all hope will be over regarding David Moyes retaining his position as Manchester United manager.

Ahead of kick-off the fifty-year-old has done his best to revive the squad and support and club and his long-term prospects before this April Fools' Day evening affair. 'The players have played well and looked comfortable at this level,' he says, which causes eyebrows everywhere to be raised given how rotten the team were against Olympiakos. But at least Moyes is trying. He has to. The bell rang half an hour ago for final orders at the Last Chance Saloon and the place is nearly dry. This is it. The mood, the whole ambience of the club, can change if the European champions can somehow be knocked out and United advance to the semi-finals of the Champions League.

The performance Moyes draws from his band at Old Trafford is indeed encouraging. For eight second-half minutes that delight the home crowd United take the lead through Nemanja Vidić. The team concedes when Bastien Schweinsteiger levels on sixty-six minutes, but United hang on for a credible draw. They have been cussed and unyielding and from displays like these the perception of a manager can be transformed. Given the unfancied Alexander Büttner plays at left-back due to Patrice Evra's knee injury, and Danny Welbeck misses one tie-changing chance, Moyes emerges with credit bolstered. Bayern have the away goal and are still odds-on to go through, but United have a glimmer. And so does Moyes. 'If' is a concept shied away from in football, but *if* United can do the business in Bavaria next week in the return leg, well, the spring will return to the manager's step and he will be at the strongest point of his tenure since signing on for six years last summer.

It does not happen. At the Allianz Arena United unravel after taking the lead through an Evra barnburner twelve minutes into the second half. At this moment Bayern are going out, United are in the European Cup semi-finals, and David Moyes is in fantasy land. For twenty-two seconds. This is the time it takes the Germans to equalise through Mario Mandžukić and for the men in red to collapse. Thomas Müller and Arjen Robben score over the next seventeen minutes and Manchester United are out of Europe. And David Moyes is surely soon to be out of employment.

He is all too conscious of the implications and, at last, comes the sight and sound of the alpha-male David Moyes who ruled Everton for more than a decade. The defending for Mandžukić's goal was a 'crime', he says. 'I've got a team of experienced players and it's the sort of thing you learn as a schoolboy.' This is a possibly a first public note of true anger at his players and

Chapter 11

20 April 2014, Goodison Park

David Moyes is back at Everton, the club who gave him the platform to land the greatest gig in British football and become the manager of Manchester United. Except this is a grey, late afternoon on Merseyside and the clock is nudging towards 6 p.m. Goodison Park has become a morgue for David Moyes. His arms are folded, he walks to the technical area, but there is nothing he can do. He returns to his seat. Then back again to the technical area. Back and forth, back and forth. Before half-time the skies had begun swallowing him, the clouds had swirled, and Goodison Park had tightened, squeezing the living breath out of the manager of Manchester United. Kevin Mirallas's forty-third-minute goal had added to Leighton Baines's earlier penalty. Now, every time David Moyes walks back from the lonely little box, each time he folds his arms, bows his head, he cannot escape the Grim Reaper, sickle in hand, watching him, from the crowd. David Moyes's old crowd are now his new enemy. The Grim Reaper may be some idiot in fancy dress paid by a company to be there, but this is no joke. Not anymore. Manchester United are losing the eleventh of thirty-four league matches under David Moyes, and David Moyes is losing the last threads of any plot he may have had. And he is losing his job. Very soon.

It was not meant to end like this, but then not much does end how it should. But not like *this*. Not for David William Moyes. Not in the tenth month of a six-year contract. Not back at the club where he became an established member of the managerial fraternity, and where they are now all laughing at him. An Everton manager of eleven years and now a figure of fun for the what-comes-around-goes-around merchants surrounding him inside Goodison Park. Time is running out. The seconds ebb away. Then Mark Clattenburg, the referee, decides it is over and blows his whistle. It is ended. United never came close to making a contest of it. David Moyes shakes hands with Roberto Martinez, the man who took over from him. The man who has made Everton into a more creative, attractive side. The man who took his job, the job that he had for more than a decade. The job that felt like it was a job for life.

Now it is down the tunnel to do the post-match media, passing people who used to work under him, who were formerly the staff of David Moyes, until last May. He nods to this one, shakes hands with that one. Keeping a brave face on as he can hear the crowd singing and laughing, happy because Everton have just done the league double over his Manchester United. It hurts.

This is the one thing that cannot be shown, cannot be talked about, cannot be admitted. The raw emotion, the pain and the anguish, the damaged pride and the self-doubt. Then having to walk into the press room, the press room at Goodison Park, and face the questions. Switch to autopilot and give answers; sound measured. Sound in control. Sound like this Manchester United team will be turned around next week. Sound like the future can be bright again. But at this moment the future has shrunk to this cramped space on the lowest level of the old stadium and David Moyes cannot see much else, really. He cannot envisage anything else at this juncture other than this. The sight before him. Inquisitors with questions, wanting answers. Questions. Questions. Answers. Answers that are wanted all the time. This is all. This is all David Moyes can see.

Fourteen hours after the defeat, Manchester United announce David Moyes has been sacked. 'The club would like to place on record its thanks for the hard work, honesty and integrity he brought to the role.'

Seventeen hours later, Ryan Giggs is appointed interim manager for the remaining four games of the season. He wins two, loses one, draws one.

BOOK THREE
Louis van Gaal

Wayne Rooney is Wayne Rooney and Michael Carrick is Michael Carrick. These are different people.

– Louis van Gaal

Chapter 12

The Unveiling

Louis van Gaal strides into the Europa Suite at Old Trafford as The Right One. He had better be after the debacle of The Chosen One. David Moyes never asked for the sobriquet. But there it was daubed in glaring letters on the big banner at the Stretford End, staring down at him in every home game as his Manchester United took the agonising, season-long plunge that led to his dismissal. How errant the title proved. Now is the time of The Right One. And here he is, at the dais, in the room in the South Stand used for big occasions. Where the Champions League and Europa League press conferences are usually held. Except that after Moyes's failure there is no Champions League football in the upcoming season. Or Europa League. There is no European football at all.

The Europa Suite is packed and waiting. Waiting to hear what Louis van Gaal will say and how he will say it. After the David Moyes unveiling in this same venue a year ago that featured a lot of 'hope', there is a new feeling. A new expectation. An expectation that this manager will be different. He has to be. On and off the field. With the players and with the media. Van Gaal speaks in a declamatory style that makes his replies sound like the final word. On anything and everything. His Dutch accent comes with a tinge of Germanic sternness that can make him sound pompous, though Van Gaal has a fondness for a straight answer that all football journalists love. *All of football loves*. He also favours a long pause when speaking so it is hard to know when he is finished. This only adds to a faint sense of tension whenever Van Gaal is present. The Dutch have a reputation for speaking plainly, directly and brusquely. Three qualities to gladden any reporter on the Mancunian beat and any Manchester United fan. The news from his homeland is that he likes to eat hacks for breakfast. After the Moyes debacle this, too, will make the United devotee warm and fuzzy.

This guy can manage. He is one smart cookie. Like Sir Alex Ferguson, Louis van Gaal is a one-off, an original. He is no identikit gaffer gushing management guff and other verbal stodge as fig-leafs for the mediocrity of the abilities lurking within. Ed Woodward hired him because of a c.v. that states he is as close to definite success as is possible in the precarious world of football. This is no mere track record, more a glittering Yellow Brick Road that shows the Champions League, a Uefa Cup, two Uefa Super Cups and the Intercontinental Cup, plus the annexing of league titles at all of Van Gaal's four previous clubs. Three are continental aristocrats: Ajax, Barcelona and Bayern Munich. The fourth is a tiny Dutch team – AZ Alkmaar:

evidence of Van Gaal's ability to alchemise winners whatever a club's pedigree and status.

The sixty-two-year-old's standing as a *bona fide* managerial giant is sealed by his success being achieved in three different countries, Holland, Spain and Germany. Van Gaal is intent on adding England to his record. This is the Dutch footballing Don's way. The challenge is to make United the fifth team in a fourth nation he has led to the league championship. Van Gaal is not ruling out clinching the Premier League in his debut campaign, but qualification back into the Champions League is the minimum requirement. Having signed a three-year deal Van Gaal will not countenance failure to add a twenty-first crown for United during his time at the club. Yet there is a nag, as there always is. With David Moyes it was about ability – he won nothing in eleven years at Everton – and with Louis van Gaal it may be his temperament.

At just after 3 p.m. on 17 July 2014, as Manchester bathes in twenty-six-degree Centigrade heat and hazy sunshine, Louis van Gaal peers out at the television cameras and radio mikes as he prepares for his unveiling as the nineteenth permanent manager of Manchester United. Van Gaal, resplendent in club blazer and tie, is alone. Karen Shotbolt, the United media officer, may be alongside, but there is no top brass. No Ed Woodward. The executive vice-chairman, following the unhappy hiring of Moyes, is a relieved man. He is a relieved man to have landed the manager known as the Iron Tulip. He is a relieved man because Moyes has gone and he has in place the manager who continues to fly through a stellar career. Five days after the Dutchman led Holland to third place at the World Cup with a 3–0 victory over Brazil, the executive vice-chairman can recede into the background and allow Manchester United to become the Louis van Gaal Show.

The hiring of Van Gaal for the new term promises far more than Moyes could deliver. But make no mistake. Ed Woodward also has to deliver. And on this mid-July afternoon, where is he? Where is Woodward on this day-of-days? Like a lot in the football soap-opera, the non-stop burlesque, the cabaret that never sleeps, it hardly matters. Yet it does. As the media conference develops, Woodward's absence seems prescient – a smart move – given the awkward nature of Van Gaal's opening utterances as the new manager of a club with global ambitions. One which trumpets '659 million fans' worldwide. And has an insatiable commercial operation that will be the first to set up a Manchester United franchise on Mars once life is confirmed there.

Van Gaal requires no time to indicate he is his own man. The questioning of the club's commercial desires he is about to offer up confirms he may be a loose cannon. Likewise when Van Gaal criticises the length and breadth of the upcoming tour of America. Some way into his introductory conference, after batting away similar questions, he is asked again: 'Would fourth place and a return to the Champions League for next season be acceptable this year?' The answer comes reluctantly, Van Gaal conceding: 'For me, the challenge is always to come first, not fourth.' He says this despite being cautious about Manchester United's immediate prospects under him. He adopts the quite grown-up position that he first wants to learn about his players before making any kind of prediction. But what else can Van Gaal say? The manager of Manchester United cannot declare: 'Fourth this year would be progress after last year's seventh.' This is the truth, but the headline writers would have a field day. 'Moyes II has landed'. 'Van Smaal's limited ambition'. Yet while Van Gaal may have made a concession he has at least done so with the cutest answer available to him. This is the kind of skill Moyes lacked. Van Gaal's register is in the positive, the definitive. Of the 'always'. Of the challenge to 'come first, not fourth'.

The Dutchman is less guarded – or perhaps he is just calculating and smart – when he twice aims fire at the United money-making machine. The day before had been his first in charge of the world's largest club. Yet even as Van Gaal was starting to realise the scale of United's commercial operation, and deciding it needed taming, the club announced a Japanese company, Nissin, as the latest 'global partner', taking the number of sponsors to more than sixty. These latest backers are noodle-makers and they sit alongside soft-drink companies, tyre manufacturers and high-end watch merchants. Whether or not Van Gaal is aware of any of them appears immaterial as here, a day later, he launches a broadside at the club's perpetual commercialism. 'I cannot give predictions because you never know,' he says. 'It's the biggest club in the world and within two days I know already how important Manchester United is . . . But also how important the sponsors are and I have to work and prepare a team and I have to adapt to this big club. It will not be easy but when you see my career you see what I have won. The future shall show if I can do it again . . .'

Almost immediately he feels the need to repeat the point: 'But it is difficult because the greatness of this club is more than other clubs. And this club is guided in a commercial way and it is not always possible to meet commercial and football expectations. It is the biggest club because of world renown, but in sport you are never the biggest unless you've proved it every season . . . Barça were number one in Spain, Ajax number one in the Netherlands and Bayern Munich number one in Germany, and now Man United number one in England and I hope I shall fulfil the expectation.'

Phew, quite a statement, in which Van Gaal not only name-checks the previous continental giants he has managed, but also casually asserts their status as top of the pile in their respective countries. Not sure what Real Madrid would say about Barcelona being number one in Spain, but this is the Van Gaal-style. Anything the Dutchman says would have made instant headlines. He could have discussed his favourite colour, noodles in Japan, or the aeroplane he flew in on, and the front and back pages would have been cleared.

He has not finished, either. Right at the end, another bombshell. To a question about whether Wayne Rooney will be his captain, Van Gaal says, unprompted and almost as an aside: 'Michael Carrick was injured which is a big blow because he is an experienced player. It is important we have experienced players, but not only age and football experience but as a human.' As the manager stands up to leave he is asked how serious is the injury to Carrick, the squad's one genuine high-class central midfielder. The reply is that Carrick had surgery this morning and is likely to be out for three months. At the very start of the Van Gaal tenure this is a real blow, though the prime story remains his stated ambition to go for the title and his beef with the commercial operation.

The Louis van Gaal Manchester United is up and running and is precisely what the doctor prescribed after the dour dog days of the Moyes tenure. Van Gaal had started the unveiling by saying: 'First of all, thank you to Sir Bobby Charlton because it's a great honour to come into this stadium and be guided by him. I saw him play so I know what he means to Man United and English football.' The question now is what can the Iron Tulip mean for Manchester United? The answer: to be the Wizard of Oz of English football. In an instant. A flash. Return the club from the black-and-white world of David Moyes to the fantastical Technicolor land of Sir Alex Ferguson and Sir Matt Busby. The land inhabited by the Busby Babes, where red-shirted superstars play football from the galaxies and win title upon title. The land where the glory of the 1968 European Cup win, and 1999 Champions League triumph, runs on a never-ending loop. United are lost and need to find the way back to the land where Busby, Jimmy Murphy, Duncan Edwards, Denis Law, George Best, Sir Bobby Charlton, Sir Alex Ferguson, Bryan Robson, Eric Cantona, Roy Keane, David Beckham and Cristiano Ronaldo all reside. This is the storied club of the Munich disaster, three European Cups and twenty league titles. Of glitz and glamour and operatic storylines. Of the grand gesture and the common touch. Of history, heritage, pedigree and dreams, always dreams, and dreams of dreams.

Instead, it has turned into the club who finished seventh last season under Moyes. The club who after the end of Ferguson's twenty-six-and-a-half-year reign is experiencing the tremors of a first, quivering uncertainty for a generation. Insecurity stalks the Theatre of Dreams. The squad requires major surgery. Away from the pitch the club is grasping for identity and direction and stability under the new regime. New-Age United is a club in desperate catch-up mode to modernise in the wake of Ferguson's departure. The rush is on to embrace the digital social age by finally opening a Twitter account while overhauling its Facebook, Instagram and website operations. Moyes was the man appointed to oversee all this but failed. He could not handle the heat. So into this state of flux, and into a town where a second Premier League title in three years has been claimed by the 'noisy neighbours' at Manchester City, has walked Van Gaal. He will be allowed more time than Moyes because of his c.v. But not too much more. United fans are twitchy. Life has been miserable for them for the past year or so. Van Gaal is charged with re-establishing the club's domination.

Can he do it? Before the unveiling, Mehmet Scholl, reserve team manager under Van Gaal at Bayern Munich, described the Dutchman as a 'genius coach' but also offered a warning. 'He's very strict and severe. So the players have the chance to follow him or they are out and he takes the next players.' Scholl was far more scathing off the record. And he also said United's talisman and best footballer, Wayne Rooney, could be in for a shock. 'There are twenty-six, twenty-seven players and he [Van Gaal] is looking for the fourteen to follow him – fourteen, fifteen, sixteen to follow. His thing is not the motivation ... His thing is really working on the pitch – that's brilliant. And that's how the players learn. Some of the players, I can tell you, like Rooney, I don't think he has to learn anything more. So that will be difficult for him if the coach says, "You have to do it in a completely different way. Whatever you did until now, change it".'

So how will this go down? Will Van Gaal rub everyone at the club up the wrong way and provoke instant alienation, or will he be a little subtler, more charming in his approach than his reputation might suggest? The second intriguing question is the style of football. One prominent Premier League manager has observed that though Van Gaal wins trophies by the schooner-load, his teams are functional. Always have been and always will be. How will that go down with the United support who expect their favourites to perform like the gods of entertainment *and* win football matches?

Van Gaal's arrival is a start. His presence means stardust again swirls around Team Showbiz. The swagger has returned. He took mere seconds to do what David Moyes never dared: question the dominant institution of British football. Van Gaal is instantly showing he does not care about anything apart from number one: himself. All that matters is being able to operate in the best conditions to succeed. United should be grateful at having landed the arch-perfectionist. The manager's history shows he is a winner, and the always cocked body language, the lack of self-doubt and the impassive features offer the look of an operator accustomed to triumph.

This is the former school teacher's style. And, according to some, this is because he can be a killer. The Manchester City chief executive, Ferran Soriano, who was previously in place at one of Van Gaal's former clubs, Barcelona, said of him: 'If you treat your people badly, they remember. One day you make an error and they kill you. I've seen this in many clubs. Louis van Gaal has been a very good coach in many clubs but his style is very difficult. The same thing happened to him in Barcelona as in Bayern Munich. He is very tough, people don't like him, but he wins. And one day you don't win – and when you don't win, everybody who is angry with you will come back to you and try to kill you.' Van Gaal knows this. His master-plan is simple and is the same as Jose Mourinho at Chelsea, Rafael Benítez when at Liverpool, and Sir Alex Ferguson before him at United. Win while he can, do all the killing, make as many kills as are possible before becoming The Killed. Keep on winning. Keep on killing. Don't stop. Don't ever stop.

Tomorrow is Friday, 18 July, and Louis van Gaal will board the club's private jet for Manchester United's pre-season tour of the United States of America. There is money to be made and matches to be won and footballers to be assessed. By the time Van Gaal flies home with the squad in early August he will be far wiser about his starting XI and who he needs to erase. He knows how. He is ruthless. He will need to be.

Orders of his are being executed back in Manchester. The dude has been in the job less than a week and already he has acted more decisively than David Moyes. He has also decided that what was good enough for the great Sir Alex Ferguson is not up to Van Gaal's standards. Earlier on Tuesday morning, Van Gaal's first major task as manager is put into action when the first-team training pitches at Carrington, next to the Jimmy Murphy Centre, start to be ripped up so that the grass can be re-laid with the Desso surface that has been used at Old Trafford for the past year.

Now here, in a cramped press room at the Rose Bowl, after a scheduled thirty-minute drive took two hours, Van Gaal again unloads at what he views as a bloated summer itinerary. His mood is hardly helped by the fact he is sitting at a table on a platform in what is little more than a broom cupboard. The florid hue of his visage seems even deeper as he contemplates the tour schedule. After close to a week here in Los Angeles, United will fly on to Denver, then Washington, DC, and Detroit for the three-game International Champions Cup tournament, with the final (if reached) in Miami early next month becoming the fifth match of the tour. The whole shebang is a money-maker, of course. Van Gaal's way would be to have a shorter programme and, maybe, a base from which to fly in and out of. But not this summer. Not when he has to hit the ground sprinting and without any preparation time for a gargantuan job made even more exacting due to the demands of the just-finished World Cup. Some might call this taking on a challenge that would, under normal circumstances, only be accepted by a desperate man or a madman. But there is already a conviction that Van Gaal possesses the exact mix of talent *and* zaniness required.

'The tour was already arranged and I shall adapt and United will do everything to apply to my rules, but I have said that already,' the manager says. 'This is the first time I am late for a press conference, but it is the Los Angeles traffic, so I am sorry for that.' The apology is a curiosity. It is difficult to imagine Ferguson deciding the best strategy would be to say sorry to the media. One adjective to describe Van Gaal might be 'complex'. Another could be 'confusing'. There may not be too much difference between the two. Here he is apologising to journalists in Pasadena. Yet this is the man who has consistently clashed with the media throughout his career. When at Barcelona Van Gaal had a particularly fractious relationship with the local hacks who covered the Catalan team on a daily basis. He blamed them for his departure at the close of the 1999–2000 season, saying: '*Amigos de la prensa. Yo me voy. Felicidades.*' This translates as: 'Friends of the press, I'm going. Congratulations.' That is one way to exit Barcelona. Maybe the deeper truth of the contradictions Van Gaal is not afraid to display is that any man, woman or child would be shown to be inconsistent if they were exposed to enough public scrutiny. Rare is the person who does not change his or her mind occasionally.

Van Gaal's reputation as a managerial great with an edge includes a disdain for reporters and silly questions. The Barcelona experience was hardly a rarity. His peccadilloes regarding the fourth estate extend to a lack of patience if journalists offer statements rather than questions. Even if these are silly they are preferable to a statement, though the hack may still be jumped on.

For tomorrow evening's match the four-hour round-trip through the traffic will have to be repeated. All the travelling is not 'positive for good preparation', states Van Gaal, when there are 'commercial activities and dreadful distances, having to fly a lot and jet-lag'. He is certainly not holding back. Still he has already been promised that next summer the tour will be reined in as 'they have said that to me and I am very confident that it shall be'. Van Gaal's persona suggests Ed Woodward had better keep to this or become embroiled in a lively debate at a future date. Already making the club bow to his demands for next year's summer tour is a pretty interesting development. It is about to become better. A whole lot better. When speaking to MUTV Van Gaal goes further, actually questioning if United are 'too big'. It is difficult to believe he actually uttered this and it has an undercurrent of humour.

The *raison d'être* of the Glazer family's model of ownership is for United to become a non-stop money-minting operation and its own benign state. A self-contained, self-governing entity which is bigger than any one figure or employee. Van Gaal or, indeed, Ed Woodward are mere custodians who may hold the highest office but who revolve around the club. It cannot be the other way round. Van Gaal's complaints come despite the tour being a maximum 13,471-mile trip, assuming United reach the final in Miami on 4 August. Under Moyes last summer, when United toured Australasia and Asia, taking in Thailand, Australia, Japan and Hong Kong, the club made a 24,000-mile journey. In 2012 – ahead of Ferguson's final campaign – they covered 22,000 miles when visiting Durban, Cape Town, Shanghai, Oslo and Gothenburg. That cannot have been too arduous as

United went on to claim the thirteenth title of Ferguson's reign.

But, no matter. Van Gaal tells MUTV, the club's own in-house broadcast organ: 'Maybe it is too big a club. Not only in a sporting sense but also commercially. We have to do a lot of things that normally I don't allow . . .' This is absolutely brilliant. During his time, Ferguson became so choleric with MUTV that he refused to speak to them. Twice. Actually blanked the club channel. Felt he had been turned over, betrayed by the station. Once was in 2005 when a presenter criticised Ferguson's tactics in a European Cup game at Villarreal; the second occasion came six years later when a MUTV interview led to an FA charge for questioning a referee. Imagine that – the Manchester United manager effectively banning the club's own television station. And this an institution so blindly loyal to the club that it is nicknamed fondly by some in the media as 'Pravda'. But now the first Manchester United manager from the continent breezes into the club and seven days in chooses to inform its own broadcaster that the club might be too big. He then follows up with the casual observation: 'I have to adapt to this big club but I think also this big club has to adapt to Louis van Gaal. I hope we can have some balance to that.' What Van Gaal is saying is both reasonable and ridiculous. Football, in a nutshell. Woodward may well have laughed on hearing this. Privately, of course. And only if alone.

The only area where Van Gaal's bullishness is absent regards the team and where he can take it this year. As the Pasadena night grows sultry, Van Gaal is asked if United's seventh-place finish under David Moyes was an under-achievement. 'I cannot judge that because I am also new in the Premier League and when you see the Premier League there are also a lot of clubs capable of playing higher-level football . . . To be the champion in the Premier League is much more difficult than in the Netherlands or Germany. Because in Germany you don't have so much money. I have to wait three or four months and give you a clearer answer.' The three-month wait is a theme Van Gaal will cultivate until, in a quelle surprise reaction, when this deadline arrives and United are still fumbling under his management, he decides the media are being silly for holding him to it.

Now, when two of United's expensive summer signings are paraded in Pasadena, they are consigned to the role of mere footnotes. Already, this is par for the course. What is to be expected in the Iron Tulip Show. Here is a manager who on arriving at Barcelona in 1996 declared: 'Louis van Gaal is the star now.' But to be clear. Luke Shaw cost £30 million from Southampton and is the world's highest paid teenager on £100,000-plus a week. Ander Herrera's fee from Athletic Bilbao was a cool £29 million. And they are sitting up there on the table as, at best, extras. They will, however, be pushed to the front of the stage in the coming days by you-know-who as he criticises both of them for differing reasons. For the time being they offer the usual platitudes. 'I don't feel any pressure to come in for [Patrice] Evra. He has been great for the club for ten years, so hopefully I can carry that on,' says Shaw quietly, of the departed left-back. Despite having only just turned nineteen, Shaw is a mature character who already seems to understand that despite the big transfer fee and mammoth wages the challenge for him is only now starting. 'There will always be pressure, but I try not to focus on that, just on my own game on the pitch. With the new gaffer, you have to impress in training and that is what I am looking to do.' Shaw is being billed as the Manchester United and England left-back for the next fifteen years. He is soon to be dubbed overweight by Van Gaal. Herrera, a slim pass-and-move midfielder, who was one of the lead actors in the Moyes–Woodward transfer debacle twelve months ago when he was close to joining, says: 'I can promise to work hard and be a good professional, but there are other midfielders in the team. Between all the players, I am sure we will help the team, but not only me. There are a lot of midfielders and they can play well like me.' His inability to pass straight is soon criticised by Van Gaal.

The media cannot get enough of the Dutchman. Neither will the United support after tomorrow evening. LA Galaxy are to be routed 7–0 in a display of, if not liquid football, then still pretty juicy fare. But before this, one of the privileges of tour life is about to be enjoyed – a level of access to United's pre-match preparation that does not happen at any time during the regulation season. The entire final training session before the match is open. Outside in the warm evening, sitting behind a goal for the first time, Louis van Gaal's style and interaction with his players is witnessed. It is intense. There are traces of the former school teacher, except Van Gaal is more eccentric headmaster whose unpredictability is obviously quietly frightening the Manchester United players despite many being high-class professionals and serial trophy-winners. It is as if they regard the Dutchman with the same level of awe and respect as Sir Alex Ferguson. This is the searing difference between David

Moyes and Louis van Gaal. Moyes, for all his pronouncements of Glaswegian *gallus*, could not hold this bunch of millionaires in his palm as Van Gaal is doing effortlessly here. Moyes was a tracksuit coach but this guy takes the notion of the hands-on manager to a different dimension. He bellows at his players in what seems chaotic fashion, seeking out Phil Jones for a hearty high-five following one impressive finish. There is also a rather loud telling off for poor old Luke Shaw after he unloads a particularly weak shot. The temperature may be hot but Van Gaal's enthusiasm and energy levels are close to the red as Chris Smalling also earns some praise and a hearty smile. It all appears a little intimidating. The Dutchman positions himself next to the right-hand post of the goal and berates and praises each player as they attempt to finish. To say the squad look bemused and awkward – like first-year trainees at the club – would not be an overstatement. But there is also total and utter respect written across the players' faces, whether it be Wayne Rooney or a youngster like Reece James, the twenty-year-old who has yet to make his senior debut for United. 'Aura' is another word for what Van Gaal is showing here in Pasadena. It is instant and impossible to ignore. It has already impressed Ryan Giggs, his assistant, one of the many prominent figures at the club who did not feel quite the same way about David Moyes last season.

The day before there is an audience for the press with Ed Woodward at the Beverly Hills Wilshire for an hour or so. The venue is a deserted bar on the ground floor of the hotel and as usual the hot issue is who United might buy this summer to facilitate the major rebuilding job Van Gaal has to do. The manager has lost three of United's established back four in Patrice Evra, Rio Ferdinand and Nemanja Vidić, who have left for Juventus, Queens Park Rangers and Inter Milan respectively. This cannot be viewed as anything other than a lack of planning on United's part. All of these players were in decline during the last two or three seasons and it was never news they would be leaving. Sir Alex Ferguson is culpable. He should have bought at least one established central defender plus a replacement for Evra before he retired the previous year. It is one of the major problems David Moyes inherited and one that is now passed on to Van Gaal. The Dutchman's answer is to switch to the three-man central defence system that will be witnessed for the first time against LA Galaxy and which will baffle the United players in their opening four matches of the season. United's fitness boffins expect the injury-plagued Jonny Evans, Phil Jones and Chris Smalling to have their rudest seasons in health terms to date. But this prediction proves awry. When the term starts the trio are part of a nightmarish injury run that, by December, reaches forty-one differing problems.

There is also a glaring gap in the manager's squad in midfield, despite Herrera's arrival, plus a sizeable question mark over the wide operators, Antonio Valencia, Nani and Ashley Young. And then there's Danny Welbeck – where might he go? Ditto Tom Cleverley, a midfield lightweight. Oh, and how about Shinji Kagawa, Anderson, Darren Fletcher, Anders Lindegaard, Wilfried Zaha and a few others? Woodward states that Van Gaal is free to break the world record transfer fee should he wish. 'I stand by what I said – there is no budget. We are in a very strong financial position. We can make big signings. That doesn't mean we go and throw money around. Louis is the manager . . . Louis is the one who makes the ultimate decision about who he wants in the squad. I'm not going to force-feed him with a player he hasn't selected.'

To the Dutchman's complaints at his unveiling about United's commercial pursuits, the executive vice-chairman responds: 'We are a different sized club. You have not experienced what being a Manchester United manager is until you have been Manchester United manager.' This should be read as exactly what it is. A polite but firm 'Deal with it, Louis'.

Woodward's willingness to offer a straight answer is a feather in his cap. If asked a similar question about Sir Alex Ferguson, Woodward's predecessor, David Gill, would have done anything to avoid addressing the situation. Instead, Woodward always tries to give a clear response.

The cash Van Gaal can spend dwarfs that available to Arsenal's Arsène Wenger. Jose Mourinho at Chelsea and Manuel Pellegrini, the Manchester City manager, are also in charge of relative poor houses. Should Van Gaal wish, United could break the world-record £86 million Real Madrid paid Tottenham Hotspur for Gareth Bale, and still have £100 million with which to play. Uefa's Financial Fair Play regulations, which relate to revenue and turnover and not incurring a high loss through spending, have left United as the big winners due to the massive income Woodward is generating for the club. Next summer United will be even flusher with the start of a world-record kit deal with Adidas that is worth £750 million over ten years.

*

This is a plotline for another day. There are always a plethora of pressing issues at United. The club is a jam-packed metropolis of stories that are forever morphing and developing and refusing to go away. A current narrative strand is who Van Gaal will appoint as his captain now Nemanja Vidić has left. Robin van Persie was the Dutchman's leader for Holland at the World Cup and Wayne Rooney was promised the position by David Moyes during negotiations for his new contract. Yet Van Gaal's answer at his unveiling was to hint that Michael Carrick was a contender. He would have been a left-field choice, but only because the experienced midfielder, who turns thirty-three this week, has not been on anyone's lips. The more he is considered, especially given Van Gaal's answer – 'My philosophy is not just the football player but the total' – the greater sense the appointment of Carrick makes. But he is out for up to twelve weeks with an ankle injury so is not in the frame for the time being.

It would seem to be between Van Persie and Rooney. Van Gaal is close to Van Persie, an off-field friend he attended matches with while the forward was recuperating from injury ahead of the World Cup. He fits into the 'not just the football player but total' of Van Gaal's 'philosophy' – a word and concept the manager is to mention almost every time he speaks publicly. Van Persie is intelligent, shrewd and can see the bigger picture. He is a family man, in his thirties and has already enjoyed a supreme career. This is also true of Carrick. Away from the actual action both of these footballers impress as much. Rooney would seem to be behind by this measure. His personal life has featured colourful episodes, yet the forward is the most natural leader of United – a firebrand presence in the mould of Roy Keane. Since the Irishman left nine years ago, the armband has gone to Gary Neville, who was vocal but no Keane, and leaders in the passive mould like Ferdinand, Vidić and the deputy, Patrice Evra.

Bryan Robson, a great leader of the club, is available to offer an opinion on the captaincy. He is present at the next stop on the Manchester United circus, a sponsors' event in West Hollywood at the Mondrian Hotel at 8440 Sunset Boulevard. This is an opulent affair that crystallises where Manchester United see themselves in the world. Around a pool area that looks out over the hills of LA free Champagne and wine is on offer. The women are in expensive evening attire and the men glide around the place like models. Everyone is looking to see if they are being looked at to see if they are being looked at. Around the corner is Fox Studios and Paramount Studios, with Dodgers Stadium, Rodeo Drive and the Getty Museum also near to this prime slab of real estate perched on the Sunset Strip.

But Manchester United are not here to dream. They're here to make money from dreams. Into this scene walks Robson, the 'Captain Marvel' who hung on long enough to be a member of the 1992–93 and 1993–94 Premiership-winning teams. In addition to who should be the next leader of Manchester United, he can address the leadership vacancy with England. Steven Gerrard's retirement means Rooney is also being talked up as the next captain of his country. 'There is no standout England captain,' Robson says. 'Even a few years ago, you had the likes of John Terry, Rio Ferdinand, Gerrard and Frank Lampard who could have been captain. There was a decision to be made over which one you would go with as captain because they were all strong candidates. Yes, it does worry me a bit for England's future.' This is a surprise. Where is the United-centric backing of Rooney? It eventually comes. 'You look at it and it is a difficult one. You want somebody who is a talker on the pitch, somebody who can organise and I just think it is difficult for a forward to do that. But if you look at the England set-up at the moment, the candidates are probably Joe Hart, Gary Cahill, because he will be in the team, and Wayne Rooney. And the only one who really stands out is Wayne. If Wayne was to be selected as captain, it might give him a real boost where he really feels he needs to lead by example.'

Eight days after Louis van Gaal took over, the manager watches the first United team he has selected trounce LA Galaxy 7–0 on a humid night in Pasadena. The match may pit the glamour MLS franchise against the world's biggest club, but it remains a friendly. And yet 86,423 attend. Here is the pull of Manchester United. Van Gaal intrigues everyone as he names Darren Fletcher as captain and not Rooney. He appeared the obvious candidate considering Van Persie is resting following Holland's World Cup campaign. The match features two goals for the twenty-year-old Reece James on his debut, but it is nearly delayed as the manager and his squad come close to arriving late after being caught up in traffic. Again.

This opening game is also the first sighting of 5–3–2 or 3–5–2, a formation that is to become a prime subject for debate and analysis. Tonight it has Luke Shaw and Antonio Valencia as the wingbacks, with Chris Smalling, Phil Jones and Jonny Evans as the centre-backs. Van Gaal is understandably happy and keen to talk about the system. Of the switch to 5–3–2 he says: 'It was not just the goals, but the beautiful attacks. When you want to change a system, you must start at once. We don't have time to prepare for other things. The other system they can play is 4–3–3 and they have played it for many years.' This is a puzzle because United, really, have been in a 4–2–3–1 shape in recent seasons. 'I can change back if the system doesn't work. With the quality of the players we have, I can play 4–3–3 with three strikers on the bench, but want to play with two strikers.' Privately, though, Van Gaal is unsure if he can play 4–3–3 at the moment because of the lack of pace among his front players. In the blizzard of shapes put out by the Dutchman when the new campaign begins, 4–3–3 is to be rare. Instead, he experiments with 4–2–3–1, 4–2–2–2, 4–1–3–2 and just about any other combination of 4, 3, 2 and 1. Also emerging is Van Gaal-speak, a unique philology that has him directly translating from Dutch to English. He finishes a contented presser with an illustration of this. 'We have four number tens, so the selection is not balanced in my eyes. I have decided to play this system because of the quality of the players. But if we lose, I can change back to another system.' It may sound awkward but everyone knows what he means by 'changing back to another system'.

The tour has moved on to the state of Colorado and the altitude of Denver. It is a hot evening as the players train. These are some of the early sessions under the new manager so there is a magnified value to witnessing them. After seeing Van Gaal's performance in Pasadena they can be filed under: 'Not to be missed.' At the Rose Bowl, in the final work-out before the hiding administered to LA Galaxy, Van Gaal scolded Luke Shaw and this drew attention to the left-back and his physique: a cruiserweight build, reminiscent of Wayne Rooney. Now, as Shaw trots around the home of the NFL's Denver Broncos, comes confirmation of the impression made in Pasadena. He looks, well, beefy. And this is a player whose game is enhanced by his searing pace, an asset that was a prime reason United bought him. For Southampton he would regularly tear up opposing defenders, and his skyward rise last season caused Roy Hodgson to take him to Brazil for the World Cup. The young defender does not make the starting XI for United's 3–2 win over Roma the next day, though he comes on at half-time. Wayne Rooney scores twice and Ander Hererra once, but United are disjointed despite the victory. There is an embarrassing moment in the second half for Ben Amos, the third- or fourth-choice goalkeeper, who is chipped from seventy yards by the replacement Miralem Pjanić to spark a late revival that nearly claims the Serie A club a draw. Sam Johnstone, United's goalkeeper before Amos replaces him at the break, also makes errors. So, too, does the young defender, Tyler Blackett. And the touch and poise of captain for the night, Tom Cleverley, desert him. Juan Mata and Rooney are also in clumsy form. So Van Gaal may have dished out his first half-time rollicking. Still, a win is a win and the party flies on to the capital of America.

A few days later in Washington, DC, ahead of the meeting with Inter Milan, Shaw is out on the practice field working alone, running along one side of FedEx Field and hitting crosses into the area from the left, before sitting out parts of the team session. Before what is the second International Champions Cup match, Van Gaal, rather startlingly, explains: 'Shaw is OK, but I am always a trainer-coach who sees individuals and what they need. He needs to be fit and is not very fit, not fit enough to do what I want. He needs to train individually until he is fit.' Given the summer Shaw is involved in, first with England at the World Cup, now straight on to this tour, the obvious question is, why is he not in prime condition? The lad is still a teenager, so he should be teeming with youthful zest. This is put to the manager. 'I cannot judge that, but I see what I see. I have spoken with him and we have made a programme for him. He agreed with me,' says Van Gaal. 'How long? That we have to see, but that I don't know. I have heard good messages from Strud [Tony Strudwick, the fitness coach], but we have to see.' This is a bit of a pickle for Shaw. The next day, before kick-off, there is further intrigue as he is not even listed on the club website as a reserve. The custom for these games is to have all players who are not in the XI on the bench. Yet Shaw does take part in the warm-up and limbers up those £30 million-priced muscles, and after the half-time break comes on for the second match in a row. United's website apparently made a mistake in not including Shaw on their team sheet, it emerges. After Inter are beaten 5–3 on penalties following a goalless draw, Van Gaal does not spare him, saying he was fortunate to play. 'He is working very hard. He was lucky. Normally we would play Reece James but he was injured. So I asked Luke if he would play. He did a very hard training session this morning but he still did very good,' says the Dutchman. This is not the best start to Shaw's United career and the fascination now is how he responds. And, indeed, how others players respond to Van Gaal's (seemingly) scattergun man-management approach.

Sir Alex Ferguson reacts furiously to Nani's red card during the 2-1 Champions League last-16 second leg loss to Real Madrid at Old Trafford. The manager also signalled his discontent with Wayne Rooney by dropping the striker for the vital tie, 5 March 2013. © *Dani Pozo/AFP/Getty Images*

David Moyes smiles happily in front of the dug-out after being officially appointed as manager. But the Scot was to find the Old Trafford hot-seat uncomfortable throughout his brief ten month tenure, 5 July 2013. © *Martin Rickett/PA Archive/ Press Association Images*

LEFT: Wayne Rooney arrives in Thailand for the club's pre-season tour. He would soon return home due to injury, 11 July 2013. © *Pornchai Kittiwongsakul/AFP/ Getty Images*

BELOW: David Moyes and Ed Woodward struggled throughout summer 2013 to strengthen the squad and it was not long before cracks began to show. © *Eamon and James Clarke/Empics Entertainment*

Moyes found it difficult to convince his new Manchester United players to buy into his tactics and on-field strategy. © *Adam Davy/Empics Sport*

LEFT: Robin van Persie was particularly hurt by Ferguson's retirement. © *Philip Oldham/Landov/ Press Association Images*

BELOW: The dismal 2-0 Champions League last-16 first leg defeat at Olympiacos was the night Moyes's sacking by the United executive became a *fait accompli.* © *Adam Davy/Empics Sport*

The Grim Reaper at Goodison Park may have been a joke but there were no laughs for David Moyes as a 2-0 loss at Everton sealed his fate, 20 April 2014.
© *Action Images / Carl Recine Livepic*

RIGHT: Louis van Gaal instantly asserted his authority on taking over. Here he faces the media during his official unveiling, 17 July 2014. © *Jon Super/AP/ Press Association Images*

BELOW: Van Gaal appointed Giggs as his assistant and wasted little time shaking up team tactics and shape, switching to a 3-5-2 formation on the summer tour of America. © *Nicholas Kamm/ AFP/Getty Images*

LEFT: Radamel Falcao was the billboard name in Louis van Gaal's Galactico era. But he flopped badly after arriving on a season-long £16m loan from Monaco. © *Valery Hache/AFP/ Getty Images*

ABOVE: Ángel Di María cost a British record £59.7m fee from Real Madrid but was the second Galactico to struggle. © *Chris Brunskill/Getty Images*

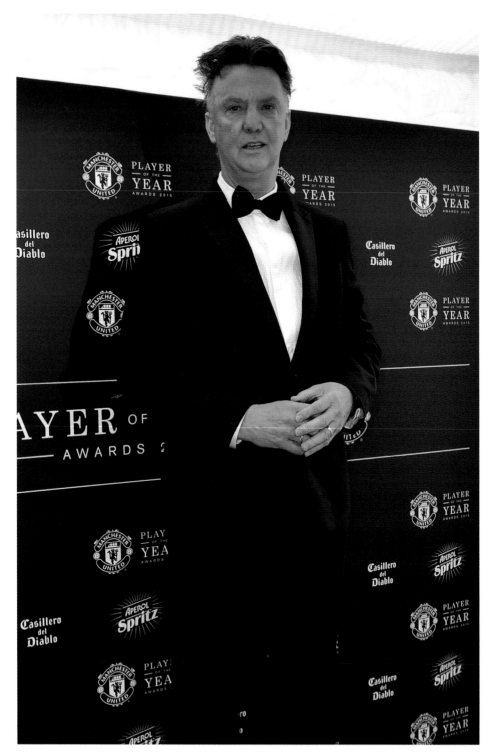

Louis van Gaal made a grandstanding speech at the end of season Player of the Year awards which indicated how comfortable he was after a season at the club.
© *Mirrorpix*

On Shinji Kagawa, a Ferguson favourite who could find no regular place under David Moyes, Van Gaal is at it again, damning him with faint praise. 'I know him from Germany and he played number ten there. I want to play him number six or number eight in our system and I have tried that. I want to try him number ten because he wants to play there. He played better there than he did the other positions.' The Japanese was indeed a touch anonymous when he came on as a replacement, though he did convert one of United's five penalties. The shuffling of positions and personnel, as well as formations, becomes a characteristic Van Gaal trait once the season starts. A realisation begins to form that the supposedly Mr Decisive may actually be a bit of a ditherer. At the moment, though, Van Gaal is still firmly in the honeymoon phase, so all the shape-shifting means the manager is viewed as a decisive man of action.

Two days earlier the chance for the first intimate meet-and-greet with Van Gaal – the only one until next summer's tour – comes when the manager holds his tour sit-down. Precisely a year and eleven days after the showdown at the Cut Bar & Grill in Sydney with David Moyes, the audience is at the Mandarin Hotel, the team's base in Washington. It is luxurious and suave and the kind of place where the lounge is gold and platinum and there is a footman for every need. There are even staff solely to polish the chandeliers. Downstairs in an empty conference room Louis van Gaal's arrival is awaited. When he walks in alongside Karen Shotbolt, and takes a seat at a round table, the buzz in the air is the omnipresent one that accompanies quizzing all the heavyweight managers. The slight doubt that can be felt is whether this vastly-experienced operator, accustomed to near-absolute primacy and control, will cede enough ground for true questioning to be allowed. Who knows what will occur. This is not the first time in the ring with Van Gaal. In May, when it became clear he was to be appointed at United, Van Gaal was preparing Holland for the World Cup at their national team's training camp at Hoenderloo, which is around an hour's drive south-east of Amsterdam in the Dutch countryside. There, despite the strict understanding that there should be no questions about the Manchester United job, entry was allowed into the complex. What unfolded was revealing about LvG The Man. After morning training Van Gaal walked through the mixed zone and, despite having brushed off a BBC reporter the day before, he was polite enough to stop and answer questions. This was the first surprise. It would have been simpler for Van Gaal to carry on walking. He had not yet officially been announced as United's manager and he had the World Cup to focus on. But no. He stopped and there was a smile and immediately the sense was of a man who was enjoying the action – who, whatever the day-to-day ups and downs, *loves* being at the centre of the action. He also softened the atmosphere straightaway with his body language and demeanour. It offered a clue about how Van Gaal gets players to respond to him. Standing there, waiting for the questions, he *knew* what was coming next but did not care. In fact, the converse seemed true. He *wanted* to be asked about the future after Holland, *his* future. There was a feeling, too, that he was waiting to see how smart or clumsy the questions would be. Van Gaal was constantly judging, constantly evaluating. Again, this quality must keep his players on their toes.

So Van Gaal waited and the questions came. They were designed to be subtle enough to ensure he did not stomp off but still addressed the reason for being there. Asked how important it was that his concentration be solely on Holland, he said: 'That is always the case that we want to be focused on the competition. One of my players [Ron Vlaar] told me in the morning that his club was up for sale – Aston Villa. So what is he thinking about Aston Villa? It's logical that everyone has their problems or maybe no problems. For example, I have no problems. You keep focused because of the training sessions, because of the team meetings and tactical meetings. And because of the passion of the players who play at the world championship and also for the trainer-coach. It's the same. I have invested a lot of time in this so you can imagine how very important [the World Cup is] for me and the players. I've been in football for forty years. In three months I'm sixty-three. So I can manage the situation.'

And with this Van Gaal was off. Here was a charm offensive *and* a glimpse of what had taken him through his career and how he would continue when landing at United later in the summer. It illustrated that his autocratic style has a personable streak running through it. The trick is to read him right, understanding when to push further and when to regroup and go again. Now, sitting in the basement of the Mandarin Hotel, the first question he is asked is the obvious one. 'Is Ferguson's legacy not a daunting one?' Answer: 'The club are thinking that I am the man who can wear this legacy.' Question: 'You stated that you joined a Manchester United that is "broken". Can you expand on that, please?' Answer: 'I don't think it is a hard word because I think when you are seventh, at that time the team is unsatisfied and without confidence, and when you are like that you are broken. So now they have me: a new manager, so new chances for the players and they want to show themselves unbelievably . . . We have to make a way of playing football that is not the same as before, and that is difficult for them. They have to perform under [pressure]. They have to decide within one second [what to do] and that is not easy.'

Van Gaal is merely warming up here, the command performance is ahead. The cocktail is being mixed: grins and prickliness. As if he could lose his temper at any given moment on any given question but, actually, may only be having a joke – may only be teasing. Or vice versa. Or none of the above. It is confusing, challenging and invigorating and what is understood instantly is how he can command a dressing room of thoroughbred footballers who have won everything and who are one-man franchises, far richer at twenty-five than Van Gaal was at that age. To see him address a group of sweaty, blowing-hard, highly-tuned players at half-time of a crucial game must be quite a spectacle. When Karen Shotbolt decides it really is time to move the manager on, Van Gaal stands and as he departs the stage offers a dazzling smile. 'Interesting eh? Interesting.'

There has been shadow boxing, sparring, a few feints and jabs but no stingers or heavy blows from either side. The main thing has been fun – it has been enjoyable to sit down and go toe-to-toe for a while. Van Gaal has a sense of mischief, and also an ability not to take himself too seriously. Two qualities he is not always credited with. The performance has been gentle, really, though there were hints of the manager who will leave a confused impression with some of his utterings in the months ahead. But despite this there is a certainty in his own brand of management methodology that floods his speech. Like his rival, Jose Mourinho, he has a self-assured plan, describing the way he coaches as being in the players' 'brains and not the legs'. He explains: 'You have seen my exercises with all the tactical [approaches] and without the tactical [approaches]. I am not for running for its own sake and I am for running with the ball, but they like that, of course. But the most important thing is they have to know why we do things and when they do, the football player is not playing intuitively. A lot of players are playing intuitively and I want them to think and know why they do something. That's a process that is difficult at first and in the first three months. It takes time. When we survive the first three months, it will be the same as for me as at Bayern [Munich]. After the first three months we were sixth or seventh, and we were third in the Champions League group. We had to win at Juventus and we won that game [4–1] and that was the turning point.' That was the 2009–10 season in which Van Gaal claimed the Bundesliga, German Cup and made it all the way to the Champions League final before losing to Mourinho's Inter Milan.

The quote from Van Gaal that really stands out – 'We have to make a way of playing that isn't the same as before, and that is difficult for them' – takes the mind back twelve months and a comparison with David Moyes at his sit-down when he said: 'There is an element of fear that has to come with managing a club like this.' Moyes talked of being scared. Van Gaal talks about the difficulty for the players having to adjust to him. Just as he maintains the formidable Manchester United must adjust to him over commercial strategy. Van Gaal does not give a flying whatsit about anything unless it can help the team. This is how it has to be if he is to manage this club. Beginning, middle, end of story. 'I don't say it's a dream to manage Manchester United,' Van Gaal says. 'Because I am sixty-two and I know what I can do and I think Manchester United know what I can do. I am not a child anymore, I know what I can do. But it's fantastic because not any coach can work with the biggest clubs.'

The Manchester United fans will lap this up after the travails and derision of the Moyes campaign. And Mourinho, the champions at Manchester City and all the rest of the Premier League will have to chew and digest it, long and hard, until the new season comes. Then the simple question will have to be answered: is Louis van Gaal going to follow David Moyes and become the second dismal failure in two years and lead to the appointment of a third Manchester United manager in three seasons? This is what Sir Alex Ferguson has done. He has left behind a fear that a palsied decline is afoot. Everyone wants to know if hiring Van Gaal is only going to take the institution further along the road to being mothballed. The short answer, from the evidence gleaned at the Mandarin Hotel on a sunshine-bleached Monday afternoon in Washington on 28 July 2014, is no. Van Gaal seems like the right man at the right time to pick United up from where Ferguson left the place, that peculiar state of being on its knees *because* of his greatness. From this perspective David Moyes has fulfilled a crucial role. Being 'the man after the man' is a cliché for a reason. Perhaps this thankless work should draw gratitude and garlands from the United masses. With no Moyes failure there would be no Van Gaal at the club now.

The Dutchman's *modus operandi* seems to be to serve notice in every act, large or miniature, that this is his Manchester United battleship now. If it is to go down he'll still be straddling the canons, saluting and grinning.

In Los Angeles Van Gaal took one look at the tour plans okayed by Ryan Giggs when David Moyes's interim replacement, and ripped them up. He deemed the training base at the StubHub Center in south LA too far away from the Beverly Wilshire Hotel and ordered staff to book the nearby Holiday Inn so the players could rest between double sessions. He did the same in Denver and now in Washington. Van Gaal has been tinkering with training times and daily routines as much as possible. The attention to detail, the meticulousness, and the sense that Van Gaal has oversight of everything, is in supreme control only a few days into the job, is impressing the squad and the rest of the club's staff. Stories are emerging of Van Gaal's insistence on punctuality. One player has spoken of how a team-mate had to be covered for when he turned up late for lunch. It was an act that will have increased the *esprit de corps*. And given that this is the opposite of what was intended – Van Gaal's idea is that by being punctual the team bonds, yet in being late the bonding occurs because they are helping out a team-mate – somehow fits neatly with the Dutchman's unpredictable persona. This particular player was not unduly late, but late is late for Van Gaal. He has also adopted round tables on tour for meals to ensure a more communal feel, the manager sitting at his own top table with staff. He is building his 'total' world around the players, to produce a platform from which the 'total' player will grow. The fear and respect and fascination of the players is electric and there is a crackle whenever he enters the room. The Dutchman instantly 'owns' the space and mood.

On to Detroit. Michigan's most populous city has been hit by the hardest of times and the buildings and streets have the look of old United States, as if the 1970s are on a constant reel here, filmed in buttered sepia CinemaScope. In nearby Ann Arbor it is the day before the Manchester United of Wayne Rooney takes on the Real Madrid of Cristiano Ronaldo. If a cliché was needed to bill this then The Clash of the Titans would suffice. Open training at Michigan State Stadium – a.k.a. the Big House as the place holds 110,000 and is America's largest sports arena – is buzzing with a crowd that blends a prep-school contingent, a jock-athlete constituency and a confederacy of the younger. On the near touchline a rare sight is afforded when a real-life (and usually reclusive) Glazer (namely Avi) is spied, a sure sign that this is the showpiece event of the tour.

The following day United beat Real 3–1 in front of 109,318 fans, which considering 'soccer' is way down the nation's sporting hierarchy, and the state of Michigan has no Major League Soccer team, deserves the kind of 'wow' uttered by a former manager just over a year ago. A goal from Javier Hernández and two from Ashley Young secure the victory before a record crowd for a match in the States, beating the 101,799 who saw the 1984 Olympic gold medal decider at Pasadena's Rose Bowl. It is a result that ensures the stakeholders' dream final. Why are the Premier League, Major League Soccer and the US Soccer Federation all happy? Because the mighty Liverpool await the mighty Manchester United in the final of the International Champions Cup in Miami in a few days' time. Not that Louis van Gaal knows. In tremendous eccentric uncle-style, he asks: 'It's Liverpool in the final? OK, thank you. It's also good for English football and very important that two teams from the Premier League will play in the final. But also for them it is preparation time. It doesn't say anything [about next season] but it is better to win than lose.'

He may be out of the loop on United's next opponents, but Louis van Gaal has never been so on-message as he is now about United's commercial imperative. All of a sudden the Dutchman is hailing the enormous crowds who have watched the club on the tour and recognising that the victory takes United to Florida, the fifth state on the royal procession. Listening to Van Gaal this evening he sounds like an evangelist for a newly discovered world. 'It's amazing,' he says of the super-sized Big House capacity. 'Within fourteen days we have played for more than 300,000 fans. We also had the chance to meet the American fans, of course. These are very good points.' This is about as tender as Mr Aloysius Paulus Maria van Gaal becomes.

As always, the football is the thing and Van Gaal wants to speak about United's opening goal, scored by Ashley Young. 'I think that in the news all over the world the broadcasters will show the first goal. It was a fantastic goal. All the team has touched the ball I think.' This slice of football aesthetic came in a smoothly-slick sequence after twenty-one minutes that ends in four smart passes that allow Young to open the scoring. Darren Fletcher prods the ball to Wayne Rooney, who plays a one-two with the Scot. Fletcher plays in Danny Welbeck, who recycles the ball to Young, who slots home. This is the kind of stylish move that offers encouragement for the coming season.

The injured Chris Smalling and a still not match-fit Luke Shaw apart, Van Gaal selected what has emerged as his first-choice XI on tour. The goalkeeper is David de Gea. The centre-backs, Phil Jones, Jonny Evans and Michael Keane (for Smalling). The wing-backs are Antonio Valencia and Ashley Young (for Shaw). Darren Fletcher and Ander Herrera are the dedicated midfielders. Juan Mata the number ten. And Wayne Rooney and Danny Welbeck the strikers. Fletcher was United's best player against Real and he helped create the winner scored by the substitute, Javier Hernández, by feeding Shinji Kagawa whose curled cross was finished by the Mexican. United old boy Cristiano Ronaldo, who had a fifteen-minute cameo at the end of the game, did little, though the Portuguese was cheered enthusiastically every time he deigned to touch or even go near the ball.

United follow this win with success in Miami, where Liverpool are beaten 3–1 in the final and Van Gaal claims the International Champions Cup. Thus the US tour is the very best of starts for the manager and his new squad. And for Ed Woodward and the Glazers and United's devotees across the globe. Five victories, sixteen goals, and a Theatre of Dreams-full of $$$$s is the yield by the time the whole festival of red touches back down in Manchester.

Chapter 14

A Season in the Red

Question: Can you do better than David Moyes, Louis?
Answer (after four games): No.

The new season approaches and this is the moment for predictions about whether Louis van Gaal will be a prince or a pauper of the technical area. The manager's *modus operandi*, his faith, his managerial DNA, is all about 'the philosophy'. So now is the time to see this in action. When the real matches start and Van Gaal has to deal with the trench warfare that is English football's nine-month campaign. He also has to appoint a captain and which of the main contenders, Wayne Rooney and Robin van Persie, he plumps for will say much about not just Van Gaal the manager but Van Gaal the man. David Moyes had given Rooney the nod during contract discussions, yet judging by Van Gaal's decision to share the captaincy around on tour he may be investigating why the player came to be viewed so lowly by Sir Alex Ferguson. To put it another way, if Van Gaal is all about the player as 'human being', maybe the full Rooney persona falls short of what is required as the on-field personification of the Dutchman. In these terms Van Persie seems the no-brainer option. Van Gaal and Van Persie were as thick as thieves during the run-up to the World Cup in Brazil. Van Persie, though, understands that their professional relationship is the basis of any understanding between them. Yet given Van Persie was Van Gaal's captain at the World Cup, and after the jock-athlete slapping of hands on the touchline between RvP and LvG in celebration of the striker's swallow-dive header against Spain in a group game, Rooney would seem to be the outsider.

This need to know the 'human' behind the footballer would be given a whole chapter in the Van Gaal managerial manifesto, a tome that could be called My Philosophy (And How It Will Make Manchester United Great Again). David Moyes's equivalent work would be: My, Our, Anyone's Really, Please, Hope (And I Have A Six-year Contract To Work This Out). These are two contrasting schools. Philosophy versus Hope. Each concept can be as vague and nebulous as the other and yet there is no argument that Van Gaal is dealing in a far grander abstraction. *Philosophy* just sounds more sophisticated and intelligent than good old-fashioned *hope*. But what 'My Philosophy' actually is seems a little unclear. That is a kind way of putting it. A less diplomatic offering might be that no one has a tiny clue what the hell Louis van Gaal means. Not at this stage, anyway. He *is* trying to explain, though. The manager wants to know about the player as a 'human being' and to train their brains not legs. Of most import is that his United squad, as with all his charges at his previous clubs, 'have to know why we do things and when they do, the football player is not playing intuitively'. Back in the real world, with the *cognoscenti* and media demanding to be impressed by Manchester United, the problem is that there is no real discernible style of performance. Philosophising is fine, but what about how the team will play? Van Gaal talks of the first three months being difficult. But the scenario could be far worse: in three months of struggle Manchester United could be way off the pace and Louis van Gaal in deep trouble. After the first six league games – let alone three months – David Moyes was already in the mire. The side were twelfth and West Bromwich Albion fans were regaling him about how they could sack whom they wanted. At Old Trafford. Before a stadium full of stunned United enthusiasts.

Manchester United should – and have to, for Van Gaal's job security – finish in the top four, but this will not be easy. King Louis. The Iron Tulip. Manchester United's saviour. A more appropriate moniker might be The Man With The Broad Shoulders. The encouraging news is that the Dutchman certainly has a pair. And he is not bashful in telling everyone about them as each day, each week, shows more and more of his chutzpah, brains and ego. All these qualities are required as Van Gaal surveys a squad which still has worrying holes in it ahead of a season in which the team could conceivably struggle again. The challenge is to fix the mess left by the doomed David Moyes's tenure and somehow make Champions League qualifiers out of last term's seventh-place failures. United's players are lining up to claim a twenty-first title can be won, but their manager markedly is not. Van Gaal would never say it publicly, but fourth place will do just fine at the close of his inaugural campaign.

It is 11 August and three weeks remain of the transfer window and there is a pressing need for further squad strengthening. So far only Luke Shaw and Ander Herrera have been added. And once any new players arrive, there is the further crucial requirement for them to adapt to the manager's new shape, new process, and, yes, new *philosophy*. This is a whole lot of change. United need midfielders and defenders, and to somehow make the cumbersome-looking 3–5–2 an aesthetic delight. All the cavalier adjectives associated with United and their buccaneering 'attack, attack, attack' heritage, jar with this awkward 3–5–2. If it does not scan on the page, how can it do so on the field and bewitch opponents with a fluid rhyme and rhythm? Who can imagine 3–5–2 continuing the tradition, the charisma, of the storied ranks of butterfly-killers – George Best, Eric Cantona, Paul Scholes, Ryan Giggs, Cristiano Ronaldo, Wayne Rooney et al? Only Louis van Gaal at the moment, it seems. Yet even a cursory look at the Dutchman's previous sides suggests they are workable rather than gangs of operatic performers whose ninety-minute offerings constantly soar.

Ajax's Daley Blind is a midfielder (and utility defender) and it sounds like he could soon become a United player. 'I am happy here in Amsterdam. But if there comes another club I will have to think about it and then we will see,' he says. 'I am happy here' is the modern-day 'come-and-get-me' plea in an age of obfuscation. To understand what a footballer really means about his future examine closely what is said. If the opinion is a clever way of indicating that leaving could not be further from the truth, when actually saying nothing like that at all, then Blind's 'I am happy here' does just this. If he says: 'I will never, ever, ever leave Ajax', then maybe, just maybe, this is different. Not that Blind or any player can be blamed. In what other business is an employee the subject of speculation and questioning about where he might be working next?

The following day it emerges that Van Gaal is keen on Marcos Rojo, the Sporting Lisbon defender who starred in Argentina's run to the World Cup final. 'Sixteen million pounds', it seems, is the price for Rojo, who is a tough-tackling, left-sided defender who can operate at centre-back, is pacey, and at only twenty-four fits snugly the ideal of a Van Gaal player. Another suggestion is that Van Gaal has not yet given up on Ángel Di María after the Real Madrid forward's on-off transfer to Paris Saint-Germain has finally fallen through. On talkSPORT comes a klaxon of a hint regarding Di María. Carlo Ancelotti's assistant, Paul Clement, is admitting he could still leave the club. 'Things can very quickly change – the window doesn't close until the end of this month. But currently we have twenty outfield players and three goalkeepers, so it is not a big, big squad,' Clement says. This is about as subtle as Blind's effort. This time the red light is in the opening sentence. And this is followed up by Clement hinting that if Di María is sold, the high transfer fee can be used to invest in the greater numbers needed to ensure squad depth.

Tonight it is United's final pre-season friendly, against Valencia. In front of 58,381 fans Van Gaal is making his Old Trafford bow. He is certainly popular, at one point high-fiving fans in an endless chain when walking along the turf towards the bench, waving and beaming in his tailored club suit. Valencia are beaten 2–1, the much-maligned Marouane Fellaini grabbing a late winner (after ninety-one minutes, no less; Fergie-time) to the now not-so-ironic cheers of the crowd who have previously booed and sarcastically cheered the Belgian. A year ago David Moyes lost his first game here, 3–1 to Sevilla.

The victory is followed by some significant news: the captaincy has been announced and Wayne Rooney has been given the armband. Here is it then: a flagship statement regarding Louis van Gaal, the manager, the man, and his philosophy. Just as the effervescent Ed Woodward offers a window into the Glazers' thinking by being their chosen one, so the appointment of Rooney reveals how Van Gaal views his team, his mission, ahead of his first season. He says: 'For me it's always very important the choice of captain. Wayne has shown a great attitude towards everything he does. I have been very impressed by his professionalism and his attitude to training and to my philosophy. He is a great inspiration to the younger members of the team and I believe he will put his heart and soul into his captaincy role. Darren Fletcher will become the vice-captain. Darren is a natural leader and will captain the team when Wayne isn't playing. Darren is a very experienced player and a very popular member of the dressing room, I know he will work well alongside Wayne.'

The decision caps a startling reversal of fortunes for the lad from Croxteth: Rooney would never have been made captain under Sir Alex Ferguson. A pariah maybe, but never the leader of the band. Rooney was heading only one way under Ferguson and that was towards the exit. Now, after Van Gaal's anointment, Rooney is rather chuffed, beaming with the 'honour' of being named 'captain of this great club'. Will the decision affect Van Persie? Could Van Gaal's self-declared off-field friend react adversely? He is surely too professional. But, anyway, Van Gaal will not give a hoot. In Rooney he has identified a player who has always been vocal and a winner. Given how Rooney's status plummeted under Ferguson, and how his esteem dropped with the other players, it will be interesting to see how they respond to his promotion. The fact that Louis van Gaal has backed him will boost Rooney in their eyes. With others having departed in the year since Ferguson stepped away there is also a fresh dynamic. David de Gea, Phil Jones, Chris Smalling, Jonny Evans, Michael Carrick, Rafael da Silva, Darren Fletcher, Ashley Young, Antonio Valencia and Robin van Persie are among the players who have been at the club the longest. And apart from Van Persie, who may or may not feel slighted, the rest of this bunch should accept Rooney instantly.

Rooney does not play well against Valencia. But then neither does the side. Van Gaal calls it the 'worst' display of his six matches in charge. Throughout the match United are as tepid as they have been under Van Gaal. They managed just two chances in the opening forty-five minutes before livening up a touch after the break. The first goalscoring opportunity is a weak Phil Jones header that the visiting goalkeeper, Diego Alves, collects easily; the second a dubious penalty won by Rooney, who strikes it against the right post. As on tour, heart has been required to pull United through against the unimpressive Spaniards. The Van Gaal factor, though, means there is still more optimism than twelve months ago when David Moyes's United were beaten by Sevilla. But more is required. A lot more.

Rooney may not have glittered on his debut as captain and Van Gaal will be asked about the advisability of awarding him the honour. But this is a side-issue. The real business is that on the cusp of the new season, the second since Sir Alex Ferguson left, there is a real fascination at what is going to happen. The Dutchman's aura and résumé means he must surely succeed. If not then it will be an even bigger deal than the failure of David Moyes.

It is 15 August, just gone 2.30 p.m. in the Jimmy Murphy Centre, the building next to the first-team pitches at Carrington, and Louis van Gaal is sitting before the media throng ahead of the first match of the season, which is at home against Swansea City. The disappointing Valencia display is felt in the slight tension in the room and there is a crackle as the manager starts to speak. The pose is self-assured, his tone even, the delivery of word relaxed, nonchalant almost. In all of this, and the responses he offers, Van Gaal looks and sounds every bit the deeply experienced campaigner that he is. A man who has sat through countless press conferences and fielded hundreds of thousands of questions. He looks like he is happy to be here *and* that he would rather be anywhere else.

The first answer he offers is to a simple question. 'How ready are you?' Van Gaal is calm, yet straight into prickly, awkward mode. 'I am not ready but my squad is ready, that is more important. I am not nervous or worried. The most important thing is that my squad is ready and not I. I don't play football.' Rooney's timid performance against Valencia remains a hot topic, and Van Gaal's critique of him adds to the intrigue when he says his first outing as captain 'may have been a bit much for him'.

What may really be *too* much is the season-long challenge to cope with the role of Manchester United manager that begins at 5 p.m. on Saturday after a shock-inducing 2–1 defeat by Swansea. It is their first opening-day home defeat in the Premier League. And it is the direst possible start as United attempt to regain a Champions League position. Remember, they have no European football this term to test resources and stamina. This is the first season there is to be no midweek continental lights shining on Old Trafford since the 1989–90 campaign. That is a quarter of a century ago. For United this is the ultimate embarrassment. Since English clubs were allowed back into European football following the ban after the Heysel Stadium tragedy of 1985, United have been omnipresent, winning the now defunct Cup-Winners' Cup in 1991, the first season back, and two Champions Leagues (1999 and 2008). They also reached two more finals of the premier competition, in 2009 and 2011. Ferguson was always honest about the club's performance in the European Cup, believing that a total of three triumphs was not enough for United. He was correct. But what the knight guaranteed, at the very least, was that United would be a factor year in, year out in the Champions League. Moyes could not even drag the club into the Europa League and it was this, really, that cost him the job.

So let no mistake be made. This cannot happen for a second successive season for all kinds of reasons. Van Gaal understands this and will state it throughout his first year in charge. A top-four finish and the reclaiming of Champions League football is the bare minimum required. This is what he has been instructed to achieve and what he dare not fail to pull off. There is prestige attached to Champions League football. There are blue-chip sponsors whose deals have lucrative incentives triggered by participation. And, being in the competition acts as a magnet to attract the star talent who can help the club actually compete for the trophy.

Thus, when the Old Trafford masses, excited by the brave new dawn, see their beloved red men go down to Swansea – Wayne Rooney scores United's goal – a major inquest begins. Afterwards Van Gaal actually employs the adjective 'smashed' when referring to how the defeat will affect the players' confidence. Yet the master of philosophy shows no lack of faith in his preaching: 'We have to know it is only one game of many games and you shall not be the champion at this moment, you shall be the champion in May.' Champion in May? That's brave. There's more of the cod-pugnacious stuff. 'I have said before that because of our wins in the United States and against Valencia the expectation is so high, and I have seen in the first half a lot of players very nervous, making the wrong choices, and that is a pity. These players have to get used to that expectation because this is Manchester United. You have to cope with that pressure. I have said to them in the dressing room, "I cannot say you didn't do your very best, unbelievable work, fantastic mentality, but reaching the level is difficult, not only running but using your brain and then you can play like a team". In that, we have failed today.' The problem is that many of these players were bulls in the opposition's china shops under Sir Alex Ferguson and now Van Gaal is bewailing how they have to become accustomed (again) to the 'expectation' of representing the club.

In the context of Moyes's awful campaign, and Van Gaal being heralded as the Zeus-like saviour, the sight of him abandoning the three-man defence he worked on all summer and reverting to four at the back – as he does at half-time – is far from reassuring for fans. What must this do to the players' confidence in their new manager, too? This is the unnerving balance the Dutchman has to strike: he has to be decisive and back himself to be able to change course during training or during a match, but the change has to work. Against Swansea, discarding the three-man defence to revert to the normal two centre-back system obviously does not. The twenty-year-old Tyler Blackett, who has been at United since he was eight, made his debut alongside Chris Smalling and Phil Jones as one of three centre-backs. At the break United are 1–0 down and Blackett's baptism of fire becomes hotter as he is told by Van Gaal to get his head around playing with Smalling as one of two centre-backs in a flat back four. The youngster ends up on the losing side. Any effect this may have on Blackett is collateral damage, of course, but what might this have done for his confidence? Is he one whose spirit may have been especially 'smashed'? Jesse Lingard also suffers the nightmare of making his debut and suffering a twenty-fourth-minute knee injury, and is not seen in United colours again during the season.

Another take on this is that Van Gaal has been warning that time is required, he signed a three-year deal after all, and that not too much notice should be taken of the unbeaten run in pre-season. Back in the here-and-now Premier League world, the supporters, neutrals, armies of pundits, amateur tacticians, psychologists, football shamans, soothsayers, sages and laptop twitter warriors all want to know what this loss means.

And they want to know now. After the match, Van Gaal admits he needs better players. 'That is not a question because I knew that before this game,' he says. This last comment becomes worth recalling when no more defenders are added in the January transfer window despite the manager's stated acknowledgement that 'we need defenders'.

He adds: 'It is also the question if we can play like a team and if we can reach the [right] level. Today, we didn't reach that level. When you don't play like a team, when you miss the chances, it is very difficult because every team shall create chances against us because we are playing with a big space behind us.' The last few words are trademark Van Gaal. What is he really saying? 'We are playing with a big space behind us.' Is he blaming the defenders, the midfielders or everyone? Or is he admitting he got his tactics and selection wrong? He is and he isn't. Pick through anything a manager says and does and a strong case can be made that everything is his fault or – a kinder term – responsibility. The alternative view is that professional players are actors of the piece and are the ones who should, who *have* to, take responsibility for the on-field stuff. All of it. Otherwise why are they paid millions?

So, the question is, who does Van Gaal consider better players? Why were Barcelona's Cesc Fabregas and Bayern Munich's Toni Kroos not signed? Apparently the manager did not fancy one or both. Which is a head-scratcher. Fabregas is a Premier League-hardened goalscorer who knows all the midfield byways. Kroos has just won the World Cup with Germany and is a prince of schemers. But closer examination might reveal that neither player actually fancied moving to Old Trafford, and that suggestions otherwise were purely speculation. This is where United's absence from Europe may be against them. Fabregas chose Chelsea and Kroos went to Real Madrid: two clubs currently looking forward to Champions League football.

Even so, it does not stop the recently-retired Paul Scholes weighing in with his opinion. The former midfielder is having a party every time he pontificates on United. On this occasion he says: 'Louis van Gaal is a manager who has the status and the personality to be in charge of Manchester United. The problem for United when it comes to challenging for the title this season is that, to my mind, they have not signed enough players to change the squad radically to win the league. Fabregas and Kroos were the two names that I believe could have made a significant difference. Both have gone elsewhere.' Some may paraphrase Scholes here as: Louis, you ain't winning the Premier League (and with decisions like these . . .)

Another midfielder who is not of interest to Louis van Gaal is Arturo Vidal. When it boils down to it a combination of Juventus's asking price – £45 million-plus for a twenty-seven-year-old with scant sell-on value in three or four years' time – and a knee problem, and the Dutchman is put off. But there is little doubt that when one hundred per cent fit the Chilean's hard-tackling and dynamism from midfield is what is required. So, the wait for a maestro to conduct United central areas continues.

Instead, the first post-tour signing of the window after the tour is the defender Marcos Rojo, who so impressed Van Gaal at the World Cup. Rojo's Argentina defeated Holland on penalties in the semi-final of the tournament in São Paulo and Rojo's performance then helped convince Van Gaal he should move to buy him. His left-sidedness is of particular import to Van Gaal, who has identified this as a problem area lacking in the squad. Rojo can help provide the 'balance' his new manager desires. This is all theory, though. As usual, how he performs is all that really matters.

So far Van Gaal has added Luke Shaw, Ander Herrera and Rojo. Three times as many players as Moyes managed last summer, but still not enough. How good any of them will be is an unknown. Even Rojo, despite being voted into the World Cup Team of the Tournament, has been playing for Sporting in the Portuguese league, a competition which has little in common with the Premier League. The need for more signings is made more urgent by an already dominant issue: Van Gaal has serious and ongoing injury problems. Before the Swansea match he revealed that nine of his first-team squad were ruled out. Lingard's knee injury takes the number unavailable into double figures.

For United's squad, the loss to Swansea has them back in David Moyes land. This is not where any of the players wish to be. Not after the first match of the season. Optimism may not be crushed just yet. But it has taken a severe battering. Heads are being shaken and there is a sense that 'this surely cannot be happening to us again, can it?' The expression that encapsulated the Moyes season was the stunned, open-mouthed stare on the faces of Rooney, Michael Carrick, David de Gea, Rio Ferdinand, Nemanja Vidić, Patric Evra: the champion players of the club who were unable to quite believe what they were living. How they had suddenly been caught in the wrong film and could do nothing to affect its ending? Ferdinand, Vidić and Evra are gone, but for Rooney, De Gea and the injured Carrick the nightmare thought is that the nightmare could be about to repeat itself. It is only one match, of course. Yet the way confidence seemed to drain instantly from the side is worryingly reminiscent of the disaster of last year.

The XI who started against Swansea were: De Gea, Jones, Smalling, Blackett, Lingard, Herrera, Fletcher, Mata, Young, Rooney and Hernández. De Gea and Rooney apart, this bunch lack X-factor quality. They did not leap off the page when the team sheets were produced ahead of kick-off and they certainly did not correct that impression on the pitch. Michael Carrick may be the chief loss among Van Gaal's injured players. But even if the midfielder had been available the sirens would continue to wail about the gap in this department. Herrera is unproven; Mata is a playmaker, so no central operator. And Fletcher's best days are behind him. If the manager had landed a Fabregas or a Kroos, they would have filled this hole and would surely have been able to control the game against Swansea. A big-time, big-gun, big-moment, big-occasion midfielder is the oil in the team machine. The element that makes the side a side in all senses. They are lubricant *and* high-octane petroleum. A Fabregas or a Kroos. United players can never say anything publicly about team matters, but privately they must all be wondering what will happen if the transfer window closes and central midfield continues to be the weak link. They have all concentrated on keeping their place in the side. But this is made far easier if the team is winning, and with a weak centre there are sure to be more losses than victories.

The defeat by Swansea left Van Gaal visibly stunned and

baffled at how his players had crumpled on home territory. Itmeans he is already facing the hot lights of interrogation ahead of the second match, the away trip to Sunderland. This is Van Gaal's introduction to the always-prodding-pulling-pushing-provoking-never-yielding storm-in-a-press-room commotion of the Premier League. He has lost one match and allied to the manner of the display means it is game on for the media. Van Gaal is in tetchy mood. The result has changed him from 'king to devil', he says. This seems a surprise to the Dutchman. Which is a surprise. It may not be balanced, or even grown-up, but this is the way it is. Just as the defeat made Van Gaal appear a little lost, so his incredulity seems naïve. What else did he expect? The P-word gets an airing. 'You have to believe in the philosophy that we make again a big club, but it needs time and it's not an overnight job,' Van Gaal declares. Never mind the media, tell that to the players, the fans and the club igwigs.

Things are certainly moving faster in the transfer market than under Moyes. Before the game it emerges that local lad Danny Welbeck can leave if he wants. Here is the classic dilemma of the football fan. The die-hard enthusiast may detest seeing the departure of Welbeck, a United supporter and a boy from Longsight. But on the other hand this is a striker who struggles to score, the not-always-quite-up-to-it young fellow who has pace and is industrious. And that's about it. Oh, and tends to do better for England. Many United supporters do not care a fig for the national team. Only Liverpool and City do they care less for. Welbeck being allowed to go suggests eighteen-year-old James Wilson is preferred to him. While this is a kick in the teeth for Welbeck, it is a double-whammy for Wilson's career prospects and Van Gaal's reputation as a promoter of youth. The fans will lap up this part of the Welbeck scenario.

But many will shudder at what also transpires now: the Glazer family indicate they will not sell the club for at least five years. Even nine years into their ownership, during which time trophies galore have been won, and footballing talent like Cristiano Ronaldo and Wayne Rooney graced Old Trafford, the Glazers are still detested by a sizeable constituency. And that constituency will not wish to hear that the Americans have no plans to walk away anytime soon. The ballpark sum of debt heaped on the club since Malcom Glazer bought United in 2005 is £800 million. The residual anger felt towards the six-strong family (five brothers and one sister who now control United following their father's death in May) flares up after the Swansea defeat. Some of the supporters blame the owners for the summer's transfer activity that has stalled at the purchase of Shaw, Herrera and Rojo. The modern-day equivalent of stepping outside to sort this out is done by these fans taking to Twitter and venting their fury. The GlazersOut hashtag is used more than 100,000 times and there are tentative plans to protest against the owners at United's next home game, against Queens Park Rangers on 14 September. In the nicest and politest possible way the Glazers will not care. And what would be of interest is to discover how many supporters are actually ambivalent about the Glazers' ownership, or do not give a damn at all as long as the club continues to exist as a winning machine. Because this is a section that also exists, but dare not speak up due to the domination of the anti-Glazer brigade. The debt is now down to around £295 million, small change to a club who has just landed that near-difficult-to-believe £750 million, ten-year kit deal with Adidas.

The Glazers' popularity or otherwise does not concern Van Gaal. He likes them. As with Ferguson before him, the Dutchman is only interested in football and being able to focus on managing the club. The owners allow him to do so. In fact, he has been pleasantly surprised by how much they trust the manager to get on with the job. There is regular communication between Van Gaal and America. Avi, Joel and Bryan, the most hands-on of the family, have impressed the Dutchman with their business acumen and the shrewd eye they bring to decision-making. They are intelligent people. And the feeling is mutual. The Glazers were impressed with Louis van Gaal, the man with the demeanour and 'the philosophy' when they discussed the possibility of him taking over in the spring. And they remain supremely confident that they have got this appointment right after the Moyes embarrassment.

For Van Gaal to be granted at least £150 million to invest in his first summer is a princely way to be backed. He knows a player and how to spend money in the market. Being told there will be the same level of cash available in future windows is warming, too. But this leaves the manager no excuse. He has to deliver. The Glazers are discreet. They are never heard from. They are only occasionally seen at matches. They understand that the football comes first. The manager is about to take a plunge into the market in grand style. The Glazers did not blink when this was proposed. They have backed him. They will continue to do so. As long as he wins. This is the Dutchman's end of the bargain. And it is just fine. When Van Gaal realised all of this he understood this was the dream job. Just as David Moyes did.

Chapter 15

Galacticos on Mancunian Way

Saturday, 23 August 2014 is a notable day for Manchester United *aficionados*. The club is back in (again) for Real Madrid's Ángel Di María and the fee is to be a British record £59.7 million. This mega-deal signals that the post-Sir Alex Ferguson Manchester United are trying to fast forward through innocence, growing pains, youth and adolescence to come of age. He-who-can-never-be-forgotten never will be. But dukes are bared and Ed Woodward's first headline foray into the transfer market for Louis van Gaal is to corral Di María for sixty million large ones. The manager wants Di María as he is a game-changer of record. His pace and trickery and football intelligence fits into the Van Gaal philosophy. Di María is talked up by Van Gaal publicly and seems more of the manager's player than the first two summer arrivals, Luke Shaw and Ander Herrera, who were identified before he took over.

By the close of the transfer window, the purchase of Di María and the final-day deal for Radamel Falcao will be written up, imprinted in the rough draft of history, as The New Galactico Era. It marks a turning point in the grand tradition of United rearing the club's own players. A look outward to the vistas rather than inwards to the fields of Carrington. As with all histories, this is not quite correct. Or, rather, like all histories, the yarn would benefit from a little more complexity. The truth is that United have always had a rich tradition of buying the best in show footballers – a few recent names would include Bryan Robson, Eric Cantona, Cristiano Ronaldo and Wayne Rooney – and this did not stop the club continuing to develop and hothouse their own talent. So in acquiring Ángel Di María, United may simply be paying far more than ever before (a cool £22.6 million more than the £37.1 million spent on Juan Mata last January) for a footballer. Yet what Louis van Gaal is definitely not acquiring is a solution to the seemingly never-ending central-midfield issue. Di María is a pacey winger by trade. A player who turned May's Champions League final for Real Madrid is more of an upgrade on Ashley Young, Antonio Valencia and Adnan Januzaj. This is what the evidence points to, anyway. He is an oven-ready, proven performer.

However, there is no doubt the Argentine would have stayed at Real if only they had wanted to keep him. This may not augur well as Di María tries to settle in. In a rather puzzling move he pens an open letter to Real fans saying: 'Sadly the time has come for me to leave, but I would like to make it clear that it was never my wish.' This is not the best way to introduce himself to United supporters. Admitting publicly that he never wanted to go means he does not really want to be at Old Trafford. The honesty is praiseworthy, but the cold truth is that Di María is a professional, signed for an astronomical fee. Only five players have cost more. If he agrees to join he agrees to join. Pining for the club that he has just left, and who deemed him surplus to requirements, is not a smart way to think to the future. It will cloud how he views Manchester United and his fortunes at the club. The letter can be read as Di María being homesick already for Madrid before he has been in Manchester two days. This cannot be healthy.

On Sunday United stumble to a disappointing 1–1 draw at Sunderland. Afterwards comes the revelation from Louis van Gaal of how desperate he is to find a solution to the problem in central midfield that is seemingly the cause of his side's lack of flow and pace. 'Kagawa – I have tried to play him in that position in the US and he could not fulfil my wishes and my philosophy. We have spoken about that and he is more of a number ten. Mata was playing at number ten [at Sunderland] and I thought I had to change the other players, which is why I chose to bring on Januzaj.' Van Gaal has just put Shinji Kagawa's United career in a critical condition while illustrating that Ángel Di María is a £60 million red herring because, though his quality places him in the elite gang of players below Lionel Messi and Cristiano Ronaldo, he is no virtuoso of the middle. This auditioning of Kagawa for the role shows the manager's view of Tom Cleverley, Marouane Fellaini, Darren Fletcher, Anderson and Ander Herrera, and illustrates where Van Gaal really needs to strengthen. This weakness went beyond being an oddity, a freak occurrence, a few seasons ago. How can any club, even a pub football team, so obviously lack anyone suitable for central midfield? Since Paul Scholes faded as a force United have been unable to source a replacement. Doctorates could, and maybe should, be written about how and why. The draw at Sunderland proves Van Gaal right, though perhaps not in the way he would have wanted. Confidence has been smashed by that opening-day home defeat by Swansea. 'Here we go again, please, *please*, surely not' all connected to the club inwardly wail. Sunderland were lucky not to be relegated during the previous season, yet Louis van Gaal's Manchester United seem unable to strike any kind of terror in their ranks. This is precisely the feat David Moyes performed at the start of last season. Somehow, almost instantly, he made the club a stooge for the opposition, in the process dismantling the aura built up by his predecessor. With every passing match Sir Alex Ferguson is appearing more and more of a phenomenon, something never felt more than on the evening of 26 August in Milton Keynes.

The New Galactico Era – Di María has arrived but does not play at Stadium MK – begins with the twenty-times champions, three-times European Cup winners, eleven-times FA Cup winners, four-times League Cup winners, one-time Cup-Winners' Cup winners, one-time Super Cup winners, one-time Intercontinental Cup winners, one-time Club World Cup winners, two-time Premier League and FA Cup Double winners, one-time Premier League and League Cup Double winners, one-time Premier League and European Cup Double winners and one-time Premier League, European Cup and FA Cup Treble winners *losing* 4–0 in a Capital One Cup tie to MK Dons of League One.

What has been witnessed is difficult to fathom. This is a third match without a win, a second defeat in three. There have been two goals scored and seven conceded. Four of those goals were put past United by MK Dons, opponents who last season had more defeats in the league at Stadium MK (ten) than the eight they won. Already, Van Gaal has serious problems. This is an abysmal night for the manager and his philosophy. The team are toothless and are dumped out of the League Cup at the first possible stage. The misery is compounded by United only being in this early round due to the plunge under David Moyes, and the failure to qualify for Europe. Yet Moyes was only a penalty shoot-out semi-final loss to Sunderland from reaching the final of this competition. How United can be humiliated 4–0 by a third-tier side requires an inquest. Karl Robinson's men are quicker, hungrier and simply far better than their gilded opponents. How far might Van Gaal's men fall after this? The club has gone, in less than eighteen months, from winning the championship by eleven points to a wet Tuesday in Milton Keynes, and being knocked out in the second round of the League Cup for the first time since 1995.

After the debacle of David Moyes, how can this be? Say it ain't so, Louis, plead 659 million Manchester United fans. 'It cost also a title,' the manager says, after pulling his pants back up, emphasising what the hope of winning this trophy represented. How about triumphing in a match, first? Ángel Di María is due to make his debut at Burnley on Saturday where a packed and braying Turf Moor will be rocking, and Van Gaal will be hoping the search for a victory ends at the fourth attempt. Injuries are continuing to mount. Shinji Kagawa became the latest crock when he wandered off the Stadium MK pitch with a head injury. So there is mitigation. But this gathers no friends or understanding from fans if United lose. There is a league table that is depressing to look at. Then there is the wall-to-wall coverage of what is going wrong, and why, and what it may mean, that the faithful have to grin and bear each and every day.

Optimism has been shattered, the honeymoon violated. There are even sniggers and doubts expressed in the media about Van Gaal's credentials. Others are citing circumstances. Either way, it is on: the hand-to-hand combat between the fourth-estate guerrillas and Van Gaal has officially started. The Dutchman's insane in-the-membrane-retraining-of-brains thing is receiving serious traction. It has become a favourite. Retraining brains! Of high-end pros! Really! How new-fangled! And possibly foolhardy. After the Burnley game Darren Fletcher is asked about it. Van Gaal will be pressed on it. Everyone will be.

The real problem Van Gaal wrestles with is the underlying issue of what can be termed the 'subtle mess' bestowed on United by Sir Alex Ferguson and which was only exacerbated by David Moyes. Ferguson left two ageing centre-backs in Rio Ferdinand and Nemanja Vidić, plus the also venerable Patrice Evra. This is seventy-five per cent of the first-XI back four. If Moyes had culled all of them in his sole summer he may have had a chance. But he did not. By the time all three departed at the end of last term they had outlasted Moyes but still stayed a year too long. This is one fault-line in the squad. It joins the fissure in midfield and continues into the attack where Robin van Persie, who is thirty-one, is a striker who is injury-prone and entering the days of his career when everything seems a little laboured, a little from memory.

Van Gaal is having to rebuild the club amid the white noise of each day's ceaseless breaking news, exclusives, flyers, gossip, innuendo, tittle-tattle and the general madding of the unpredictable fancy. Louis van Gaal would rather not have the second life of the manager. The Media Life. The Public Life. The Second Life. No gaffer would. The Dutchman bills himself as the trainer-coach and this is his arena, his natural habitat, working with the squad. He adores the feel of sod underfoot as he takes to the fields of Carrington to retrain brains and feet and implant his schemes and blueprint and philosophy. With whistle hanging around his neck, assistants on hand, and the dank and invigorating Manchester wind, rain and shine, the practice pitch is fertile land for the Iron Tulip.

What is more important? The work and the sweat? Or the PR and the press? Did the latter kill David Moyes and help Sir Alex Ferguson survive the four barren years at the start of his reign, between 1986 and 1990, and the three without a league title in the early 2000s? There is a counter argument. This suggests that there is a *prima facie* case that the real stuff of the Manchester United manager is before all. Out there where it is filmed and noted and tweeted and Facebooked and Instagrammed and endlessly replayed. Where every word is dissected by the fans-cum-amateur pundits and the professional journalists. In the crucible of the social and the traditional media. And into this arena Louis van Gaal must tiptoe like a lion, pad forward like a rhino, show his wares or hide them away. One false move and he's dead. He must be one cool dude. The Fonzerelli who can float and think and charm, keep it all in-house and under control, even when Manchester bloody United are being patronised publicly by up-and-coming thrusters like MK Dons.

The focus should be on getting it right on the pitch. Yet the morning before the important Burnley fixture the breadth of Louis van Gaal's considerations are glimpsed with information that impacts directly on the quest to spend and build his ideal squad. United's status as high-end payers means to balance the books they need to offload a clutch of fringe players. The numbers are difficult to comprehend. The midfield misfit Anderson earns £80,000 a week, £4.16 million until his contract ends next summer. This is around the same wage as Danny Welbeck, the club's prime asset in the fire-sale, as good money will be received for his transfer. United want £20 million; he will end up going to Arsenal for £18 million. Nani, meanwhile, is paid £115,000 a week and joins Sporting Lisbon on loan as part of Rojo's purchase. United have agreed to pay the winger's salary while there – a trifling £4.14 million for the season – because the Portuguese club is a potato-skin-soup-imbibing pauper in comparison.

The figures keep coming. Ashley Young earns £115,000 a week, a £11.9 million salary over the final two years of his deal. Javier Hernández, the Mexican striker who is interesting Valencia and Juventus (he is to end up at Real Madrid on loan), has two years left on his weekly terms of £88,000, a total of £9.15 million. Shinji Kagawa, who is tempting former club Borussia Dortmund, becomes £70,000 richer every seven days. So, too, Marouane Fellaini, though his ankle injury means United cannot offload him in the present window. Both Kagawa and Fellaini have two years left on their contracts, so United are due to pay them £7.2 million each. Tom Cleverley, a target for Aston Villa, is one of the lowest earners, drawing a basic wage of £30,000 per week, though his deal is incentivised and can be markedly higher. Cleverley's contract expires in May so any terms Villa offer would have to be attractive or he could wait and leave then as a free agent. If United were to sell Welbeck, Young, Hernández, Anderson, Kagawa and Cleverley before the end of the transfer window, they would claw back a total of £463,000 a week. With the potential departures of Nani and Fellaini in the future, this figure could reach a staggering £646,000.

Despite having all this to keep a handle on, and despite the memory of the disastrous defeat at Milton Keynes still being fresh, Van Gaal remains bullish ahead of his third Premier League match – the visit to newly promoted Burnley. 'Maybe you can support Louis van Gaal when you believe in him? OK?' he suggests. What an individual. A one-off who was a modest midfielder who never played a first-team game for Ajax (Johan Cruyff's presence was a factor). His best success was at Sparta Rotterdam where he came to, no surprise, dominate the team and club before the former PE schoolteacher began the rise into the front rank of managers. To sum him up in rough, broad-stroke fashion, Van Gaal is smart and thinks he's smarter than everyone else. And so he is. In his world. This can also be an Achilles heel, but if Van Gaal knows it – and he surely does – he could not care less.

He brightens when speaking of the £59.7 million man who could make his debut at Turf Moor. 'He has impressed me.

The first training session was with all the boys and he was very impressive,' Van Gaal says of Ángel Di María. 'The second was a little bit less so but he has to adapt to the culture and the players.' Which is what Van Gaal is doing, too. Adapting. Enjoying adapting. Enjoying the ride. This what he is about. This gives him his glow. His shine.

There is sunshine at Turf Moor on Saturday afternoon, but there is not much in Louis van Gaal's heart. There cannot be. His Manchester United team are ponging the place out. Again. The oddly muted, tamed quality of the side under David Moyes seems to be the Scot's lingering, unwanted legacy. Burnley's ground of corrugated roofs and sightlines of the Lancashire moors cost around a twelfth of Ángel Di María's record fee. The forward with the heavenly name is about to come off sixty-nine minutes into an impressive debut where he has been United's best player, zipping back and forth along an inside-left channel from a deep-lying berth. He is replaced by Anderson. This is a microcosm, something to place in a time capsule to pinpoint the mélange of Manchester United as a club at this precise moment.

Anderson, the Brazilian United are desperate to offload, should be nowhere near the reserve list for any match, never mind coming on to participate in one. Yet the midfield-deficit gets him on to the pitch. It is his last appearance for the club. He is still only twenty-six. He leaves for Internacional in his hometown of Porte Alegre in January. He arrived in 2007 as the Golden Ball winner at the 2005 Under-17 World Cup. Three years later he seemed to have proved he had really developed by winning the Golden Boy gong for Europe's best under-21 footballer. All that followed, though, was decline. Sir Alex Ferguson, perhaps feeling a little embarrassed at his judgment, offered one of those moments when he went against the self-trumpeted principle of 'keeping it all in the dressing room' by laying responsibility for buying Anderson with his brother, Martin, the United scout. Martin had claimed the midfielder was better than Rooney. In Ferguson's autobiography, the knight wrote: '"For Christ's sake, don't say that", I told him. "He'll need to be good to be better than Rooney".' The whole Anderson tale, his existence at United, is a mystery and an enigma, a tome-worthy subject for another day.

Against Sean Dyche's Burnley, Van Gaal again fields a three-man defence, manned by Phil Jones, Jonny Evans and Tyler Blackett. It is Blackett's third consecutive league appearance, though he was spared the MK Dons mauling. What is witnessed is a bumblingly feeble display. The Van Gaal defensive trident are too far apart, marooned from each other and the rest of the team. The match ends 0–0 and, and as the saying goes, United were fortunate to score zero. Afterwards, around the back of the stadium, Van Gaal stops to speak for Monday's newspapers, and he is asked: 'Are you concerned it is taking time to retrain players' brains?' The question insinuates the delicate and always wavering balance of managing a team as large as United with Van Gaal's 'philosophy', which is not just being queried but is near to being mocked. The Dutchman weighs the proposition. 'When you put the question then I have to have concern I think. But when you are doing that after two weeks I think it's a little bit early.' The answer might suggest Van Gaal is indeed wavering – using the word 'concern' encourages the impression

– but the tone of his voice and his demeanour point to the opposite. How long can this last, though? 'We have to rebuild a new team . . . this needs time and only when I have to repeat myself every week when we are losing points, you are tired of my answer but also the fans shall be tired and that's not a good way to discuss that.'

It is still sunny in Burnley, a lovely late August day. The three-centre-back system and how disjointed and unsuccessful it is continues to be a major issue. Is it, Van Gaal is asked, 'about the two strikers' it allows the manager to field? Today the front two have been Wayne Rooney and Robin van Persie. 'It's also dependable about the two strikers and the type of midfielders we have in midfield because they are playing midfielders – and not fighting midfielders or hard-working midfielders, more technical tactical midfielders – so when you have that and also [need] support, and that you can give with our defenders, but also with five. When you see today we played more three in the back and five in midfield,' he says, confusingly.

Darren Fletcher, Van Gaal's vice-captain, is also talking. Three games into the league campaign, here is the first chance to quiz an actual player on the manager's methods. Fletcher, one of the more intelligent footballers on the circuit, is asked about Van Gaal's belief in 'retraining the brains' of the players. Smoothly the Scot says: 'You get the heart and the desire and sometimes you need to think about it more. We get that but we have always had that . . . It's something that isn't new to us, the new manager has just spoken of it publicly to make us aware of it.' Fletcher will be gone in January.

From nine available points the Van Gaal project has yielded

United two and fourteenth place. The clear skies and endless rising sun of summer and the American tour, beating Real Madrid and Liverpool and all that, are gone. What is left is the same old Manchester United of last term under David Moyes. This lot may be worse. That is the fear among fans and the chat in the press room. The sense is mushrooming after this latest rhythmless display at Burnley where a side headed by Wayne Rooney, Robin van Persie, David de Gea, Phil Jones, Jonny Evans and Juan Mata should have blown away Danny Ings and company. This may be the natural level of the players Louis van Gaal has at his disposal. America may have been no help. Winning all five matches on tour has clearly fooled the manager and everyone else about just how uneven the squad's quality is.

There are also questions about Van Gaal. United finished seventh under David Moyes and the verdict returned suggests this made him a hapless manager, considering nearly the same squad started the season as champions. Van Gaal has the résumé to back him up but maybe, say some of the whispers, the three years out of club management have left him a manager out of time.

Transfer deadline day is like the opening scene of a high-concept flick called The Radamel Falcao Incident that stars a gorgeous-looking Colombian footballer who jets into North-West England with magic in his boots and Lazarus in his eyes to make Manchester United rise again. Following Ángel Di María's arrival, the superstar striker becomes the second Galactico and confirms this new era of blockbuster footballers at the club. Falcao costs £6 million for a season-long loan from Monaco, plus £10 million in wages. That makes a cool £16 million, or £2 million more than Daley Blind's permanent transfer fee when he lands on 1 September.

From the moment the terroriser of defences with sleek black Tarzan hair and matinée-idol looks touches down in Manchester later than scheduled at around 5 p.m. on 1 September, there is a new sensation in town. There is a belief that after four winless matches Louis van Gaal's team is at last ready for lift-off. Falcao is to be paid £190,000 a week and this is apparently tax-free. As United deny matching his net take-home of £10 million a year, Monaco may be agreeing to pay the fifty per cent tax that ensures the centre-forward suffers no loss of earnings. Given the awful start to Van Gaal's tenure, here is a statement of intent. The feelings are mutual. Falcao cannot wait to become the main man in the script that is being written for him. This would never have happened under David Moyes. His marquee signing was Marouane Fellaini: even in the hair-stakes the bushy follicles of the Belgian cannot compete with the Vidal Sassoon smoothness of the Colombian's barnet. But the drama! The intrigue! Flying in late! Touching down! An hour after scheduled! The megastar salary of £10 million net! The sheer last-minute seat-of-the-pants, high-rolling, big-dipper thrill of it all!

For a prologue, this opening scene is irresistible. This promises to be a smash-hit of a movie whether the twenty-eight-year-old succeeds or not. And Radamel Falcao Garcia Zárate does not disappoint. Manchester United is never dull and the former Lanceros Boyaca, River Plate, FC Porto, Atletico Madrid and Monaco predator is perfect casting for English football's Hollywood of the North.

Yet the context, the sub-text, the *backstory*, is that Falcao is also a bit of a punt from United. The Colombian is tentative, nervous even, due to the serious knee injury he suffered last January and which ruled him out of the World Cup. Having been offered to Manchester City, Arsenal and just about every high-ranking club in Europe, only United made a serious play for him. He will prove a nice guy, popular among his team-mates and one of the few players who will offer a wave to strangers at the Aon Training Complex as he drives around in his white 4x4. But on the playing side, something is missing that Falcao spends all season trying to locate.

His arrival, however, is further evidence for those who foresee the beginning of the end for a trumpeted youth policy last spied in vigorous health at Old Trafford on 6 May. Then, Ryan Giggs, the interim manager, gave full debuts to James Wilson, eighteeen, and Tom Lawrence, twenty, in the 3–1 defeat of Hull City. Indeed, Wilson scored twice. Van Gaal, though, has a proud record of harnessing potential. Edgar Davids, Patrick Kluivert, Xavi, Toni Kroos, Thomas Müller . . . the list of stars of the recent and current European scene developed by the Dutchman is longer than United's search for a decent central midfielder. But does the £150 million-plus acquisitions of Di María, Falcao, Marcos Rojo, Luke Shaw, Ander Herrera and Blind not inform everyone what Van Gaal thinks of the current crop of United's young thrusters? Or will Falcao, Di María and the rest of the new gang of six go the same way as the £37.1-million Juan Mata and the £27.5-million Marouane Fellaini to make it more than £200 million splurged on players still to make their presence known? Maybe these are the wrong questions. Maybe what needs to be asked is what chance do Radamel Falcao, Ángel Di María, Marcos Rojo, Luke Shaw, Daley Blind, Ander Herrera, Juan Mata, Marouane Fellaini, Wayne Rooney, Robin van Persie, Phil Jones, Chris Smalling, Ashley Young, David de Gea and the rest have if first of all they are having their grey matter realigned to override the high-functioning instinct that has driven their talent to the zenith of their profession? After nil victories from the opening four matches one answer may be 'less than zero', especially as one growing theory is that Louis van Gaal's playing corps may not have the requisite grey matter. This was a question Van Gaal bridled at outside Turf Moor when it was posed. Now is the time to wait and see.

At least Van Gaal has managed to bring in six players, a six hundred per cent increase on the sole footballer signed under David Moyes, twelve months ago. This may suggest that Ed Woodward has become smoother in the market. But the real gift to the executive vice-chairman's manoeuvres is having the Van Gaal name behind him. Van Gaal 6, Moyes 1 is a resounding scoreline, especially when there is no Champions League football with which to entice recruits.

It is an international break. There is no Premier League action for a fortnight. But there is no cessation on the actual Manchester United business of Being Manchester United. The corridors and offices, lunch and dinner dates remain filled as the next piece of strategy is thrashed out. Despite the £150 million-plus just spent, the message from high up to the manager continues to be that more funds are available in the January window. 'Carry On Spending, Louis!' this very English movie might be titled.

The acquisition of Falcao and Di María, in particular, is a sweet statement for the club and fans. And further succour is offered by the firm message from Old Trafford that there is to be absolutely no discarding of trust in young shavers. The promotion of James Wilson by Van Gaal into the first-team squad is cited as evidence.

Woodward is speaking to investors in the club via a conference call as the latest accounts are published. They show that David Moyes and his coaching staff walked away with a total of £5.2 million when they were ousted, and that United forecast the cost of failure to qualify for the Champions League as potentially as much as £50 million in lost revenue. This proves to be the most loquacious Woodward is all season. 'Our budgets assume a third-placed finish, as is ordinarily the case. The 2013–14 season was a very challenging and disappointing one. But under Louis there is a real feeling at the training ground that we are at the start of something special. I'm confident with Louis as our manager, with a clear philosophy and a reinvigorated squad, we will get back to challenging for the title and trophies. Commercially we continue to go from strength to strength. The record deal with Adidas underpinned our attempts to compete for the next decade. The £750 million deal is a record, not just in football but in all sports. This is the culmination of four years of hard work. We had offers from more than twenty companies around the world.'

The kit contract, signed off in July, a few days before Van Gaal officially began, is indeed a watershed moment: £750 million over ten years represents a Luis Suarez a summer for the next decade. Serious money. Yet given Louis van Gaal has spent north of £150 million, compared with the £27.5 million David Moyes did last summer, the Dutchman does not have the excuse of not being able to strengthen his squad that was the very reasonable explanation open to his predecessor. Falcao, Di María and company have to work. If not the team has to still be successful. Or Van Gaal is in trouble.

Relief. Manchester United and Louis van Gaal have conjured up their first competitive victory. At the fifth attempt. Single malts all around for this alchemising of method – philosophy – into the material matter of three glistening points. Queens Park Rangers have been downed 4–0 at Old Trafford and the Iron Tulip is again a deity. Ángel Di María, one of the few bright spots against Burnley, has again sparkled, scoring the opener. The Argentine is the star in an all-round display that has him thrilling the 75,355 crowd with artistry that also sets up goals for others. Ander Herrera, another new boy, also registers, and the mesmerising attack-play of Di María suggests £59.7 million may be a bargain. From inside the United half, and with the ball apparently in telepathic communication with his boots, Di María runs at the visiting team in a shimmering act of dribbling that ends near the QPR area and a crafty ball inside to Wayne Rooney. This removes two defenders and allows the captain to unload. The shot is repelled but the ball is recycled to Herrera, who gives Rob Green no chance for a debut strike. This is what the congregation want. This is what it needs. The mainlining of adrenalin that flows through the system from player to fan and back again. When Herrera takes a step and from outside the area bangs a cannonball finish past Green, the surge from the Stretford End to the men in red crackles and whiplashes as if the club has just been given CPR and is bolting upright again at long last.

There is a thrill all Sunday afternoon among the crowd that moves in exhilarating waves fuelled by a joyous feeling that the twelve-month purgatory may be over. This is precisely what having Manchester United in the blood is about. The stadium is getting rapidly and gloriously drunk on the elixir being served up by Louis van Gaal's merry band, who are making the struggles and doubt of the previous four matches a distant memory. If this is the potion the new manager can mix there can only be rude health, sunshine and days of adventure ahead.

There are boons everywhere. Tyler Blackett again starts and appears accomplished, the young defender underlining the depths of riches the manager has to plunder. Nine players may be on the injury list, yet still Van Gaal could name as substitutes, Radamel Falcao, the Galactico's Galatico; the world's highest-paid teenager in Luke Shaw; Adnan Januzaj, now the wearer of Ryan Giggs's number eleven shirt and the supposed next main man of the United XI; plus Darren Fletcher and the battle-hardened Antonio Valencia. After sixty-seven minutes, and with United cruising at 4–0, Van Gaal releases Radamel Falcao for his debut to reinforce an attack already comprising Robin van Persie, Wayne Rooney and Ángel Di María. QPR may be weak opponents, but the only way now seems towards the stars. This is the dizzying way of football's instant changes in perception.

In the aftermath of the win, Van Gaal's 'philosophy' suddenly becomes more appealing. And it is the didactic approach that again shines through. He sees himself as a moulder of player and team, consistently talking of 'evaluating' himself, the XI, the set-up of the club, the road marked out on his map. For Van Gaal, 'the most important thing is I'm seeing the players not only as football players but as human beings'. However, his philosophy is perhaps summed up in the two-sentence quote that follows the almost obligatory question: 'Is first place still possible?' He responds: 'Yes, it is always possible. Because we have to play a lot of matches and we are not so much behind as you know.' In other words, 'We will hang in there. Always'. True. And truer still after the demolition of QPR. Rooney and Mata also score *and* from the start the manager throws away the three-man defence for the first time to return to the four-defender backline with which player and fan all seem more at ease.

The manager is in a jocular mood post-match, and his sense of well-being moves him to speak of his spouse, Truus. 'This is special because it is also my wife's birthday,' says Van Gaal. 'She said the biggest present shall be victory. We gave it to her.' Yet he is still focused, admitting that 'we can improve', with the unsaid bit being that this was QPR who are bound to be relegation strugglers. And there is criticism of Ángel Di Maria. 'When you prepare three goals and make the first goal by yourself then you cannot play bad. But he had a lot of unnecessary losses [of possession] so we can do better, even Ángel di María. I am analysing the game and I see things we can improve as a team.' There has been a pass completion mark of ninety-one per cent, which featured a silent assassin display from Daley Blind as the midfield metronome, the £14 million man coasting through the match in monogrammed dressing-gown fashion. The injured Michael Carrick is the head holding-midfield honcho, but he is thirty-three and Blind has shown he can be the understudy.

'This is a good start,' Van Gaal is saying. 'We are building a process and have to play in a certain style. I hope to be manager of the champion of the Premier League. If not this year, then my second or third, but I want to give the championship to the fans. I have played always attack and my teams have scored the most of the league. So I hope at the end of this league we shall score also the most. The most important thing is trajectory.' And positivity. And crucially and tellingly *perception-change*. The men in red shirts have looked a team rather than eleven blokes whose identity has been snatched. The view of Van Gaal up there on the high-wire shifts after he had been teetering from the gusts caused by the winless first quartet of games. The grim truth is that after only 360 minutes of competitive football Van Gaal was still coming into this match running out of excuses for why Manchester United were not functioning under him. Another duff display, a fifth outing with no victory, and open season on the Dutchman would not have been far away. Not now. Not for the moment. This victory and the manner gives Van Gaal the most valuable commodity only winning can buy: time.

In the living nightmare since Sir Alex Ferguson retired this is about as good as Manchester United have been. It is somehow strange, though, the performance and result. Despite all the expertise and analysis, no one can quite point their finger at why, or even how, Van Gaal's methods have finally worked. His mention of 'attack' will go down well with supporters. This is the first time that Manchester United, whose *de facto* motto is 'Attack! Attack! Attack!', have managed three first-half attempts since 22 April 2013. And that was in the 3–0 victory over Aston Villa that sealed the title for the last time under Ferguson. It has taken Moyes's thirty-four league games, Ryan Giggs's four, and now the fourth match of this season for the sequence to be broken. It is a statistic that takes some digesting.

If the mood is light due to the trouncing of QPR, by the following Sunday in the East Midlands it has reverted to the same old, same old. United are humiliated 5–3 by Leicester City, leaking four unanswered goals in twenty-one madcap second-half minutes, having led 3–1 approaching the hour mark. This is a defeat that should – and does – haunt Van Gaal. He is back to appearing a near-chump, the side are hapless as they throw away three more points. Tyler Blackett, a quiet individual who cannot be described as a member of the dark-arts school of defenders as he is more positional than a car-crash tackling player, is sent off with seven minutes remaining. He will be suspended and becomes the latest member of the squad to be unavailable to the manager. The league table on Monday, 22 September can be filed under 'look-away-now' for all United fans, at best to be revisited five years hence for one of those 'do-you-remember-when-Manchester-United-spent-£150-million-and-were-twelfth-after-five-games-with-just-five-points?' kind of moments.

Forget the QPR result, and signs of the team gelling, the thinking has gone full circle. In this gasping age of the second-by-second football whirl Van Gaal appears a manager out of place. The three years since his last club managerial appointment at Bayern Munich seem to have rendered him a lumbering Diplodocus to the ruthless Killer Shark that is Chelsea's Jose Mourinho. Suddenly the 3–5–2 system of America, and which began the season disastrously before Van Gaal discarded it, can be viewed through the prism of the shape being abandoned as long ago as the early 2000s when coaches swapped a striker for an extra body in midfield. How Louis van Gaal and his tactics and philosophy were exposed by the Leicester manager Nigel Pearson is a puzzle. Pearson is not near the top of any list of coming Einstein managers. He is fifty-one and rather rudimentary. Van Gaal is the man whose c.v. boasts a European Cup, seven titles in three different countries, and who has a reputation for being a tactician supreme. Yet he has just taken his Manchester United side to Leicester to be outfoxed by Pearson. On Saturday West Ham United are the visitors to Old Trafford and Van Gaal and United are already in must-win territory.

The uneven results show the difficulty of bus-loading-in a coterie of new players and trying to artificially implant them instantly into the team. Especially as the leader of the gang, Louis van Gaal, has hardly been at the club any longer. More and more the lack of foresight and preparation for the time when Sir Alex Ferguson was no longer the big guy seems negligent, a dereliction of duty. Ferguson himself should have started to rebuild the squad – his words on resignation about leaving the organisation in the best health to continue his gilded years were just not correct. The defence he bequeathed was leaky and erratic under Moyes. A similar staleness and quality-deficiency beset the midfield and attack. A second season on from Fergie, only in the goalkeeping department, in which the excellent David de Gea is continuing to improve, can the United squad be deemed in robust health.

Sam Allardyce, the West Ham manager, misses few tricks and he has enjoyed himself by saying: 'There was a complacency by United in not going out and delivering the signings David [Moyes] felt he needed. Now there's a panic on.' Bringing up David Moyes, and introducing the word 'panic', is a neat double whammy. But this is where United and the manager are, six matches into the term. The inescapable truth is that *five*, yes, *FIVE*, goals were allowed through the Manchester United rearguard at Leicester and that must shine a bright light on the lack of a strength in the defence. The vultures are again circling, hopeful of some prime carrion. The bare fact is the supporters are embarrassed. And no manager wants to embarrass supporters because there is only one way that can end if it continues. Van Gaal knows this, of course. Number one in the Manager-Huckster Playbook is 'keep the fan onside'. Especially the fan in the stadium. The one who attends each week. Lose him or her and hear the hearse chugging down the road.

Van Gaal has had slow starts with clubs before and they have gone on to win the championship. The manager offers an explanation why. 'We give a lot of information and you have to work out that information. There shall be a moment in the season when this information is too much, maybe at this moment it is too much for the players. You have to be yourself, you have your own identity, but that is very difficult because we are starting with a new team, a new relationship between players so that's why it needs time. But I don't want to say that all the time because at the end all the fans are very tired of hearing that sentence.' Continue to lose and he will need a new sentence. Van Gaal still appears and sounds like he is in control, that he is writing the plot rather than the plot writing him. But the reality is that despite him having had slow starts before, and success coming, this is still about faith. Can he hold his nerve? Even if he does, will it make any difference to the actual results? This is the Premier League. A competition the Dutchman is learning about all the time. He is on work experience *and* fighting to survive in a real-time world that keeps unfolding before him with all manner of surprises and incidents.

By 2 November Louis van Gaal and Manchester United will be ten matches into the Premier League season. Between the 5–3 disaster at Leicester and then are matches against West Ham United, Everton, West Bromwich Albion, Chelsea and Manchester City. Make no mistake, the squad still believes in Van Gaal. And it is important that this belief is not eroded. Left orphaned since Sir Alex Ferguson walked away, and finding no comfort in David Moyes's brief incumbency, the players want this man from Amsterdam to be the one who will make them winners again. They know if Van Gaal gets it right for them – which means the players getting it right for him – the medals and glory will come once more. But it is this way round. Manager-to-player. Master-and-servant. This is what is in Van Gaal's hands. A potent force if he can harness it. If not, then the players will be forced to turn to another man. The club to another manager.

Chapter 16

A Purple Patch

Late September has been reached. The six freshmen have had time to settle in, the squad is used to hearing all about the manager's philosophy in each and every training session, and so now is the time for Louis van Gaal to prove everything will gel. That whatever formation he deploys works, and that the results – and scintillating performances – are to be routine. This is why he was employed. A purple patch of the deepest hue would shut just about everyone up.

On Saturday, 27 September at Old Trafford the team sheet is awaited eagerly to discover where Wayne Rooney will operate against West Ham. Van Gaal said in the week that his captain 'can play in more positions, he's a multifunctional player', while praising Radamel Falcao as the main striker. Here Van Gaal is agreeing with Sir Alex Ferguson that Rooney need not always be deployed in attack. And, that Falcao is better in this department. Under Ferguson, Rooney's selection further back was a demotion. Under Van Gaal it is, too. But as the striker is his captain, and has the 'special privileges' of wearing the armband, which means he will always play (bar an act of God), there should be no murmurs of discontent from Rooney. Thus far, Rooney, as with the rest of the squad, is chirruping from the right song-sheet. 'I'm happy to play out wide – I can do a job there and I can do a job up front. It depends on the situation of each game and what the manager wants me to do,' is the Liverpudlian's verdict.

When the XI is announced the captain is again in midfield – though he plays more as a number ten than a traditional deeper-lying operator – with Falcao up top alongside Robin van Persie. Fifteen minutes of the second half of what ends as a 2–1 victory have gone when, wherever Van Gaal believes Rooney should be positioned, his leader ensures he will not be seen in a red shirt during October. The captain has been sent off. The Rooney Misdemeanour unfolds near the centre-circle as he decides to halt a West Ham attack by chopping down Stewart Downing and receives the sixth dismissal of his career. This is not great. For Van Gaal, for the side, for Rooney. Especially as after an early opener from him, and a second twenty-two minutes into the contest, United continue the slipshod defending and confidence-deficit that killed them at Leicester. There is a real struggle going on before the home crowd, who watch with fingers over their eyes, and it seems that the Rooney red card is, perhaps unconsciously, influenced by this anxiety. With United down to ten men, West Ham have enough chances to pull United back from their two-goal lead just as Nigel Pearson's side did last weekend. Kevin Nolan has a finish ruled out for offside – probably correctly. The backs-to-the-goal defending Van Gaal's desperate side are forced into is rewarded by a memorable clearing header from Paddy McNair, the nineteen-year-old Northern Irishman making his debut. The end to the contest has been heart-stopping for the home support, but a win is a win, given the start to the campaign.

Afterwards, there is a wait to see if Rooney talks, and secondly how he reacts to the sending-off. This is the Rooney of his maturing, elder statesman years and the striker does indeed desire a chat. He is in contrite mood. He will not be appealing. 'No. I understand it. I knew at the time that I misjudged it. It is a red card and I don't think it will benefit anyone to appeal against the decision.' Rooney understands, too, there may be a view that he is returning to the temper-laced days of yore. 'I expect people to say that, but at the end of the day, I was trying to break up the play,' he offers. The same note of acceptance is sounded by Louis van Gaal in the corridor behind the directors' box when he offers his thoughts for the Monday newspapers. His mood might have been pretty different if United had not claimed what is only their second victory of the season. After contemplating the need to have a 'more friendly way' to make a cynical tackle – as the manager suggests how his captain should do it next time – comes a comment that is as close to a public exhortation of man-management the reserved Van Gaal may offer. 'He is for me an example for the squad,' he says of Rooney.

Before the Everton match, the Premier League table shows United in seventh position, with eight points after six matches. It also shows eleven goals scored and nine conceded. This shows the balance to be awry despite all the money spent by Van Gaal.

Ángel Di María and Falcao are the fresh, exciting new blood at the front, but at the moment the team is top-heavy. Marcos Rojo and Luke Shaw were specialist defenders bought in, and Daley Blind can also operate at the back, but defence continues to be the weakness. In full feisty mode Van Gaal defends the rearguard as a unit by saying defending should 'begin in the striker's position', though he admits the need for improvement. This comes with the rather leaden statement that placing the blame for all the goals conceded on Di María and the rest of the attack is because 'the media are writing it's because of the weak defence, but no. I have explained I want to improve your knowledge of football also'. Which is altruistic of the manager.

Whatever Van Gaal's view it remains odd that for a side whose manager likes to tire the opposition by pass and pass and pass and pass and, yes, one more pass, please, and then, *and only then*, we can go for goal, that this caution is not being underpinned by a more watertight back-line. 'The defence begins in the striker's position,' Van Gaal states. 'All the teams are mostly scoring goals out of counterattacks against us and free-kicks and corners – not that they make their goals like we do out of building up, first, second, third and fourth phase.' And fifth and sixth and maybe eleventh phase. Ferguson was maybe a three- or four-phase man, at the very most.

On Sunday, at Old Trafford for the early afternoon kick-off against Everton, the defence is again shaky. Near half-time, and leading through Di María's third goal in five games, Luke Shaw concedes a clumsy penalty by taking down Tony Hibbert. Leighton Baines, who has never missed a penalty in the Premier League, steps up and smacks the spot-kick to David de Gea's right and the Spaniard makes a dazzling save. Shaw hugs De Gea, referee Kevin Friend blows for the break and United float into the dressing room on a perfect psychological breeze to listen to Louis van Gaal's interval words. In the second half the leaky defence continues to need De Gea, who is putting in a man-of-the-match display. And then it happens. Finally. Character development/hero arc in The Radamel Falcao Incident. The Colombian scores his first goal in his fourth run-out for the club, finishing from close range on sixty-two minutes. He enjoys his celebration, a primal scream renting the Manchester air as he wheels away in ecstasy. Falcao has been off the pace, but the match ends 2–1 and Van Gaal has his first set of back-to-back wins. The Galacticos are working, the contributions from Falcao and Di María instrumental in United's twin victories. Old Trafford is buzzing again. The fans absolutely adore Falcao and here today, in the flesh, they have seen him strut his wonder stuff. Van Gaal says 'he needed that' of Falcao. 'I have talked with him because I thought he was forcing himself too much to score a goal. I can understand that, but now he has scored it will be better after the international break.' The team can enjoy another two-week pause with United on eleven points and up to fourth. 'We are not playing good but we are already fourth in the table. What is coming when we are playing well? We have to do it ninety minutes,' the manager adds.

Sir Alex Ferguson decides this is the moment to offer his first public words on Louis van Gaal. And lo and behold these are supportive. Ferguson tells MUTV: 'He's not been getting the results that are expected but when I came to the club I didn't get the results I expected myself at the beginning. What we needed then was Sir Bobby Charlton, [chairman] Martin Edwards and the board to stick by me and we had a great spell after that.' Ferguson picks out how Van Gaal has given debuts to Tyler Blackett, Paddy McNair, Tom Thorpe, Saidy Janko, Reece James, Jesse Lingard and Andreas Pereira. Ferguson even addresses how his presence at the club may loom over Van Gaal. 'There's a bit of that and obviously the press don't miss an opportunity to focus on me during a game.' Ah, the press. Sir Alex is sorely missed by the Fourth Estate. Actually, he probably is . . . But Ferguson is wrong here. The one narrative that is not being worked upon is the one about Van Gaal peering over his shoulder at his predecessor-but-one. Ferguson is stuck in the Moyes 'era'. This new guy is the cat who warned that Manchester United would have to adapt to him.

United are next in action at West Bromwich Albion on 20 October, a Monday evening. Ed Woodward, whose hustle in acquiring Di María, Falcao, Shaw, Herrera, Rojo and Blind has got the critics off his back for the time being, is about to re-enter the consciousness. The Radamel Falcao Incident takes a dark turn as Van Gaal drops him for the first time. It will not be the last. Woodward, sitting in the nice seats at The Hawthorns, appears to swear at one point during a match pulled from the fire by Daley Blind's eighty-seventh-minute equaliser. Another new signing doing the business for Van Gaal. Some reports claim the executive vice-chairman said, 'What a fucking waste of money' about a particular player in an episode that explodes into the classic arc on Twitter: a night of hue and cry and then the whole thing is instantly forgotten. Woodward did not actually say anything about a player, though he may have complained about a pass being wasted. This microscope taken to Manchester United is said to still bemuse Woodward over a year into the job.

The draw shows the unevenness of United. It is an inconsistency that, though expected in this bedding-in process, is concerning the manager and his players. Van Gaal has to accept some culpability here. Falcao was given only three starts before the Dutchman decided he deserved to be dropped. This cannot help a footballer who needs to rediscover his best play following a serious knee injury. He can only hope to do so in matches. The Colombian was used as a substitute at West Bromwich, four minutes before the other billboard summer signing, Ángel di María, was taken off by the manager. This comes after both players had scored in the previous match, against West Ham. Di María has completed only one full ninety minutes in five outings since starting his first match, against QPR. The manager's policy here, again, is affecting the player's ability to relax and settle into the side. Despite it being reasonable to require time for the team and club to settle under the Dutchman, there is still a near-febrile atmosphere around the place. The truth is the big fear is of a jam-tomorrow culture settling at United long-term. This became the mantra of David Moyes: the six-year deal, building for the future and how Manchester United is the kind of club that allows time. Forget the P-word, the T-word is the most potent one at the club. It may take Time for Louis van Gaal to create his Philosophy, but he had better do it quickly. Or else.

Jose Mourinho, the former protégé of Louis van Gaal, is bringing Chelsea to Old Trafford for the biggest match of the campaign so far. Before the game Van Gaal is in good form, revelling in the moment, and reminiscing about his experiences with Mourinho, whose antics he makes clear do not ruffle him. 'I'm made from a little bit of iron . . . a shield, an iron shield,' he says, lowering his hand down before his face as he talks, as if there is indeed a shield there. He then adds slightly provocatively: 'You have to ask him, why he, Mourinho, reacts like he reacts, not me.' But Louis and Jose are firm friends. This stands out when Van Gaal says: 'Sometimes we SMS but when we see each other we feel the warmth between us and our families, so that's nice. He is a very modest and emotional human being.' There is an intriguing amount of honesty and openness here, a disarming tenderness. Ferguson had this in him, too. The ability to show the real person in an unlikely public moment. The shutters are supposed to go up when the media persona appears. But here and there, if listened to closely enough, every now and then a Ferguson, a Van Gaal, will display their ease with themselves by being themselves in public, and this enhances them.

Sunday, Old Trafford. The dying embers. Chelsea are leading 1–0 from a fifty-third-minute goal by Didier Drogba. United's response has been poor. They are being out-thought and the spritzer levels seem down. In his seat, where there is rare movement, Louis van Gaal is thinking – he will say later – 'we lost our heads'. Then, miraculously, after Branislav Ivanovic's red card at the end of normal time, out of nowhere Robin van Persie rockets in a left-foot finish that grabs a point. He wheels off on a run of celebration and rips off his number twenty shirt. Is there some luck here as United's reaction to going behind has been insipid? Maybe, maybe not. But the way the place goes completely bananas is cathartic and may be the moment – the latest in the desperate hope that it can be, *at last* – that Louis van Gaal's Manchester United discovered where the kryptonite for opposing teams has been hidden. This is the style of dying-breath goals akin to how Sir Alex Ferguson's teams used to kill all-comers. The whistle blows, the match ends, and Van Gaal is saying of Van Persie: 'He did a stupid reaction after the goal. You can be excited but you don't have to pull your shirt off because then you have a yellow card. It is not so smart.'

The point against the title favourites could still be the fillip United require. This is where the team are: looking for positives everywhere, any shaft of light that might sound the herald back to a permanently bright future. They are ten points off the pace set by Mourinho's men. The Chelsea game is ten days after the three-month deadline Van Gaal set for outsiders to judge his team and philosophy. Chelsea may well have departed Old Trafford wondering if United aren't heading in the right direction, and that now, finally, Van Gaal is in business. Manchester City, at the Etihad Stadium, are up next in the derby. Bring it on is the rallying cry from manager, players and supporters.

Later in the week, at a sponsor's event at Old Trafford, the captain is seen apparently limping on to the pitch for a photo shoot. Wayne Rooney! Injured! He has just returned from his month-long suspension and, if true, this is dire news. Yet the next day, 29 October, is a good one for United followers as their on-field general feels 'hopeful of being fit' for the derby. This is Wednesday. It means the build-up, the razzmatazz of the local squabble is under way. Manchester City are six points behind Chelsea in third place, though the champions have played a match less and if United can defeat them, well, proceedings would become interesting.

Across town, the uber-sober, perma-calm Manuel Pellegrini is admitting to working on tightening his rearguard, but not of tinkering with the game-plan to deal with Rooney. 'We really don't change our way to play for some player or other player. If it's not Wayne Rooney it will be Ángel Di María, Juan Mata or Robin van Persie.' Pellegrini's tactical inflexibility is the weak gene of his managerial DNA. Van Gaal is diametrically opposite. His genetic make-up courses with ruses and cunning and tactics. The Dutchman confirms the captain is fit. 'Rooney was not injured, the media was writing that. He was never injured. Maybe his shoes were too tight, that is possible, but he was never injured. That is all I can say to you because he is my captain and he shall play.'

There is a moment of levity when Van Gaal slips into German to recall how Bayern Munich did not have a derby opponent during his time there. But when returning to the *subject du jour* he claims he is not 'jealous' of the riches in the City squad that include Sergio Agüero, Vincent Kompany, Joe Hart, Yaya Touré and David Silva. As a side-issue it would be an interesting experiment to discover how Van Gaal would play these players and how they would play under him. Better than Pellegrini is the suspicion. Both managers, though, sound the same register. A win would take United to within a point of City, and Van Gaal declares: 'We are waiting on that boost because that can give you more than only the result.' Pellegrini, meanwhile, believes that the beginning of a City-surge is nigh. 'We continue with our target for this season – to try and defend our title and to continue in the Champions League. It's very difficult to know what will happen in the future.' All very true, but where is the fizz, the call-to-arms, the 'we'll fight them on the streets of east Manchester'?

The match turns up the curiosity of a United back four of Antonio Valencia, Michael Carrick, Paddy McNair and Luke Shaw. Two midfielders and two comparative novices. This follows Chris Smalling's foolish dismissal after receiving a second yellow card for felling James Milner with only thirty-nine minutes gone. So United are down to ten men for nearly an hour. This forces on Carrick for his first appearance under Van Gaal following the ankle ligaments injury he suffered within twenty-four hours of the manager arriving in July. Sergio Agüero scores what proves the only goal on sixty-three minutes. The referee, Michael Oliver, waves away three credible penalty shouts for City. And United have a real go towards the end but lose. This means that at the ten-match mark Van Gaal's side have only thirteen points, half the number stacked up by Chelsea. United are down to tenth position, having won just three times, lost three times and drawn four times. There have been sixteen goals scored and fourteen conceded. These are concerning numbers. Forget about the title, Van Gaal is facing hand-to-hand firefights if he merely wishes to finish fourth and gain the Champions League qualification the Glazers and Ed Woodward have demanded. It is 2 November and the promised land of May and the final Premier League table, with United sitting snugly above the club finishing fifth, requires a faith of imagination to picture.

*

The former Fulham man, Chris Smalling, becomes the latest of the Van Gaal cadre to be slated by his manager. He is labelled 'stupid' for his sending-off. Interesting approach. Sir Alex Ferguson rarely criticised one of his own. Jose Mourinho is the same. So Smalling joins Shinji Kagawa (now back at Borussia Dortmund), Luke Shaw, Ander Herrera, Wayne Rooney, Robin van Persie, Phil Jones, and in the future Ángel Di María, Antonio Valencia and Radamel Falcao in being upbraided on the record. Apart from showing any kind of sensitive side, a penchant for reading proper literature or a love of music not in the canon, this is the grand non, non, non in elite professional football. You do not slag off your players where everyone can hear you. But Van Gaal does this. And does it in a fashion that does not seem to have 'lost the dressing room' – that catch-all football truism that may not mean anything anyway because it doesn't make a load of sense in the first place. How do you find and not lose the dressing room? Win games. That is it.

So this is Van Gaal. He is a shake-up merchant, not an arm-around-the-shoulder kind of guy. He stirs up players, his employers, his club (United's a commercial monster), the media. Himself, probably. Here he shows the major difference between the men and boys of the managerial game. Moyes had hope. The real operators have originality of thought. Call it imagination. All the best have it. The ability to think differently, off the cuff. Sir Alex Ferguson was a master of this. Was there a more wrong-footing management move than his signing of Laurent Blanc from Internazionale in summer 2001? Or Henrik Larsson in January 2007 for a less-than-three-month loan from Helsingborgs? Or Michael Owen from Newcastle United in July 2009? These were all counter-intuitive dances that fought complacency. Such deals showed the potency of true intelligence – imagination. What Ferguson did was to introduce a poetry of thought into a sport dominated by fish-and-chip thinking. He subjected the familiar to re-examination, caused a review of how to consider Blanc (past it at thirty-five, of course), Larsson (thirty-six, certainly over the hill), and Owen (twenty-nine, definitely had it). All three became renewed, suddenly the sprightly coming football men of their youth with a fresh ticket to the rarefied air of elite play. The way in which they had already been packed and boxed away was shown to be wrong. A laziness. A waste. But only because of Ferguson's vision. He forced Blanc, Larsson and Owen to look at themselves in the mirror and see a reborn player. Forget whether these were good or bad or prescient decisions from Ferguson. What they most certainly proved was the aesthetic, the romantic, the poetic eye of the Scot as manager and man.

Imagination is what Ferguson had in abundance and David Moyes lacked. Van Gaal? There is no doubt he has imagination. There are countless illustrations. The introduction of the goalkeeper Tim Krul for Holland's World Cup quarter-final penalty shootout that won the tie against Costa Rica and a place in the semi-finals. Brilliant. Lucky, as well? Sure. But what is luck? How about the way Van Gaal lagged behind in his first seasons at Barcelona and Bayern Munich, both teams appearing as awkward as the Dutchman can under questioning? But who won La Liga in 1997–98 and the Bundesliga in 2009–10? These triumphs were twelve years apart. Yet the same aesthetic, the same pictures of how the season would be, a kind of imagination of faith, emerged before Van Gaal and then occurred. And this is why United's faltering start to his first campaign does not seem to trouble him and should have no effect on how the club may go next year. This is the theory. This is his story and he's sticking to it.

A criticism of Van Gaal's style has surfaced that suggests he appears to be making it up as he goes along. He may be. He may not be. It does not matter. To him, anyway. Something, somewhere in his make-up will ensure it works. From Wayne Rooney downwards, the players continue to believe, as they must. What they see, which the displays do not show, is how the manager is on the training ground: totally and utterly convincing. Unwavering in mood and focus. There is no nature where he is concerned. It is all nurture. The brilliance is in making it appear as if he is making it up as he goes along while all the time the results will be taken care of. More courage. More *imagination*.

This is what makes Van Gaal sure of himself. Like Ferguson. Like Mourinho. Confident. An illustration comes in the press room at the Etihad Stadium after the derby defeat. Van Gaal is admitting he feels 'lousy' for the fans. It is mentioned that United's thirteen points is 'half Chelsea's points tally'. So, how does he assess the deficit? This is a classic hack question, the kind Sonny Liston, the former world heavyweight boxing champion, meant when he said: 'Newspapermen ask dumb questions – they look up at the sun and ask if it is shining.' In an instant Van Gaal says: 'Yeah, but I can count also. So that's not so difficult.' That's it. Dismissed. Off you go. The question is legitimate but the questioner is left feeling impertinent for posing it.

David Moyes was given a six-year contract and was sacked inside twelve months. Van Gaal is asked why he feels he has assurances. It is the closest-to-the-bone question yet – being mentioned in the same breath as Moyes is a first and shows bravery from the questioner. Van Gaal does not bridle. 'That is only the belief in yourself and the players and the staff. I cannot speak for him.' On the paltry points tally he is highly critical of the team and himself. 'I feel myself very lousy for the fans in the first place, and also the board because they have a great belief in me, my staff and my players. I said from the beginning when we won every game in the United States that the process shall take more than one year – it will take three years.' So Van Gaal is not saying three months any longer. This refit could take three years. This puts him further into Moyes territory. The Scot liked to hug his six-year contract as evidence he would be given time. He could hardly be blamed. Six years *was* a hell of a long contract. The thinking behind *that* decision continues to baffle. Why not give Moyes ten or twenty years, or the twenty-six-and a-half years Ferguson served?

Van Gaal can still offer a quip about the injury list that has become a standing joke. Ahead of the Crystal Palace game, when discussing Marcos Rojo's shoulder injury, the manager laments: 'The human body has been made by God, not by me.' Everyone takes the opportunity to laugh.

The run is now three games without a win: 2–2 at West Bromwich Albion, 1–1 against Chelsea and that 1–0 defeat by Manchester City. This is not the stuff of fantasy. This is not the stuff of red-shirted swarms taking visiting teams back to the Stone Age at the Theatre of Dreams. This is mundane, at best. A state of affairs that is making the vultures salivate. There is nothing majestic about Louis van Gaal's Manchester United. Or the Manchester United of David Moyes. The Manchester United of no-Sir-Alex-Ferguson. This team plays with the gusto of a funeral march. In the Great Man's long reign, once he had won his first pot, the FA Cup in 1990, the longest stretch without a trophy was under twelve months. Thus when Louis van Gaal says he may need 'three years' to take Manchester United back to the zenith, he is being utterly unreasonable in the context of the mores of the polite society constructed by Sir Alexander Chapman Ferguson. Three years! 'We shall win a lot of matches in a row,' Van Gaal says. Those thirteen points from the opening ten matches are United's poorest yield since the 1986–87 campaign. That return got Ron Atkinson sacked and brought in Ferguson.

The signs of unease are beginning to appear not just in the media but from within the team. There is a niggling sense that life at Manchester United is not what the big guns signed up for. It is implied by Robin van Persie's confession that Sir Alex Ferguson's retirement has indeed set the striker back. This is no bombshell. Rio Ferdinand's comments, two months before, that Ferguson leaving 'took the wind out of everyone's sails' but 'the person it hit more than anyone was Robin', had, according to Van Persie, 'some truth in it'. The Great Man really is proving a difficult spot to expunge.

Anyway, it's Old Trafford! It's Crystal Palace! Never mind the unspectacular opposition, feel the easy three points. Correct? Not really. This is hardly total football. United are hoarding the ball but are disjointed. Again. Rojo's injury and Smalling's suspension means Van Gaal goes for the eleventh centre-back pairing in his twelfth competitive match as manager. This time he pairs Paddy

McNair with Daley Blind, who is moved from midfield. This is only McNair's third start, his debut coming in the victory over West Ham at the end of September. A midfielder originally from Ballyclare Colts, the nineteen-year-old still has the innocence of adolescence. Around the training ground he can look like a sixth-form student or a fan in a United tracksuit, wide-eyed as he is about to be given a tour of the place, rather than a real-life, up-and-coming young star of the first team. But that is what the Northern Irishman is. He has an elegant style reminiscent of Alan Hansen, the former Liverpool central defender who was a supreme reader of a match and who was able to see the pass. A single Juan Mata goal after sixty-seven minutes settles the game, though it might have been more as he also hits a post late on. There is a scare for United when Yannick Bolasie's cross hits Luke Shaw and might have fallen to United old boy Fraizer Campbell. Later, McNair shows the inconsistency of youth that Van Gaal has mentioned more than once, allowing a long Palace ball to bounce. This time, Campbell pounces on the error but his attempted lob sails over David de Gea's goal.

Next up, after the latest international break, it's Arsenal. Since the great team led by Patrick Vieira, the men from north London have usually been a comfortable proposition. Now, who knows? The win against Palace is the first for a month and the team are not dominating as should be expected from the £150 million-plus outlay. Will they ever? The mood around the club and among the players is certainly happier. That is the message coming from the dressing room. The conviction is that the umbilical cord that ties the manager and his charges is a lifeline Moyes never had when results soured. Remarkably, from the tenth place after ten games, United are suddenly within touching distance of where they want to be. Van Gaal looks content. 'We are now two points behind fourth place, so it's in our hands. I am happy.'

The break for the international fixtures means there is time for more analysis and there is much to be done on United. The shape-shifting nature of Louis van Gaal's United teams are unprecedented in this manor. If David Moyes had continually changed formation he would have suffered scorn. The shape against Palace was the fourth match in which the single-striker approach, with a four-man defence, was used. Van Gaal started the season with 3–5–2, which lasted four games. Next came 4–4–2 for four outings. Now this latest formation. All in the first twelve matches of his reign. This is adding to the sense of a message muddled and uncertain, which is not a brilliant scenario for the players. And, despite being the manager who talks of a clear vision, Van Gaal still remains unsure of how the side should play. So, too, do his players. The 3–5–2 of the summer tour seemed a bold move then. Van Gaal persisted with it initially when back home, but that feels a long, long time ago. Now it's chop and change, chop and change. Retrain brains. And switching positions, as Ashley Young and Antonio Valencia, to name two who have had to move from winger to wingback to full-back, is no way to establish rhyme, rhythm and accord. The Dutchman's goblet of genius seems empty each time he drinks at the moment, precisely when he could do with an overflowing chalice.

The comparison between Van Gaal and David Moyes at the same point in their tenures is inescapable. Both are guilty of finding different ways to lose the thread, to start messing the job up. Sir Alex Ferguson's successor was The Man with the Fixed Blueprint. Louis van Gaal is The Man with Too Many Plans. Football is supposed to be the simple game. Pass and move. Move forward. Repeat three or four times. Now try to score. United's players must be confused. Van Gaal warned this would happen at the start, so the squad cling to this. It's been the same pattern everywhere he's been, the Dutchman continues to say. But 'how soon is now?' must be the question. There is a sense of this in the Palace game where Rooney and Fellaini stray from the game-plan, falling back deep to cover for the gaps in defence. Van Gaal did not correct this until half-time. It seems strange to allow a whole forty-five minutes to pass with two of his experienced players disrupting the strategy. Slightly staggering even. And then afterwards he criticises *them*. These are the kind of details that can prove costly. Neil Warnock's team should kick themselves for failing to capitalise. This is more evidence that the unclear messages are continuing. There is an increasing sense that while Mata's winner secured three points it also papered over a large amount of confusion within the ranks.

The Battle of the Galactico's Wounded Knee is about to begin. The denouement of the first act of The Radamel Falcao Incident is the reveal of the full challenge our hero has to overcome: the left knee he injured badly in January, remains delicate and requires frequent icing. The plot races into the second act with this catalytic challenge. Can the lion heart overcome the suspect joint that may have blunted crucial pace and edge to establish himself as not only a first-team regular but the leading man of Louis van Gaal's Manchester United? Second acts have a habit of becoming far worse than the hero could possibly imagine. And on Monday, the nursing of the knee is made public, the revelations an instant Twitter smash-hit, every detail pored over. Now Falcao not only has the concern over the ongoing treatment that consists of applying ice after every training session and match to mitigate further damage, but also how this will be digested in the wider world. Falcao is a popular figure and by all accounts a gentleman. But the rest of the squad is surprised by the extent of the problem, though it was something he flagged up when signing. His anxiety is shown when he reacts to the revelation on Twitter, saying in his native Spanish: '*1 tonto especula, algunos pocos más tontos sin objetividad replican, para que millones crean mentiras. Nefasto lo de esos pocos.*' The translation is, 'One fool speculates. A few others lacking objectivity respond and millions believe lies. It is disastrous what a few fools can do.'

The tweet reveals how sensitive the Colombian is about his current position at the club. The state of Falcao's knee is crucial to his future because United hold an option to take him permanently from Monaco. As well as his knee, Falcao's form will also be closely observed. This has not been great: there has been a solitary goal in five appearances, and he has been dropped since the trip to West Bromwich a month ago. To make matters worse he is now unavailable due to a calf problem. The Colombian has settled well into the fabric of the club and is a good and conscientious trainer, but he appears unable to turn on the form when it comes to match-day.

On Saturday, United beat Arsenal 2–1 at the Emirates

Stadium and the focus of the build-up, Danny Welbeck, does not score or 'come back to haunt' United. Van Gaal was in full *je ne regrette rien* mode beforehand. 'I have already said what I think – he was not a line-up player, he was more a substitute than a line-up player and he was already with different coaches not a line-up player and then with Mr Van Gaal the world is changing?' Come March and FA Cup quarter-final time the world will be a starkly different place for Mr Van Gaal. The non-line-up player is in the Arsenal starting XI who knock United out of the competition on a Monday night at Old Trafford. And the scorer of the winning goal is Mr Daniel Nii Tackie Mensah Welbeck.

David Moyes has joined Real Sociedad and Monday brings news of his first game of professional football as a manager, 216 days after that darkest of dark days at Everton. It is a goalless draw with Deportivo de La Coruña, after which the man who would (not) be king after Sir Alex Ferguson, says to the gathered media, some of whom are from these shores: 'Sorry for dragging you out for a 0–0.' Back in England, Ryan Giggs, Louis van Gaal's number two and player-coach under Moyes, is asked about last season. 'It was disappointing overall, but you have to look forward and learn from your mistakes, look to improve all the time. It was a tough year for everyone, but I hope David does well. It's a great chance for him and a great challenge to be coaching in a different country, which probably not enough British managers do. It's brave and I'm sure he's excited and I hope he does well.' This is the final word on the Moyes–United 'era'. Apart from when Moyes mentions in future utterances the mantra of needing more time.

Giggs, a relatively unemotional and quiet man, proves *au fait* with Van Gaal-talk. When might his beloved Manchester United claim the crown again? 'It is a process,' he says, slipping in a P-word, perhaps hoping it would not be noticed! 'I mean, I think everyone will agree Chelsea are head and shoulders above anyone else, but it's a process and you just have to try to keep improving and see where that takes you.' The same P-word again! Cheeky! Of his boss, Giggs adds: 'He obviously demands a lot, he's somebody who's got plenty of experience, likes to play attacking football.' Attacking football? Did Giggsy not mean to use another P-word? As in, 'Possession-based football', because this is what the LvG United are doing a lot of, but with little rapier.

Bayern Munich are in town for their Champions League encounter against Manchester City and Van Gaal visits The Lowry Hotel where they are staying to see old friends. Later the Dutchman is spotted in the first-floor bar area, dressed in an expensive-looking tan-coloured suit, with his wife Truus, and speaking to Marcus Horwick, Bayern's chief media officer. It is a visual reminder of the esteem in which Van Gaal is held in Bavaria. He went close in 2010 to leading Bayern to an unprecedented Treble of Bundesliga, German Cup and Champions League before Jose Mourinho's Inter defeated them in the European final. Ferguson, of course, achieved the English equivalent feat with United in 1999 when claiming the Premier League, FA Cup and Champions League. The present mob have a lot to live up to. But the relaxed air Van Gaal carries with him is permeating the players, though they understand they still have to perform or they could be the next to be criticised in public. Moyes hardly, if ever, did this and still suffered bad results and a lack of faith, receiving little loyalty in return. The Van Gaal mystique seems to allow him to bag any of his players openly and the inverse is true: devotion from the gang increases.

Take the Friday briefing for Hull City's visit to Old Trafford. Robin van Persie was replaced at Arsenal having managed only thirteen touches, and Van Gaal has no compunction about questioning the man he made captain of his Holland team, and who is supposedly an away-from-the-game pal. 'Every player in my selection has to fight for his position and I shall always take the best of the players, and it must also be suitable for the mix of players,' Van Gaal says before describing Van Persie as 'very bad' against Arsenal. Falcao is fit again and available. To a question about whether the Colombian can start to meet expectations, the manager says: 'I hope so because we have him on loan because of that.'

Against Hull the next day Chris Smalling, Wayne Rooney and the maligned Van Persie are the goalscorers in a 3–0 win for United. This is a third victory in a row and United impress. The team shape continues to be a conundrum: today it is a quasi-4–2–2–2. This has Ángel Di María in attack alongside Rooney, Ashley Young at left-back and Van Persie in midfield. This must surely have made the captain chuckle given his travails at being yanked in and out of attack to midfield. But who cares when the side is winning? Besides, Van Persie adds the third after the break and suddenly the manager appears to be a man of great foresight. Falcao comes on for Van Persie and misses a good chance, but only the Colombian dwells on this.

In the context of how this season has gone, the team is flying. These three victories mean United are up to fourth position, eleven points off Chelsea. This is a yawning gap, of course. If Sir Alex Ferguson had allowed such a deficit after only thirteen matches a major incident room would have been set up at Old Trafford. But those were different times. Already. Eighteen months after the knight retired, lagging such a huge distance behind the leaders is considered progress in these parts following the season under David Moyes.

Afterwards Van Gaal corrects talkSPORT's Manchester reporter when the Dutchman is asked if his 'methods' are taking place: 'It is not methods but philosophy.' There is laughter in the room. The journalist takes his gentle upbraiding well. Philosophically. The mood is bright. The mood is the colour of the Dutch national team livery. This has been United's best showing of the season. Di María pulls up injured and Rooney also looks to have hurt a knee near the end. But these are about the only negatives to be found. Van Gaal is not content, though. He has an agenda to be aired. 'I cannot change that because I don't think it's good for the football players that they play within two days another match. In the December months, it shall be like that. I also have a wife and kids and grandchildren and cannot see them this Christmas. But I want to work in the Premier League, I have to adapt and I shall adapt.' Classic wrong-footing by Van Gaal, expressing his concern in his own particular way, shoehorning in a mention of marital bliss, extended family and a pastoral concern for his players. The funny thing is that he does seem genuinely concerned for the players. This is not just a moan about exhaustion.

Three days later and Rooney is out for the visit of Stoke City because of the knock he suffered towards the end of the Hull game. His is the forty-third injury or illness of Manchester United's season. A high number. 'I had to change my attack again so it's unbelievable – it's the truth. Di María [who is also injured] cannot play and Rooney cannot play,' says an unhappy Van Gaal. James Wilson has been drafted into the XI for only his second United start. 'Yes, of course, a big opportunity,' says Van Gaal. 'I would have brought him already on Saturday but he was ill. He has the opportunity to show himself tonight.' Wilson's inclusion means Falcao is ignored as his predicament worsens. He is surely fit enough now to start but is on the bench. How can the dashing idol drag Manchester United up to Mount Olympus if he is sitting and watching? The twelve-minute cameo he is afforded when coming on for Wilson is no use either. This is a low point, a nadir. Here is the tension, the drama of The Radamel Falcao Incident, but our hero could do without it, really. Can he resolve his crisis by somehow developing new skills at the ripe old age of twenty-eight? Can he be reborn as a crafty number ten? Or, if his pace is not blunted and, actually, he just needs a decent run in the team – *so come on, Louis, be fair and pick me, please* – can he force his way into the XI and show those quick-to-judge critics? If these ifs are resolved he will discover his true capabilities and become not only the hero of Manchester United's resurgence but a universal figure, a man for all ages, for everyone, everywhere. This is the way of Hollywood. Falcao's way at Old Trafford already seems a dead end. He does lack pace. He does not appear a player who could become a high-class number ten.

He cannot get a run of games. And, Van Gaal's football *modus operandi*, a slow pawn-to-king-four of a march up the chess board does not create a flurry of chances for the born predator that is Falcao.

This is a side-issue to the main question of United's form. Stoke arrive on a cold December evening. The evidence is becoming unignorable: Louis van Gaal has something going on. Marouane Fellaini, who is enjoying a revival under the manager, opens the scoring after twenty-one minutes. A fine header from a smooth Ander Herrera cross. The fans are in good cheer, singing the 'Twelve Days of Christmas' ditty that features only Eric Cantona as in 'Four Cantonas, three Cantonas, two Cantonas and an Eric Cantona'. However, by half-time, Steven Nzonzi's equaliser has dampened the festive spirit a touch. After the break Fellaini, Herrera, Van Persie and Wilson are all over Stoke before Juan Mata makes the breakthrough. The Spaniard's curving high ball towards Marcos Rojo is missed by a bunch of Stoke defenders and bounces past Asmir Begovic to give United a lead on fifty-nine minutes they do not relinquish. The strut and swagger is visible among Van Gaal's players throughout. United are again resembling the once familiar unforgiving threshing machine. This fourth consecutive victory is re-casting Van Gaal as a managerial great once more. The fickleness of the expert views that fill the media and the fan-zones is shown up. The plodding, man-out-of-time-and-place merchant who cannot decide on formation, whoever thought that? Later, Rojo's girlfriend posts a photograph online to prove it was his final touch from Mata's ball for the goal, but no one in red really cares.

Fellaini is a peculiarity and as good an illustration of the vagaries of managing this club. Tall and gangly, and no renowned curator of a ball, he became an emblem of all that was wrong about David Moyes as Manchester United manager. But now he is causing a startling suspicion to emerge that he may be a Louis van Gaal lieutenant. Imagine that. After being a favourite to be sold – Napoli were sniffing around in the summer. Fellaini went to see Van Gaal as the transfer window was nearing its close and was told he had a chance of a future at the club if 'he worked hard and proved it'. Coming out of the meeting the impression was that if Fellaini scrapped hard he might do enough, at most, to be considered a decent squad player. For the diehard United fan even this is a heresy. If Van Gaal begins viewing Fellaini as a go-to man, what would this say about how the manager wants the team to play?

Afterwards, in the mixed zone, which is near the players' tunnel and is set up for players to stop and speak, should they wish, there is no one around apart from a security guard and Daley Blind, who is recovering well from a knee injury. Robin van Persie, David de Gea, Ander Herrera, Michael Carrick and James Wilson walk through and offer polite apologies. Then comes Chris Smalling, who does stop. United are in fourth position after fourteen matches with twenty-five points, eight behind Chelsea's. 'Yes, we can beat Southampton and Liverpool,' the defender says of the next two opponents. Fellaini appears and he believes the championship challenge is very much on as United are 'waiting for a Chelsea mistake'. For all the criticism Fellaini has had aimed at him since signing, there is no trace of bitterness or smugness now he is beginning to turn things around. Everything is intelligent and articulate, and delivered in a surprising whisper considering the size of the man.

The Friday press conference ahead of the Southampton match touches the realms of torture. Radamel Falcao's situation requires some answers – James Wilson was preferred as a starter against Stoke – and Van Gaal is not keen to offer any insight. The tension around the subject is palpable. There is near-silence over the issue, and there is a sense the situation has gone past mere settling-in pains. Van Gaal does not care for any player's sensitivities. 'I'm not interested. He has to follow my philosophy. Do you understand that? Yeah, I'm here because of that.'

There is added interest surrounding Van Gaal's relationship with Ronald Koeman, the Southampton manager. Koeman was Van Gaal's assistant at Barcelona, the younger man's first coaching appointment. That was in 1998. Six years later Koeman was Ajax coach when Van Gaal was made technical director. From here the relationship dissolved. Koeman is a more instinctive manager than Van Gaal. Despite not being employed to coach at Ajax, there came a famous incident where Van Gaal intervened during training to tell Zlatan Ibrahimovic to attack the post more. The manner in which he then triumphantly greeted the Swedish striker's subsequent goal from the ploy right in Koeman's face meant there was no way back. The tensions have now eased. But Koeman's success so far in his first season at Southampton in guiding them to third position, a point and a place better than United, despite the obvious difference in transfer budget and player salaries, creates ample opportunity to poke fun at United's form and for Van Gaal to get a little uptight. The point is put to him, and in full bristling mode he remarks: 'Do we know how many players we lost?', apparently missing the point. 'I don't think money is the question in this.

When Manchester is coming clubs are always asking more money and we have to pay. Do you think Southampton pay too much for players?' Some may have the violins out for Van Gaal and United here. Manchester United suffer because they have *too much* money is the Dutchman's argument. Swiftly on to the next question. 'Can you put the record straight because a lot has been written about the Koeman bust-up at Ajax?' Answer: 'Why are you asking the question for the fourth time when I have given a clear answer. Why? Why? It is only your interest to ask.' Because it is the job. Punters wish to know. The football world is tuned in. It's all part of the managerial psycho-drama.

Southampton are defeated 2–1 at their ground in what is a hit-and-run mission, United barely deserving the victory given them by Robin van Persie's double. Van Gaal is not much happier than he was before the match. The team, remember, has won its last five Premier League matches. However, there is some mystery about their recent success as United are no finely-tuned orchestra. This is what Louis van Gaal gives to his employers: scrambling results when there seems no way to be able to do so. Under Moyes the last five league matches might have been lost. Last season United's record against direct rivals was poor. The Scot led a team who lost home and away to Liverpool, 4–0 on aggregate. He drew and lost against Chelsea, the overall score 3–1. He lost home and away to Manchester City, 7–1. Only Arsenal were beaten, 1–0 at Old Trafford, and held goalless away. The record also shows up the lack of goals against United's competitors. There were only two. Van Gaal has thus far drawn 1–1 with Chelsea at Old Trafford, lost 1–0 at Manchester City, and defeated Arsenal 2–1 in their backyard.

Pre-Liverpool, who are next up, the injury news from a more relaxed Van Gaal is that he only has 'four players' out: Shaw, Smalling, Di María and Blind. And 'Falcao could make a return'. Van Gaal nearly joined Liverpool in 2012 as director of football, though he does not want to expand on this. This is probably wise because Manchester United and Liverpool fans do not enjoy the most cordial of relations. United are in a welcome third place, eleven points behind Chelsea, who stand on thirty-nine, and along with second-placed Manchester City have played a game more. Are United in the championship race? 'That I said when we were thirteen points behind. We now have a better possibility because I don't think Chelsea shall lose so much,' he responds.

Despite third place, veiled criticism of the side's style of play has started to come from within the team. Jonny Evans, the Northern Irish defender who has been at the club since a boy, dared to say after the Southampton match that United 'want to be playing better football, we also know we've got to entertain our fans as well'. This points to the lack of thrill there can be watching this Van Gaal side. The manager thinks about it and demurs. What else can he do? 'I'm not agreeing because against Hull City it was a fantastic match and we won 3–0 and could win 6–0. It was very entertaining. The supporters that I've spoken to after the match were excited about the match. No, we are not consistent. We are looking for that. I think we have flair enough.' The Hull display was three games ago and is the exception rather than the rule. This demand for wins *and* show-time football must exhaust the manager. Unless Manchester United shine every ninety minutes then a public flogging awaits.

The Liverpool game goes like a dream for Van Gaal and United. They shine, they glow. It is a 1.30 p.m. kick-off at Old Trafford and within twelve minutes the fans are enjoying themselves as Wayne Rooney beats Brad Jones. United never look back. By half-time it is 2–0, Juan Mata has headed a second, and supporters are singing to Brendan Rodgers that he's 'getting sacked in the morning'. This is party central, an early Christmas present. Rodgers's men are being handed a hiding right before them. Robin van Persie's seventy-first-minute strike makes it a handsome 3–0 victory, a sixth consecutive three-pointer for the resurgent United. David Moyes's United lost by the same scoreline in this fixture here last season. Van Gaal becomes a folk hero. The fans can go to work smiling and desperate to bump into any Liverpool supporters they know. The win keeps United in third place with only a game to go before Christmas. They are ten points ahead of Liverpool and eight behind Chelsea. The formation has been another new one – 3–1–4–2 – that has Wayne Rooney in a deep-lying role. It has worked like a fantasy for Van Gaal the strategist.

It is 14 December. Saint Nicholas is due down chimneys soon and the final match before the big day is Saturday's visit to Aston Villa. If this becomes the seventh three-pointer in a row United will cement third place into the New Year. Given the awful start of thirteen points from ten matches, it shows just how Van Gaal has transformed things since then. The manager is hardly batting away the possibility of a title challenge, and Chelsea and Manchester City may be peering a little nervously over their shoulders. There is a queue to get the message out. 'If we are in and around the top by Christmas or January then we are right in there with a chance,' says Michael Carrick. Next, here comes the captain. 'We have to believe we can win the title. We are eight points behind and coming into a busy period,' says Wayne Rooney. 'If we can win our games and the others have one bad result then there is nothing there [in margin].'

Villa away starts the clogged Christmas–New Year programme of which Van Gaal complained. Then United host Newcastle United on Boxing Day, visiting Tottenham Hotspur two days later, before travelling to Stoke on New Year's Day. Four matches in eleven days could mean a harvest of twelve points if all are won, and Rooney adds: 'If we can keep picking up points and winning games, then hopefully the other teams will drop points and we can be right in there going into the second half of the season.' What follows is a pocket-treatise on Van Gaal and, by implication, David Moyes. About his new manager Rooney is glowing. He and the rest of the squad like how Van Gaal has taken charge. Though the sideways tactics are different to Ferguson's gangbusters approach, this is not the point. The point is Rooney, Juan Mata, Radamel Falcao, David de Gea, Robin van Persie and everyone else are playing *for him*. As Rooney says: 'Everyone can see he has an aura about him. He has experience. When things weren't going great for us earlier on in the season, he knew what he was doing, he knew the form would come back and that we would win games. There was no panic, he stayed calm because he has been through it all before. Thankfully the lads have believed in him and what he has said.'

This last sentence is the difference between Van Gaal and Moyes and illustrates how the whole show rests on trust and confidence. The whispers about the Scot started almost from day one. The 'lads', as Rooney calls them, just did not fancy him. The respect Moyes had for Ferguson and the club veered too close to deferential. Awe may have been manageable but overawed? Van Gaal is certainly the opposite of deferential. Awe? Forget it. Though he is, of course, respectful of the institution he works for and the manager who revived it. But the Iron Tulip is more respectful of his own ability and what he can do – what he will do – for United. What's more the players have been dazzled by the Van Gaal chutzpah in tearing up everything they knew before under Sir Alex Ferguson. Moyes insisted on taking the training sessions and threw himself around, but ended up cutting a quasi-desperate, amateurish figure. The Van Gaal methodology is even more hands-on – it is hands *and legs-on* – yet the way he stalks the players in training, watching them, stopping to berate or praise or go all demonstrative, while often holding a clipboard, whistle dangling around his neck, may make him seem eccentric. But deep within the psyche of the professional footballer, where the base need is to be taken care of and told everything will be all right, the United players are responding to a man whose charisma has them all wanting to please him. Then there is the replacing of the grass at Carrington's first-team training pitches with Desso, the planting of more trees to provide shelter from the wind, and the installation of HD 'spy' cameras so that the players' every move and every facial twitch is monitored, even down to how they are reacting to instructions. The precision Van Gaal demands means his players are told off if they are even a yard out of position.

Rooney continues: 'It was a massive change when the manager and the new staff came in. It was a lot for us to take in and adapt to the things around the training ground and on the pitch. He is a great manager. He is great with the players. He is honest with the players who are playing and those who aren't, which is great. We have a great team spirit. We all want to be successful. As long as we keep working we won't be far away.' Mature words from Rooney. And United are blooming again. In the round. Individual cases are individual. A certain supreme occupier of the United number nine shirt seems to have already become an old lag in the eyes of Van Gaal. There are eight days until Christmas and Radamel Falcao has scored only once. This is not megastar principal male stuff. The only goal was the winner against Everton on 5 October, two-and-a-half months ago. The centre-forward decides the time is right to get a message out. On Sunday, against Liverpool, Van Gaal gave him only twelve minutes, and as his agent Jorge Mendes is 'very strategic' in his counsel and advice, according to another United player's representative, he may be behind the timing of Falcao's utterance. 'From my point of view, yes,' the Colombian says when asked whether he would like the loan converted into a permanent transfer. 'But obviously I have to analyse the situation, see if I play more and see what decision the board takes. But from my point of view, I really want to stay.'

Michael Carrick's return to the United line-up has coincided with the run of six straight league victories since his first against Crystal Palace. This is worth raising with Van Gaal ahead of United's trip to Villa. 'I think you give too much honour to Michael Carrick,' he says. 'He is my captain so he brings a lot of experience but also a lot of composure. I can use him in different positions and that I like. Because he is my captain, he can transfer my philosophy on the pitch . . . I have three captains, but of course there is a sequence. Rooney is one, Carrick is two, Fletcher is three.' This is the first anyone has heard about Carrick being a captain and ahead of Darren Fletcher, though as the latter is almost certainly out of the club in next month's winter transfer window this is no major surprise. And the choice of Carrick – again ahead of Van Persie – is another indicator of how the manager is thinking. It is another snub for Van Persie who, after his World Cup exploits, cannot have expected to be second fiddle to Wayne Rooney as the gun striker and behind Rooney, Carrick and even Fletcher in the armband-wearing stakes. This is some fall. There are unconfirmed rumours the pair may have had a falling-out, which may explain this. The truth, though, may be as simple as Van Persie being past his peak and Van Gaal, with his cold, clear vision, has spotted this.

So, United have won six league games on the trot. This is the purple patch required, the run needed to bolster confidence in the manager's attempt to rebuild the club. Such a run as this has not occurred since Sir Alex Ferguson's final, championship-winning season of two years ago. Asked if Van Gaal is more 'bothered about performance', the manager says: 'I am not only focused on results. And when I speak with Sir Alex he says, "Not any problem, you have won." But for me it's also the performance that's very important because when you perform you shall win more and that's what I want to show to the fans and the players want to show that.' Louis van Gaal lecturing Sir Alex Ferguson on style over substance. The man whose Manchester United side is so far emerging as a functional outfit telling the man whose teams were filled with swashbucklers that victories are not enough.

At Villa Park the run of consecutive victories ends at half-a-dozen as United draw 1–1. There are great scenes for Falcao as he *does* start and *does* score. It is the equaliser and the point could prove crucial in the final analysis and could make the Colombian's loan worth it for that alone. If Manchester United gain a much-prized top-four finish, and return to the hoop-la of the European Cup, the £16 million paid for the once-feared forward will be a bargain.

Chapter 17

The New Year Coming

The winning streak may be over but nineteen points from twenty-one is what Ed Woodward was talking about when he hired Louis van Gaal. One prominent gentleman of the football fraternity is impressed by Manchester United and offers the manager an early Christmas present by praising him, the team and, hold on a minute, Wayne Rooney, too. Step forward Sir Alex Ferguson, once of the Old Trafford hot-seat. 'Rooney's back flying, and Rooney will always get you a goal. That's always an advantage with a team that's got a goalscorer,' he reckons, which is praise indeed considering the toxic relationship the pair have endured lately.

Then it's on to Van Gaal. 'I don't know how he can expect to be getting the best results with the injuries he's had [in his squad]. And when he gets the best players back you watch United,' says Ferguson. 'Because he's a great coach, he'll do well. I'm not interested in what's happening with the players he's brought in because they'll need time. When I took Patrice Evra and Nemanja Vidić in the January of the same year they were all over the place – it took five months to get used to playing for Manchester United, the culture, the history of the club, and these new players will be exactly the same.' Ferguson has a point. United are currently third in the Premier League and playing with renewed vigour in attack. It won't last long, though, will it? It never does. Does it? Or will it?

In what may be his last public words for a while, Ferguson offers a précis of his time at the club. 'Many people have different interpretations of what I've made Manchester United over the last twenty-six years, with great players, Rooney, Ronaldo, Cantona, Keane, Robson, Schmeichel. There's too many to talk about. But, honestly, I think the spirit of Manchester United has come from the '92 team. I think that gave everyone at the club, not just the supporters, myself, my staff, the directors, Bobby Charlton who was brought up in the Matt Busby era ... it brought back the history of Manchester United, no question.' History. Pedigree. Heritage. Nostalgia's for the future.

'Tis the night before Christmas Eve and it is 4 p.m. in the Jimmy Murphy Centre and there is a tinkle of jingle bells as Louis van Gaal strides in with a bottle of grog in hand. Newcastle United are the visitors on Boxing Day, but before business drinks are offered and Van Gaal raises a glass of the red stuff and toasts us. 'Cheers and much love to your family, that's also important,' and after imbibing, offers a quip. 'Not a bad wine, our sponsor?' This is the latest bravado performance before the gathered media. The run of success is six victories on the bounce and a draw. But even during the early-season

Ferguson also stalked the technical area and the assistant referee and fourth official. A lot. To try and intimidate and win an advantage for the team. Van Gaal almost never leaves his seat on the bench, which seems a surprise for a man who is so keen on winning and focused on squeezing every angle to do so. 'I don't see any influence from me when I am there shouting,' he says. This is a thought-provoking statement considering the number of touchline lieutenants of the English game who are constantly up and down. But this is how Van Gaal works. He has his own way and makes others consider their way. The players, Van Gaal's bunch of high-earning success merchants, are particularly impressed by this. They thought no man could impress them as much as Sir Alex Ferguson. Louis van Gaal is coming pretty close. Here, Van Gaal's theory is that having spent the whole week ahead of match-day preparing, once it gets to the game it is largely up to them. This ceding of responsibility is appreciated by his players and is part of Van Gaal's 'philosophy': he wants them to be the agents of the side's destiny as much as possible. It is a telling Van Gaal incongruity: train, teach and control as much as possible so that in the end they do not need the lectures and can take over. However, the manager admits that 'sometimes they can't read that, but then you have half-time or you have a change [a substitute]. You have trained them to read the game by themselves. It is like a child, you educate'. Stupendous. Who does not feel like a child in Van Gaal's presence? That is what separates him from all the rest. He is pleased with Ferguson's praise of him, though he is not, of course, going all puppy-dog and panting about it as what The Great Man has said 'gives you that pressure that you have to get results. And it's not so easy to win Premier League matches'.

Old Trafford is packed for the Boxing Day visit of Newcastle. Going forward United are fluid, the attack of Radamel Falcao, Robin van Persie, Juan Mata and Wayne Rooney ensuring Alan Pardew's side crumple in the second half. But the rearguard is unreliable and still causing the frustration Van Gaal feels at the team being unable to dominate from start to finish. He goes with a back three for this match and there is some case for the defence in the rejigs the manager has had to make. The Phil Jones–Paddy McNair–Jonny Evans combination fielded in this eighteenth Premier League outing is the twenty-second different combination, including substitutions, due in part to the number of injuries the squad has suffered. United's opening two strikes in the 3–1 win come from Rooney, who plays behind Van Persie and Falcao. Both goals display how good United can be when roving forward with the ball. The first is a slick Juan Mata pass to Falcao whose superb volleyed touch to Rooney meant all he had to do was finish. The second again featured Mata playing in his captain to score, before Rooney showed why Van Gaal likes to deploy him in midfield, unloading a diagonal pass on to Van Persie's head for the third.

But the failure to dominate, unlike the 3–0 win over Hull City a month ago which has become the touchstone display for Van Gaal, is foremost in the manager's mind. Draws follow against Tottenham Hotspur and Stoke City, and in early January Van Gaal offers a new phrase, a pleasing epigram, ahead of Manchester United's long trip to the South-West to face Yeovil Town in the FA Cup third round. Reminded of the humiliation at MK Dons in the League Cup, Van Gaal says: 'Also in Ajax and Barcelona I have lost against a second division club. It's not only in England like that. It's a . . . how do you call it? A gladiolus game, the dead of the gladiolus. You are dead or you receive the gladiolus flower. It's like that. Of course, we have to win against Milton Keynes, but we have lost.' Newspapers love a new phrase, anything, really, that adds colourful language to the copy. The football hack must be a distant relative of Jackson Pollock, such is the delight with which the palette is refilled. 'A gladiolus game, the dead of the gladiolus. You are dead or you receive the gladiolus flower' – is lovely. Van Gaal is also admitting that the FA Cup is United's best hope of a pot this season. United are as good as Van Gaal's reliance on flower-power as Yeovil are beaten 2–0, but this is a story with *nonpareil* to what the manager can announce a few days later.

In the week Victor Valdes signs as the back-up goalkeeper to David de Gea, on Friday the lights are dimmed at the Jimmy Murphy Centre and a hush descends as Van Gaal – *wait for it!* – declares the squad's long injury nightmare is over because Ashley Young is the only player now unavailable. Hallelujah! Search out the bunting. Raise the flag full mast. Declare a holiday. Van Gaal is in a wonderful dismissive mood. Someone asks if David de Gea is the 'best goalkeeper in the world right now?' This is a dream of a tap-in of a question for any manager. Apart from one. *Au contraire*, goes Louis van Gaal. 'I can only say what I am watching, and that is Manchester United. I cannot see the whole world. You cannot either, in my opinion. I can only say that David de Gea has developed himself in the six months that

I've been here very much. I'm very pleased with his development.' Van Gaal is possibly ensuring De Gea is kept grounded. But it jars as the manager can. Yet he moves from this off-hand manner of a hardly public exercise in the man-management of his star goalkeeper to pointing out the individual humanity of two of his other players.

'Wayne Rooney is Wayne Rooney and Michael Carrick is Michael Carrick,' he says, indicating a comprehension of how their respective characters must be handled independently. 'These are different people.' One reading of this is to picture how Confucius, Lao Tzu and the Buddha have got together at a Premier League blue-sky thinking session and thrashed out the eleventh commandment about players, about the human that resides within the football kit: *These are different people.* A secondary reading is that it is all a little confusing and confused. Such is the Louis van Gaal way. Hang in there and it will all become clear. Until, that is, the next moment of brilliant confused muddled-ness.

Southampton hand United their first defeat in twelve games. It is the South Coast club's first league victory at Old Trafford for twenty-seven years. The only goal came once the visitors sensed at half-time that rather than allow United to come on to them by defending deep, they should take the initiative. After the break the switch in mentality works as Dusan Tadic's goal enables Ronald Koeman's team to leapfrog his old adversary's and push United into fourth place. Afterwards Koeman says: 'I am not surprised we won today. We have organisation. We have eleven clean sheets in twenty-one games. If we keep the spirit and the organisation, we can keep in front in the table.' It could almost be Van Gaal speaking.

United's manager, though, is not happy when sitting down to face interrogation. The killer fact is that after this defeat Manchester United have thirty-seven points from twenty-one games, and despite the recent run of good form, this is the 'same points as last season' at this stage. 'Yeah,' begins a tense Van Gaal. 'So you have waited on the moment you can put this question. The moment I have the same points as David Moyes.' Van Gaal is pushed on the progress of his team. 'That is what I am always saying, we have to be better, we have to improve. That is why we are working very hard. We didn't choose the right solutions in the third and fourth phase, but that is also because Southampton defended in a very small space and very well organised. They came for a draw and they got away with a victory. That is a little bit of luck and unluck.'

Considering that Van Gaal is Zeus one week and El Diablo the next depending on results, his restrain and composure is remarkable. He and other managers must surely share a laugh and a serious grumble at the constant reassessing of their abilities in today's boom-and-bust football culture. Retaining dignity in this world is some effort. Yet this does not mean the unavoidable question of whether Manchester United are making greater progress under Van Gaal than David Moyes is not a credible one. As both managers had the same number of points after the same number of games, one answer is no. Another is yes because of the sense that Van Gaal must know what he is doing due to the track record, the players' willingness to listen and respond, and the harder edge there is now to the side.

*

Van Gaal is expected to talk with Radamel Falcao on Monday, after leaving him out against Southampton. Falcao is not happy, as would be expected, though Robin van Persie has an ankle problem and this may be Falcao's way back into the squad for the trip to play Queens Park Rangers on Saturday. By this point of the season, six months in, there can be no equivocation: the signing of the Colombian is clearly not working. The numbers show he has only been granted eight starts in his thirteen appearances and scored three times. He has also just been left out of the match-day squad. To put this in context, imagine if Wayne Rooney had been dropped from the eighteen players the manager wants at his disposal for a game. Those in and around the club believe Falcao is at risk of not being taken on permanently for next season. There are other players, including those whose contracts expire in eighteen months' time like David de Gea, Robin van Persie, Jonny Evans, Phil Jones, Chris Smalling and Rafael da Silva, whose futures are also in doubt. This summer will again feature a clear-out from Van Gaal. Last year he allowed fifteen players to be sold or go on loan. There may not be as many this time, but several futures are to be decided.

Falcao's agent, Jorge Mendes, decides the time is right to intervene. 'The truth is, right now we don't know what will happen,' he says. 'What we do know is that he will play in one of the very best clubs in the world next season, whether that is Manchester United or not.' This seems an optimistic statement regarding his client's current stock value. What Falcao requires is a flurry of goals between now and the end of the season, and consistent evidence that he is the player United believed they were signing in September. This seems unlikely if the player can get nowhere near the side. Van Gaal offers an unconvincing note by suggesting that Falcao is 'generally happy'. He refuses to confirm the striker's place in the upcoming match-day squad, or even his place in the team, simply shrugging off the agent's intervention via the media. 'It doesn't interest me. You want to make a story of it. Not the fans, you.' There may indeed be a wish to make a story from this, and that is because there is a yarn here. A Moby Dick-sized one. This is a £43 million-priced Galactico who headed a new wave and a new way for the world's biggest football club when he jetted in. Yet he cannot get a place among seven reserves to sit on the bench for a match against Southampton. A match at home where United are traditionally on the attack, attack, attack and should be dying to unleash a striker of Falcao's ilk. Instead the manager selects the nineteen-year-old James Wilson, plus three centre-backs, two of them also youngsters, in the eighteen for the game.

The question of how many central defenders – three or the regulation two – are to be in the XI is alive once again after the Southampton match. It seems strange to still be talking about it this far into the season but it continues to be a hot issue. Will Van Gaal stay with the three centre-backs or decide on the time-served four-man defence as the way forward? The world has to know. 'What is the most suitable for the players you have,' says Van Gaal, coolly.

There is better news for Falcao, though. He starts at QPR. He does not score and he does not receive too much service. There is some praise for his movement, but really that is the least a top-class centre-forward should offer. However, he survives the entire ninety minutes. Falcao has entered that twilight zone of always looking across anxiously whenever the fourth official's board goes up and praying the digital number it displays is someone else's. He may not have been overjoyed to see James Wilson, a fifty-seventh-minute substitute, hit United's second after Marouane Fellaini shows why David Moyes bought him by scoring the first. This is the first game after the defeat by Southampton and a victory is the best way to bounce back.

There is a sponsor's launch in the Europa Suite at the start of the week. The managing director, Richard Arnold, 'will be joined by members of the club's first team'. After coffees and a presentation, Juan Mata is the player offered up to speak and the questioning is kept in line. David de Gea's future is the real interest. But asked about De Gea, Mata is prevented from answering and the subject closed down. This is one of the great unknowns of the football scene: how much difference does *any* story about any player and his future at any club actually make materially? Engage with the media, disengage with the media. Advantages and disadvantages. Sometimes not saying anything is actually saying far more than if the stock-in-trade footballer platitudes are allowed. To take this instance, by not allowing Mata to speak, to offer some words about De Gea, his value to the team, questions can be raised that there may, in fact, be something going on backstage. Mata, a fellow Spaniard, would have been the perfect man to allay fears. Besides, he can speak as well as he can play. On the field Mata is the ballet in the United midfield and attack, sunshine following him as he floats around a match. Away from the park Mata pens a weekly blog that has been authorised by the club and is published both on

United's website and his own. He would surely know how to handle a De Gea question.

What Mata does say is that Manchester United's attempt to gain a Champions League berth will be 'a fight to the finish'. He is not wrong. It is the same with Mata's travails in trying to nail down a regular starting spot. This is a battle mirrored by that of his countryman, Ander Herrera. The £29 million man, like a few of Van Gaal's summer recruits, is struggling. In the same bracket are Ángel Di María, Radamel Falcao and Luke Shaw. Daley Blind and Marcos Rojo are proving steadier. Herrera, though, is magnificently on-message. 'When the manager wants me to help the team I am going to be ready, of course. I am at Manchester United and we have a very good squad with very good players and it is not easy, but of course I am going to work hard,' he says. The midfielder has been granted only six league starts, the last of them two months ago. This is the life of a footballer who is paid a lot of money and cannot force his way in the team. Wait for a chance and take it. Or else. Difficult, of course, very difficult after being out of the side. And if the opportunity is not taken then the perception about why the player has been left out previously is intensified and the player has to fight again for another chance from further down the slippery slope. Each new chance – and there will be no infinite amount – becomes a one-off unofficial trial to save the player's career at the club, especially when the club is Manchester United.

Herrera is finding Van Gaal can be distant, which cannot help any player who is not in his thoughts. And with his slight frame and current inability to dominate contests in central midfield, Herrera is struggling. Even those close to him are unsure if he will make it at the club. The current thinking is that his United career is in the balance, and it could go either way. Herrera's fate is a piddling trifle in the context of what Van Gaal has to concern himself with. He has to focus on the main game. The critics are primed. They are always primed. If not they should seek alternative employment. The examination is under way. Now is the time for the Dutchman to ensure the greasepaint does not melt, the cheeks remain rouged, the costume fits, and that he is no eager and perennial understudy to Sir Alex of Ferguson. This is the closing phase of the season and it appears Van Gaal will last until its conclusion on 24 May. Which is around four weeks more than David Moyes managed.

February is a month of four victories, one loss, one draw. The start finds Louis van Gaal under another siege. This is primarily an aesthetic issue as the side continues to resemble a Moyes-vintage Manchester United but with better results. To compound this beleaguerment, Van Gaal has also fallen foul of the legal eagles at the Football Association. He has been accused of implying bias against referee Chris Foy, who was in charge of United's FA Cup tie at Cambridge United towards the end of January. It is mid-afternoon on Friday, 6 February, ahead of Sunday's match at West Ham United, and the Dutchman is saying: 'I am not angry, I am very disappointed. I am now for nearly thirty years a trainer-coach or manager and I have never been charged. And still, up to now, I don't think that I said something wrong.' When asked if he has been singled out because it is Manchester United, a favoured accusation of Sir Alex Ferguson, Van Gaal answers: 'If I say that, then I am maybe rightly charged, so I don't say it.'

There is genuine bemusement at the charge, not only at the club, but within the media and the outside world. What Van Gaal said after the goalless draw at the Abbey Stadium was: 'Every aspect of a match is against us. We have to come here, the pitch isn't so good, that can influence that you can play in another style. The opponents always give a lot more than they normally give and defending is always easier than attacking. Then you have seen the referee – it's always the same. Everywhere I have coached these games, and I have coached them with other clubs, it's always the same.' He is bound to be found guilty and to receive a punishment of the one hundred lines of 'Louis van Gaal must not do this again' variety as it is a first offence.

After a 1–1 draw at West Ham is scraped there is not much that is aesthetically pleasing for Van Gaal to crow about. And now here is Sam Allardyce, the opposing manager, labelling the Dutchman a long-ball merchant. This is about as insulting as one manager can be about another in football terms in the English game. *No manager* wishes to be branded as a fanatic of the direct stuff. It is the low-point, an anti-intellectual, philistine position and a near-impossible claim to shake off once it sticks. There is no beauty or imagination in the performance with which Van Gaal can respond. Allardyce's claim has irony and psychological cheek. Allardyce is the author of the famous 'I won't ever be going to a top-four club because I'm not called Allardici, just Allardyce'. Allardyce *is* a manager who has been forced to live with being the byword for hoof-ball, so to stick this on the Manchester United manager, who hails from the Dutch school that makes the English football hipster go knock-kneed, is particularly comical.

United managed the late draw through 'a big fella up top' tactic that features Marouane Fellaini as the BFG and whose knock-down is finished by Daley Blind for the equaliser. Allardyce's eyes are twinkling. 'I suppose in the end we couldn't cope with long-ball United,' he deadpans. 'It was just thump it forward and see what they could get, and in the end it paid off for them.' Haha goes Allardyce and United detractors everywhere. Allardyce does have a point. United's style continues to be non-descript, stodgy even. Thumping the ball up to a target man is the supposed Plan B of a team when the blueprint has failed. With apparently no plan at all at Upton Park – Di María is the number ten, Rooney a right-sided midfielder – Fellaini is thrown on after seventy-two minutes in a scramble to maintain fourth position which works. But only just. Van Gaal's team have forty-four points, but their rivals are closing in. Tottenham are fifth, one point behind. Arsenal are sixth, a further point back. Liverpool, in seventh, are only five points adrift.

By now the football, the style, the focus, the blueprint, the *philosophy*, is supposed to be sparklingly clear. The opposite is the case. Everything is muddled and muddied and now Van Gaal is being taunted by Sam Allardyce. The statistics support the West Ham manager, too. There have been 1,861 long passes played by the team in the Premier League. This is the second highest behind Burnley's 1,877. Relegation-threatened QPR, West Bromwich Albion and Leicester City make up the rest of the top five. The other end of this table consists of United's rivals at the top. Arsenal are the lowest utilisers of the long ball with 1,098, followed by Manchester City (1,184), Liverpool (1,377), and Chelsea (1,407), who are fifth.

Allardyce's comments go around the world and back again.

Louis van Gaal is so exercised by the denigration that at his next press conference two days later, ahead of Burnley's visit to Old Trafford, he reacts. Out comes a dossier, a four-page document which Van Gaal is waving, ready to prove why Big Sam is wrong. The gathered media have become a focus group. The question comes. 'This is the first time we have spoken to you since Sam Allardyce said you were a "long-ball" side. How do you feel about that?' 'What do you think? What is your opinion?' Van Gaal fires back at his questioner. Journalist: 'My opinion doesn't count for anything.' Van Gaal: 'And that's enough? You have seen the match? You have your opinion. And that's enough? You have seen the match? You have your opinion. When a colleague of mine is saying this kind of thing then, yeah, you have to see the data and you have to put the data in the right context, I believe.'

Smart in club blazer and tie, his hair neat and his voice as calm as his demeanour, Van Gaal says: 'I think the media is also coming to the match and you have a lot of opinion about me, or about the game, or about the players and now you say that you have no opinion.' This causes a chuckle. If David Moyes had tried a similar act he would have been written up as losing the plot, just as Rafael Benitez's infamous 'facts' rant at Sir Alex Ferguson was a few years ago. But Van Gaal is Van Gaal. He says: 'When you have nearly sixty per cent ball possession do you think that you can do that with long balls? Yeah, long balls, in the width, to switch the play. You have to look at the data and then you will see that we did play long balls, but long balls wide rather than to the strikers. And a ball to the forward striker is mainly called long-balls play.' It's an interesting defence. As United fans rejoice at the manager's bravura, Van Gaal adds: 'So I give you this [he is pointing at the dossier] and you can see that also the blue ones [arrows] are the good ones because long balls are mostly very difficult, that is why I began with the explanation of ball possession. I give it you, you can copy it and then you go to Big Sam and maybe he can give a good interpretation,' and he rises to his feet and hands over the evidence. This is football porn. In HD.

Yet everyone connected with the club, even the manager privately, must be concerned because as the final fourteen matches of the campaign beckon, United have emerged as a lumpen, proletariat outfit of near-zero imagination. Despite the topsy-turvy, fickle nature of the game, this is a searing and consistent, underlying truth. Why? Given the players available to Van Gaal this should not be the case. The concerns of the start of the season when United failed to win until match five have returned. But with the major difference that they are now getting results. However, these are being eked out. United have little quality and the Van Gaal who has gathered bouquets and a sackful of honours seems a rumour, a mirage. Again. Yet again. Views are forming once more that Van Gaal is past his peak, a little old. His sixty-three years have become as damning a number as the zero that represents the number of shots on target in 2015 for Wayne Rooney since his manager stopped playing him where he has been supremely successful for thirteen years. In attack.

Timing, it is all about timing. This may be the darkest hour before the dawn, but this is a dawn refusing to break. United are a point away from Southampton in third position, five behind the dastardly enemy, Manchester City. Chelsea are a gallop clear on fifty-six points, twelve in front of United, though, to any reasonable judge, this is expected. After the Ferguson-vacuum and the Moyes-imbroglio, Van Gaal is fire-fighting. When he walks into the Jimmy Murphy Centre at 3 p.m. on Friday, 13 February to preview the Monday evening trip to Preston North End in the fifth round of the FA Cup, he hardly appears a haunted man. His attire is the dapper grey suit with the expensive hue that makes Van Gaal shimmer as a football man of the world. With a devilish grin, when nearing his seat at the table, he asks: 'No ladies here?', a question that comes as a friendly barb at the male-centric demographic of the gathered media corps before him. On Wednesday evening at Old Trafford, Burnley were beaten 3–1. The perfect response to the bore-draw at West Ham, one might think. Yet Paul Scholes's latest opinion is that United were 'miserable' at times. The victory takes them up to third, but here is Van Gaal being asked to answer Scholes. 'I don't worry about it. It's not so interesting, I think, because he is one of the fans, I hope, and he can criticise.' It is a slick response, though Van Gaal does admit style is important, which will cheer United fans who are desperate for any hint that the swagger might return.

At Preston, like Manchester United's very own Samuel Beckett, Van Gaal's search for a formation will continue. 4–1–3–2, 3–5–2, 4–4–2, 4–2–2–2 and 4–1–4–1: the manager admits he is still not clear. How much more searching will he need? The current favourite is 4–1–3–2. 'This system is more attractive and I can play with more attacking players. That's the reason I am doing that. In spite of the fact that we are looking for the balance, our results are not bad and our defensive organisation is not bad; we also score a lot of goals. So, I cannot say that I am very disappointed about that.' How about Rooney, is he content playing in midfield? 'He's happy. Otherwise he should come to me and say he's not happy. He never does. He's always friendly to me. Of course, when the whole world is writing he has to be in the striker's position, he will be thinking, "Maybe, hey". He's human.'

Van Gaal goes on to say his captain is in midfield because 'no one else can do it' and that he is prioritising buying a creative midfielder. This does not reflect brilliantly on the out-of-favour Ander Herrera's prospects at the club. But on Monday, on a cold night in Preston, it is the skinny playmaker who proves to be the hero, the catalyst for a come-from-behind 3–1 win, scoring a sixty-fifth-minute goal that may ignite his Old Trafford career. Until the strike United are again dull with Herrera playing nervously and lucky not to be replaced. There is a moment – when Marouane Fellaini gallops along the right and squares the ball to Herrera, and he swivels neatly but plays a pass without looking up that finds no one – which makes him appear a panicked schoolboy footballer rather than a £29 million Manchester United player. But redemption is his, with the goal, and the team win. That odd moment is forgotten about.

Arsenal are the next opponents in the Cup next month for a quarter-final that promises spice, and a clash of the Van Gaal stew-and-dumplings stodge with the peaches-and-cream stuff served up by Arsène Wenger. 'We said before that you've got to play whoever is put in front of you and we know it will be tough, but I don't think there is ever an easy game,' Ashley

Young says of the tie. The verdict is in from the FA and Van Gaal has been formally warned for his Cambridge United misdemeanour. Whether he should have faced the charge in the first place remains the question.

A few days later and David de Gea wants a word. He needs to clear the air. Stuff has been written about him and Louis van Gaal, and the Spaniard is not happy. Everyone, everywhere, from mother and baby to gilded footballer, has an agenda they wish to posit – sell, if you like – and what the Manchester United number one is trading in this Friday, 27 February is truth. Clear, sparkling veracity. 'Everything that has been written in the press about us not getting on is a lie,' the goalkeeper tells MUTV of his relationship with the manager. Reports have appeared to the contradictory. When you lob in this pesky new contract that is yet to be agreed, and Real Madrid apparently lurking in the background doing what Real Madrid do best – always getting their man, seemingly – well, then enough of a critical mass is occurring to fuel these stories. 'I think this is the best period of my career. I am playing the best football that I've ever played. I'm really enjoying it at the moment and I'm just trying to improve with every training session and every game that goes by, giving one hundred per cent and concentrating to the maximum.' There is no mention of a new contract, of De Gea remaining at the club next season, so this clarifies little.

Ángel Di María, who is threatening to join The Radamel Falcao Incident room, also wants a word. The winger, whose rented property was the target of an attempted burglary earlier in the month while he was inside with his family, admits he has been a little off form. 'I've had a couple of games where things haven't gone as well as they could have.' Having had to deal with the break-in, his family being terrified and having to move out as a consequence, this is not surprising. By speaking now, De Gea and Di María also offer a reminder of the whirl of behind-the-scenes material that is the story behind *the story*. The season is in its final phase and both players are signalling that their futures are in doubt. The sub-plots all have one universal character: the manager. And these sub-plots are numerous and always increasing. If Van Gaal was asked to count up how differing ones are up and running simultaneously, it is doubtful he could.

Despite last Saturday's defeat at Swansea, which means the Welsh club completed a season's double over Manchester United, the club are still fourth, a point ahead of Southampton and two better than Liverpool. Van Gaal is again in perky spirits. These are quickly dampened by a demanding question that leads to various headlines about his reply. He is asked if the difference between United and the top teams is that the latter have superior forwards while none of Van Gaal's look like scoring fifteen or twenty goals this season. 'It is true because I cannot deny it, Robin van Persie cannot deny it, Falcao cannot deny it and Rooney is not playing there much anymore. But we cannot deny that at this moment we don't have a striker who scores twenty goals in the season. This doesn't not tell anything about next year and that is what I mean by these aspects, they could be having an unlucky year and I have to take account with these aspects and I have to decide, with my staff, if it is these aspects or other aspects.'

In Van Gaal's mind he was not criticising these players. But those were still his words. He is bemoaning the lack of potency from a strike force worth a combined £100 million (Van Persie cost £24 million; Falcao will rise to £50 million in total if a permanent deal is done; Rooney was £26 million back, in 2004). Bad luck is being blamed by Van Gaal in the case of Falcao, who has two goals, and Van Persie (ten). The manager accepts Rooney's tally of nine is down to being played out of position (by Van Gaal). The youngster James Wilson, meanwhile, has two. The *Guardian* headline for this yarn runs: 'Van Gaal bemoans lack of goals from his £100 million strike force'. This is tucked inside the sports section. Different papers have their own way of reporting the story, of course. Some use the back-page: 'Screwy Louis' (*The Sun*); others also have it inside: 'Van blast at hitmen' (*Daily Star*). Van Gaal's issue is that he feels words were put into his mouth as the questioner – and everyone else – discovers at the next Friday press conference when the Dutchman says as much to the correspondent who asked the question. He may have a point but it also shows how closely the coverage is read and being monitored by the club.

On Monday evening the quest to break Manchester United's eleven-year drought without winning the FA Cup is over. Arsenal hand United a 2–1 defeat, and with it end Van Gaal's hopes of claiming a trophy in his first term, as the title, by now, appears well beyond reach. This is a rousing cup tie. But United cannot win it. The disappointment around Old Trafford feels crushing. Arsenal are successful with a fluent, attacking game. United have been good, too. There is some of the old rythm. Ángel Di María, taken off in his previous two games, is playing well until he is sent off after seventy-nine minutes. This is to prove particularly costly for the Argentine as he will not be able to get back into the side after serving the one-game suspension.

Arsenal score first through Nacho Monreal before the half-hour. Wayne Rooney equalises a few minutes later. Danny Welbeck, the man let go by Louis van Gaal because he was a 'substitute, not a line-up player', scores the sixty-first-minute winner. It is that kind of night for United, for Van Gaal. Afterwards Arsène Wenger is smiling when he is asked if Welbeck might possibly have enjoyed scoring the winner. 'We want all to do well when we play against our former club to show we are great players, but it is not easy to deal with the mental aspect of it. He focused just on his game and played football the way he wanted to. He has showed mental strength.' The Frenchman, dressed in a slate grey suit, Arsenal tie and waistcoat, is measured. But he and Welbeck are surely loving it, just loving it.

Now it is Louis van Gaal's turn to face the shooting gallery. He enters in his Manchester United club suit and sits down and is asked if the result is 'fair'. The answer is a classic losing manager's take on the result. 'I think it is very disappointing when you give the victory. You doesn't lose from your opponent, you have lost from yourself.' How about the winner from Welbeck? 'Of course, a match shall be decided by goals,' Van Gaal begins, sagely. 'And also this match has been decided by goals and when you see the second goal, it was nothing so we gave it away so the man who was doing that was the best man of my team and that is also for him so disappointing. He did it not with purpose. It happens.' Van Gaal is calm though clearly unhappy with Antonio Valencia for the too-short back-pass that led to Welbeck's winner. He is definitely not feeling pally with Di María – 'not so smart of him' is his verdict on the red card.

During the match the manager was spied on the touchline for only the second time this season at Old Trafford. Question: 'Was it frustration that took you into the technical area?' Answer: 'I have to change the shape because there was one man out. It is very difficult to reach the players so Giggs was already, for more than two or three minutes, there so maybe when I go there the players are more willing to come and I could reach Ashley Young by shouting. It is very noisy here.'

The dream of glory (in the FA Cup) may be dead, but the dream of glory (by claiming Champions League qualification) can be revived. The question now is will Van Gaal survive should Manchester United not finish in the top four? No one knows, but it could become sticky for him if United limp home seriously off the pace. The club are into the last ten matches of the season. They are in fourth, two points ahead of Liverpool, three better than Spurs and four ahead of Southampton. Five of those remaining games are against teams around them. The film Van Gaal wants to star in now would be called *The United Juggernaut* as all opposition is steamrollered. Yet there is a real danger the Van Gaal project could be exposed. Or to put this another way: this is the defining moment for all the process and balance and jazz and harrumphing and whinnying and tactics-talk and formation-debate and the endless has-he-still-got-it and does-he-know-his-best-team and what are the ex-players saying? And all the rest of this kind of noise. *All the philosophising.* Now is the time for Van Gaal to prove himself. There are vast sums riding on qualification for the Champions League. A year's worth of prestige and glamour. It matters and it does not. This is football, not war. It's a game. A sport. Viewed at a distance it is twenty-two stick men and a ball on a patch of grass somewhere. It is insignificant and it is significant. This is not waking up to find the Taj Mahal in the backyard. It is waking up to find the Taj Mahal in the backyard. It is not the Taj Mahal. It is the Taj Mahal. It is Football. Football. Football.

Just gone 6 p.m. on Tuesday, 10 March the news breaks: Radamel Falcao has been selected for Manchester United's under-21s. The reserves! With the kids and the stiffs! The Galactico's Galactico! This is some fall and seems almost cruel. But Van Gaal has no time for names, reputations and feelings. This high mark of superstardom is to wear the number nine at an almost-empty Old Trafford this evening. The man with the dreamboat looks and the hair and the name. The senses reel. Nothing compares to the guff and pretension and sheer cabaret of hopes and dreams and £££, $$$, €€€ invested in Radamel Falcao Garcia Zárate. The Radamel Falcao Incident was not supposed to be about an incident like this. Surely it cannot end this way. The Theatre of Dreams has become the stuff of nightmares. This cannot be the denouement, the defining moment of our hero's story.

Falcao fails to score against Tottenham Hotspur for the Manchester United under-21 side before being substituted after seventy-one minutes on a cold evening. The Colombian looks disappointed to be selected and he looks gutted to be taken off by the coach, Warren Joyce. His withdrawal may be a precaution to ensure he is available to face the Spurs first team at Old Trafford on Sunday. Falcao is sluggish and twice blocks a team-mate's goal-bound shot. He looks, and is, miserable. Falcao has been an unused replacement in United's last two games.

On Monday, Adnan Januzaj came on as United's last substitute in the FA Cup defeat against Arsenal, to leave Falcao as a super-expensive bench-warmer. Falcao is being driven to tears by his woes at the club, according to a friend – his former agent, Silvano Espindola. Falcao telephoned him on the way to the under-21 game to confess: 'I don't know how to deal with this situation.' The Colombian has actually cried over his predicament. 'When he was on his way to the ground to play this game with the reserves, he called me,' Espindola says. 'We spoke for twenty minutes until he reached the stadium and he told me, "I've never been through something like this, I don't know how to deal with this situation. It feels weird for me".'

This comes out in rather awkward timing after Van Gaal has denied it was a comedown for the player. 'I let my players play in the second squad. I read a lot in the papers that it was a humiliation. I don't think so. It was a professional attitude of the manager, the club and the player. Falcao has not reacted like the media. That is a big difference. He didn't play the best but he tried his utmost best. I cannot ask for more,' the manager says. According to Espindola, though, Falcao is not content. 'We talk a lot. I'm not going to say that he feels happy because he's not. We've spoken many times and cried together. It's not an easy situation because every player wants to play and every goalscorer wants to score goals, that's normal.'

Falcao's travails illuminate the varying successes or otherwise of Van Gaal's £150 million-plus splurge last summer. For a cash-mountain like this, should Manchester United be ten points behind Chelsea with ten matches left? There were the Galacticos (Falcao and Di María), the seasoned performers

(Blind and Rojo) and future hopefuls (Shaw and Herrera). A potent blend was the hope. A cocktail of superstar performers, reliability and youth injected into a squad finally receiving the major surgery it had required for the previous two seasons or more. At this juncture only Blind and Rojo have been acceptable. The rest have added little. There are 900 minutes of football left for them to do something.

Chapter 18

The Way Forward at Last

The Old Trafford clock reaches 4.34 p.m. on the afternoon of 15 March 2015. Manchester United stands still. Manchester United are in slow motion. Manchester United speed up. This is the moment. This is the one. This is not Manchester United's JFK moment. This is Manchester United's LVG moment. This is Manchester United's *moment*. Sir Alex Ferguson is not forgotten but *he is gone*.

In a time-lapse concertina kaleidoscope all of that has happened since the knight dismounted the steed on 19 May 2013, the life of Manchester United flashes before the fanatical congregation inside Old Trafford as Wayne Rooney drifts into the picture like a phantom, an apparition, a spectre. He is no figment of the consciousness, though. He is real bone and straining sinew, a thoroughbred running on hard fact and truth down near the centre circle. He is about to make the place pop and go pow as he smashes through the glass ceiling that has been imprisoning the memory of what this club should and could and *will* be once more.

Rooney's fifth goal in six games comes from a shocking ball from Tottenham Hotspur's Nabil Bentaleb that goes straight to The Knockout Kid. This brings out a Rooney of yore as the captain charges at the backpedalling Spurs rearguard, biffing defenders away and stamping over the ground in a terrifying flex of muscle and intent. He makes a chump of Eric Dier, removing him from the equation by swerving left, then beating Hugo Lloris with a cool finish to the goalkeeper's right. A jubilant Old Trafford watch as Rooney runs towards the left corner flag, throws a few shadow punches, and fall backwards in jest, aping the 'Bardsley kitchen KO' which had hit the headlines that morning. The perfect end to six intoxicating seconds.

This is it, then. The moment that has Manchester United stunning the Premier League and the watching football world again and which shuts up all those who have not stopped chortling at the club since Ferguson stepped away. The mind has to be seriously engaged to find the last time Rooney scored in quite such exhilarating fashion. The answer is that not since Euro 2004, eleven years ago, has the Croxteth Kid torn straight at a defence in such visceral, primal mode before netting. Brilliant. The player supposedly finished, according to Sir Alex Ferguson, has just ripped up Spurs. It is the type of fantasy moment every football fan wants to see. And the wild abandon with which Rooney went straight for Spurs' jugular is the personification of where United supporters hope Louis van Gaal is taking them.

Afterwards the manager is asked if this was the best his side has played. 'I have to watch the video again. I have to say we played like a team and very determined. Maybe now is the game that gives us a fantastic boost. We have waited a long time for such a victory.' And display.

Finally. How Louis van Gaal needed this. It's United's twenty-ninth Premier League game of the season. Suddenly the attention to detail, the players' belief in their manager and the serial philosophising all look part of a majestic scheme that cast Louis van Gaal as a mad-genius-professor. It is that breath-taking Rooney goal that finally wipes away memories of the David Moyes dog days and announces that Manchester United are back.

To preview the match on Friday, the manager is in a sober grey suit and brown tie as he sits down at 3.30 p.m. The latest team shape the manager is tinkering with is the 4–3–3 that is his favourite. Yes, this is *still* on the agenda. A direct hit is made by the journalist who dares to say to Van Gaal: 'You have changed formations a lot. Is it fair to say you have been quite indecisive in your team selection?' Sir Alex Ferguson would have hated this question. The premise, the subject, and, of course, that he had been asked it at all. Indecisive. *Indecisive.*

I-n-d-e-c-i-s-i-v-e. This is the one thing a manager dare not be accused of. Having the courage to make decisions is the *sine qua non* of the management game. Authority over players is a willow-o'-the wisp affair of constantly shifting sands that involves virtuoso performances from the manager and in the holy trinity of training ground, dressing room and media tribune any hint is examined to see if the gaffer is losing it. Van Gaal does not blink. And he needn't have. United unleashed their best performance of the season.

The Sunday morning of the game. There is a front-page splash about the captain of Manchester United. 'Rooney KO'd in kitchen boxing bout' it screams, a large photo of the striker laid out on the floor (apparently last month) with a smaller inset of him sparring with Stoke City's Phil Bardsley, a former United team-mate. Rooney wears white gloves, Bardsley a pink set, and an examination of the video – shot on a 'friend's' mobile phone and somehow circulated – shows the striker being put 'spark out'.

But this does not turn out to be the story of the day, though. The real news is the unexpected way that United play. Finally. Not only are Spurs defeated 3–0, they are made to appear a non-league outfit by Louis van Gaal's team. It *is* the best display under the manager by several country miles, the finest since the days of Sir Alex Ferguson. On this afternoon the 'philosophy' appears crystal clear. It is like old times. Manchester United are an unstoppable force again. The decisive factor is the one that has been missing for most of the season: tempo. Suddenly the United players who have been in a half-torpor find a zest that is both unstoppable *and* intriguing. If the manager can draw nine repeats in the final matches of the campaign, Champions League qualification is a shoe-in. The victory gives United a firmer grip on fourth place, putting five points between them and Liverpool, and a further one point advantage over Spurs.

Liverpool are next up at Anfield and everyone at the club is buzzing. At the Friday presser Van Gaal, in his Manchester

United red polo shirt, is uber-relaxed. To a query about whether victory over Liverpool, who are now two points behind United in fifth place, would deal a 'mortal blow' to their Champions League qualification hopes, the manager says: 'No, I don't think so. But it helps – and it helps a lot. It helps to continue for Manchester United because after a victory you need another victory to confirm what you have done against Tottenham.'

On Merseyside it goes like a dream, a fantasy for United. Juan Mata scores two peaches, one in each half, the second a sublime bicycle kick. Two–one is the final score. Mata, Ander Herrera (who is starting to establish himself) and Marouane Fellaini are all rampant. The passes ping across the pitch and Liverpool are clueless, particularly before the break. Steven Gerrard delights all who love United by getting himself sent off within seconds of coming on after half-time in his last match against United in Liverpool colours. United motor back to Manchester ecstatic. Liverpool are five points behind. The deficit to Chelsea is eight and while the west Londoners have a match in hand, there is a sniff, albeit an odourless one, of a championship charge, given that Van Gaal still has to take the team to Stamford Bridge.

After being unimpressive for so long United have become unrecognisable. The players are liberated. They are wild and free. The insistence on precise positioning, the mental drain of recasting their brains, and the philosophy, philosophy, philosophy is starting to near fruition. The victory at Liverpool comes and goes and the player whose form makes him a lead contender for the club's player-of-the-year gongs is still yet to sign a new deal. David de Gea, like Falcao, is represented by Jorge Mendes and stories are appearing in the Spanish and

English press about his future. It seems even the club do not know definitively if De Gea will stay. He holds all the cards.

The international break is notable for two things. The Radamel Falcao Incident takes an upturn as the forward scores two fine goals for Colombia against Bahrain, the first a sweet left-foot volley, the second a right-booted finish after breaking behind the defence. And Manchester United release a special documentary on Louis van Gaal called: 'My philosophy, my life'. What else could the title be? This is all very grandiose and visions form of The Iron Tulip breaking bread with Socrates, Plato and Homer. Yet the headline given to the write-up of the programme on the club website is a touch more rustic: 'Van Gaal: I'm not a dictator, I am a flexible man'. Here is the kind of pronouncement which can, somehow, suggest its intended opposite. In the documentary Van Gaal says: 'The viewers shall not realise I am a very flexible man as they are always thinking that I am a boss in the right sense of the word. "Boss" or maybe a dictator or something like that. I am not like that. I consider my player not only as a footballer that kicks the ball from A to B but also his environment. I want to get to know him, not only as a player, but also as a human being and that is very important.' Beyond the pastoral moment, the programme finds the Dutchman in the latest show of how United – and Ed Woodward – are branding and projecting the club. Can anyone imagine Sir Alex Ferguson being the subject of a similar in-house show? 'Sir Alex: why referees should love me.' Or 'Sir Alex: Rafael Benitez is always welcome for a cuppa.' 'Sir Alex: I want to hire David Moyes again.'

On Good Friday, Louis van Gaal is previewing the visit of Aston Villa and he gives his most revealing answer yet about his working approach. To the question of whether the manager is 'surprised' at how well this first season is going, considering Van Gaal described the team as 'broken' at the start of the campaign, he replies: 'What is surprised? How I train is not so easy for players, and it is a whole process and we started at the bottom unconscious-capable, but then your next step is conscious-incapable. And then it is capable and it has to be unconscious-capable and maybe we are in the last step of that process. What I have seen the last five matches, I think so, but still we need to wait.' In other words it all has to become second-nature. But what a way to phrase it.

Robin van Persie has been injured and Ángel Di María was suspended for the Spurs game. Van Gaal played the same side for that match and the Liverpool triumph, so has he discovered his best XI by 'happy accident'? He replies: 'You can say that but I cannot say what is in the process, therefore you can think it's accidentally but I don't think so.' Hmm. At the end of a relaxed session a basket of Cadbury's Creme Eggs are passed around and Old Trafford is a happy place. It becomes even more so on Saturday as Aston Villa are beaten 3–1. This is no real surprise given Manchester United's metamorphosis these past weeks. The excellent Ander Herrera is the star man, scoring twice. Wayne Rooney sandwiches his goal in between the Spaniard's strikes on forty-three and ninety minutes. Falcao is on as a late replacement for the third match running, but one left-foot volley hits Row Z and he also falls over during the build-up to Herrera's second.

The victory takes United to sixty-two points and third place, above Manchester City whose title defence has crumbled.

Manuel Pellegrini's side have sixty-one points and a game in hand. In the corridor the manager is asked how significant going above City in the table is. 'They still have one match to go – so it's not so relevant, it's relevant after Monday night when [if] they have lost points then it could be.' City do indeed lose at Crystal Palace 2–1.

Di María has become a replacement like Falcao. It seems the new age of the galactico should no longer be capped up as it has been relegated to a footnote, at best. Di María has been reduced to seeing how Herrera and Mata have re-established themselves under Louis van Gaal and look to them for inspiration. Can Herrera be the dominant midfielder United have lacked for years? 'Positionally, he is playing better than in the beginning, so he develops,' Van Gaal says. Not a complete yes, but Herrera can feel encouraged. Van Gaal is confident ahead of the 169th Mancunian derby. 'I always believe in my team. In our game-plan. Of course, you want to win. It is a big step in the table also. When you win, the third place is reachable, and a month ago nobody was thinking about that, besides me, of course. That is good because then you are certainly in the Champions League and then we do it better than the goal was in the pre-season.' The manager is sounding a differing note to Manuel Pellegrini, who is having to deny Manchester City are 'not a disaster or a mess' as this fixture finds his side having lost three of their last four matches. Van Gaal believes United are different to the team who lost the derby at the Etihad earlier in the season. 'I cannot say percentage. I do know that we are much better now than in the start of the process. We have to wait and see if we can continue our good shape against City.'

There is a rip-roaring atmosphere at Old Trafford, the season's most invigorating, and what follows is a 4–2 hammering of Manchester City that has the delirious home supporters regaling Manuel Pellegrini after Mata's sixty-seventh-minute goal that makes it 3–1 with the old favourite: 'You're getting sacked in the morning.' This comes after Sergio Agüero's eighth-minute strike had given City the lead during an opening twenty-minute burst in which United were overwhelmed. The turnaround is thanks to a supreme first-half offering from Ashley Young, another of the rejuvenated under Van Gaal. Young, Mata, Fellaini and Herrera have all responded to the Dutchman's vow to give every player a new start. They are another indicator of why he can do the job: rebooting a footballer out of form and favour is what management is all about.

Van Gaal sends out the same XI that beat Spurs and Liverpool, and who would have remained in place against Villa last week but for an illness to Chris Smalling, who is restored today. This is beginning to look the manager's preferred line-up. Crucially, it does not feature Falcao or Di María, who cannot get back in following his red card against Arsenal. So, David de Gea, Antonio Valencia, Phil Jones, Chris Smalling, Daley Blind, Michael Carrick, Ander Herrera, Juan Mata, Maroaune Fellani, Ashley Young and Wayne Rooney are LvG's Ocean's Eleven. And after Agüero's opener Young decides to show why he is a member. This involves scoring the equaliser, creating the Fellaini strike that gives United the lead, and the pass to Smalling that confirms City's hiding.

Afterwards the sense is that the victory is no real bolt from the blue. This is a sweet sign of the times. This is the territory

United are back occupying. This is where LvG has led the club. Is this United's best performance and feeling? The question is becoming a regular. 'Maybe the best feeling but not the best performance because we started very badly,' says Van Gaal. 'More or less like against Burnley I believe, but after the assist of David de Gea more or less we are regaining our confidence and we scored a goal before the second goal, fantastic attack also. And then the second half now I have to say the second half instead of the first half, the second half was fantastic.'

There is daylight to Manchester City, and United are eight points behind Chelsea whose seventy-three points is from one game less. To have any chance at all of the championship, United will have to beat Jose Mourinho's team before their own crowd and hope Arsenal, who are a point closer and who play Chelsea next weekend, can do the same. Even then Chelsea would have to lose points elsewhere for United to have any hope. The match at Stamford Bridge is the late one on Saturday. Van Gaal has injury concerns and Jonny Evans remains banned. If he has to select Paddy McNair, Luke Shaw and Tyler Blackett, who have all not played for a long time, this is a concern. McNair and Shaw start and United dominate possession. But Mourinho harvests three crucial points courtesy of Eden Hazard's breakaway finish on thirty-eight minutes. Marouane Fellaini is neutered, as he will be next Sunday at Everton, when he is taken off. Radamel Falcao, who is named in the XI for the time since the 2–0 win over Sunderland on 28 February, hits a post, a chance the Galactico would have netted in days of old. Van Gaal nominates the display as the best of the season, which is always an odd verdict when the side has lost. Still, Chelsea are champions-elect and United did impress despite missing key players like Michael Carrick. Next up are Everton at Goodison Park, the fixture close to a year ago that was David Moyes's last before the sack. United are in third place with sixty-five points after thirty-three games, having scored fifty-nine times and let in thirty-one. Moyes's team were seventh with fifty-seven points after thirty-four games, having scored fifty-four times and conceded forty goals. The relative positions, with Van Gaal's team four places better off, is the telling statistic.

As has been the case recently Van Gaal is in fine humour for his Friday briefing. And in the red Manchester United polo shirt and tracksuit bottoms that are becoming *de rigueur*, he offers up a dollop of honesty about David de Gea, who has been voted into the Professional Footballers' Association Team of the Year. He is the only United player in it and the only one to be nominated for the PFA Player of the Year award. Still that contract is yet to be signed. Is Van Gaal confident De Gea will still be there next year? 'I am not the boss. I want him to stay. The player is the boss, he can say yes or no. You will have to ask David de Gea, not me. He has to sign. We have offered him a lot of money.' Exactly how much ranges from £150,000 a week, plus heavy incentives, to £200,000 a week. Either way, if De Gea – 'the boss' as billed by LvG – is not playing for Real Madrid next season this will constitute a surprise.

Goodison Park proves to be an uncomfortable place again for a Manchester United manager. In Sir Alex Ferguson's last outing at Everton's home on 20 August 2012, a Marouane Fellaini goal beat United 1–0. On 20 April 2014, Leighton Baines's penalty and Kevin Mirallas's strike beat United 2–0 to sound the death knell for Moyes. On 26 April 2015, goals from James McCarthy, John Stones and Mirallas again beat Van Gaal's United 3–0. This is a sound hiding. There will be no P45 for the Dutchman, but he is not happy and no wonder. United are second to crucial challenges, hoard the ball but can doing nothing with it. It is a performance from the pre-Tottenham days of last month. The manager is as blunt as usual. The team, he says, lost the match in the warm-up, and he describes it as the poorest display of his tenure. 'It was the most disappointing performance because it is the first time that I have seen our motivation, inspiration and aggression not as high as the opponent. In sport you shall always be compared to your opponent and that was the reason. I had already the feeling and my colleagues Ryan Giggs and Albert [Stuivenberg] had the feeling because the warm-up was not so good as usual.' This is unusual, to hear Van Gaal say his players never fancied it. And if he saw this in the warm-up, the subsequent result does not suggest the manager was able to avert what was coming either in his team-talk before the match or in his ability to change the contest once it had started. Everyone can have an off-day. Including the Iron Tulip.

Having appeared certainties for a Champions League berth, there is a sweat on again after these successive defeats. The unevenness of performance is this season's unwanted leitmotif. Under Van Gaal United's inconsistency is final. The days of murdering Tottenham Hotspur and Liverpool are distant. Van Gaal and his players now ask *whatever happened to the way we were?* Liverpool are seven points behind but have a match in hand and play twice before Van Gaal's side are in action in Saturday's late kick-off against West Bromwich Albion. It means the ancient enemy could close to only a point by then. 'I have told them that. I said to the players you have given light to your opponents.' Van Gaal sounds as if he may have torn several strips off his charges. He also sounds like he believes the players have been complacent. This latter crime rates pretty high, if not highest, on the list of the gravest violations of the LvG code a footballer can commit.

As Fellaini was replaced at half-time as a precaution against a red card after the Belgian was booked, and Wayne Rooney injured his left knee, this is a gloomy day all round. And when West Bromwich win 1–0 at Old Trafford on 2 May, the club has lost three league matches in a row for the first time since 2002. But Van Gaal is enjoying the luck David Moyes lacked. The Dutchman has oodles of the stuff. An illustration can be found at Anfield. Last season Liverpool had the frightening strike force of Luis Suarez and Daniel Sturridge and together they were a goal-blitz and point-machine for the club. This nearly fired Liverpool to the championship and was a potent reason why David Moyes was sacked, the Merseyside club taking United's place in the top four. This year Brendan Rodgers has had neither Suarez, following his transfer to Barcelona, or a consistently-fit Sturridge. Lucky Louis van Gaal, unlucky David Moyes. And the Dutchman's rosy fortune continues as Liverpool lose 1–0 at Hull City earlier in the week, before United's loss to West Bromwich, and so Rodgers's men are still four points behind, and kicking themselves.

Van Gaal's side have definitely fallen back into unconvincing mode. Yet it does not materially matter. In the next round of games a late Marouane Fellaini winner at Crystal Palace secures a 2–1 victory. And when Liverpool draw 1–1 at Chelsea, United's Champions League qualification is all but mathematically secured. By the time Arsenal arrive at Old Trafford on 17 May, Rodgers's team have lost to Palace and it is confirmed. To have achieved the season's target with two games left is a massive relief, particularly after last year's embarrassment under David Moyes.

Make no mistake, though. No one is jumping up and down and sinking jeroboams of the sparkling stuff at the club. Progress. That is all. This is what Van Gaal has orchestrated. Undeniable progress. From the training pitches of Carrington to the turf of Old Trafford, and at stadiums across the Premier League, the club is moving forward again. The battleship is pointing the right way and the manager in place, Louis van Gaal, should take the praise for turning it around. The off-field business of the club is again looking slick, quick and sharp. On 7 May, PSV Eindhoven forward Memphis Depay is announced as a first new addition. For a fee of around £25 million, the twenty-one-year-old will complete the transfer in the close season. Depay was top scorer in PSV's Dutch title-winning year, and this early acquisition of a jet-heeled, goal-hungry talent shows how far the club and Ed Woodward have come since the 'Marouane Fellaini summer' under Moyes. Even here the manager's superiority is seen in his direct intervention to speak with Depay and prevent his World Cup alumni heading off to Paris Saint-Germain. It was the type of clout David Moyes did not possess and which only heavyweights like Van Gaal or Sir Alex Ferguson do. This has to impress Woodward and the Glazers. Having the Van Gaal name is making the executive vice-chairman's job of landing

A-list footballers easier. To have a manager who not only pilots the players and the rest of the football stuff *and* who can morph into a quasi-chief executive role to pull strings in the market is a fillip. Especially as a successful summer of horse trading is what is required for United to have any chance next year.

For the moment, Van Gaal has done what he was asked by Ed Woodward and the Glazers. Manchester United are back in the big time and the bright lights of the European Cup beckon. However, after Arsenal's victory over Sunderland confirms United are to finish in fourth place, they will have to work their way through a tricky mid-August qualifying round before reaching the competition proper at the group stage. There is no fanfare about any of this. It is the least the club should expect, as Van Gaal notes. The failure to do so cost David Moyes his job. Louis van Gaal has managed it successfully. But there is much work to do.

Chapter 19

A Season in Review

Full time, Manchester United 1, Arsenal 1, 17 May 2015. Louis van Gaal walks into the Old Trafford dressing room. The place is like a morgue. The team had been coasting. Arsenal were impotent. No shots at all in the first half. Take a time machine all the way back to 2004 and a match against Liverpool to find the last occasion Arsenal have not unloaded on goal in the opening forty-five minutes of a contest. Scarcely credible. This is what United had done to Arsenal. *His* United. The supposed Barcelona of English football reduced to a toothless, mundane, disjointed band. But now Van Gaal is in the dressing room and not much is being said. Not much needs to be said. His players know. They *know*. They know how an axe should have been taken to Arsenal to rub out Arsène Wenger's men after Ander Herrera scored before the break. But they could not do it. They have failed. Failed him. How many times has this happened this season? It is the major worry, the big concern. They cannot close down opponents, smother them, despatch them. And if they cannot do that, if they cannot learn, then he will have to find some players who can. Because he will not stand for it. He *cannot* stand for it. Why should he?

Louis van Gaal stands in the dressing room and tells them that he can say they were unlucky. The Arsenal equaliser was a deflection. A Tyler Blackett own goal from a Theo Walcott shot with only minutes remaining. Deflected. Past Victor Valdes. Past an unfortunate Victor Valdes who had just come on to make his debut after David de Gea pulled a hamstring. Unfortunate, unlucky. Maybe next time. He could say those things. All of those things. But no. Not Louis van Gaal. He is Louis van Gaal. This is important, crucial to next year, next season. To hopes. Our hopes. The club's hopes. The *manager's* hopes. This is the aftermath of the last match of the season at Old Trafford – only next Sunday's trip to Hull City remains – and he wants them to take a message back home to think about. Digest. Do some serious ruminating. Because if Manchester United are to challenge on all fronts in the 2015–16 campaign, as Ed Woodward stated they must just three days ago, then they are going to have to shape up.

'Is the squad deep enough to challenge?' the executive vice-chairman asked rhetorically. 'The squad will be absolutely deep enough and ready to challenge on all fronts, all competitions next year,' came the clear answer. There it is. The club are depending on him. And them. The players. *He* is depending on them. Louis van Gaal. If they fail he fails and loses his job. Or is it the other way round? If he fails they fail. It does not matter. Either way he loses his job. So Van Gaal tells them. In the near-silence of the Manchester United dressing room, he says that Arsenal's late snatched draw may have been down to the third consecutive deflected goal to follow ones conceded against Crystal Palace and West Bromwich Albion but, simply, we 'have to force the luck'. Fortune – the good stuff, not the bad stuff – is always created and multiplied by hard work and a changing of mentality. Do the right things, go looking for luck and it will come. Start focusing more on how to win the narrow matches. Start thinking like killers. Kill opponents off. Think always this way. You are what you think. Killers.

But there is hope. The manager is heartened by how disappointed they are to have thrown away a victory that would have given United the league double over Arsenal. They have done the double over Liverpool for only the second time in seven seasons. But against Arsenal they have fallen short, today. Still Wayne Rooney has been missing, Michael Carrick has been missing, Van Gaal's best two outfield players absent through injury. And his other genuine star is also now a crock. De Gea's hamstring pull means he may miss that final match at Hull and so has played his last game for United if he goes to Real Madrid in the summer, as seems likely.

But that is a story for another day, it is not the story for now. What Louis van Gaal can see as he looks around the disappointed dressing room are a bunch of players who glow with the loyalty and belief they have in him. After the lost season of their careers under David Moyes they have jumped at the chance to be informed exactly what to do, when and where, in training and over the ninety minutes. To have their hands held. In the nicest possible way. Sir Alex Ferguson was cavalier and brave and luminescent; David Moyes tame and lacking any originality or brilliance; Louis van Gaal is knowing and in control and a manager who says, oh so simply to the players: 'Come with me and everything will be all right. I will lead you again to the promised land of trophies and glory and being the gorillas of this football jungle we are in.' And for that they thank him.

It has been a gruelling season but the performances against the other top teams have been encouraging. And this can be a key to next year. To unlocking where the manna of super-confidence is stored within them so it can surge into their boots and brains. They now know what he is about, and they have bought into his philosophy. They are devoted. He has been the antidote to David Moyes the players craved. *They believe.* And so must Ed Woodward, the Glazers, the fans, and the rest of the Premier League. Especially Manchester United's direct rivals because against Chelsea, Manchester City, Arsenal and Liverpool, Manchester United have been particularly impressive. They have let them know who they are again.

The slap of Ryan Giggs's head starts it. This let Louis van Gaal tell the packed Manchester Suite he is present and that the annual Player of the Year awards evening is going to be his shindig, his circus, his parade. As it should be, for he is the manager. No one here in this room at Old Trafford is going to forget this. Do not worry about that. The wine is fine and the chat and the laughs are flowing and the table where the manager sits with Giggs and the rest of his coaching team is close up to the stage, the front-row seat, the bird's-eye perch, from where he can see everyone and everything, just as he likes it. And after the playful slap of Giggs, which the club legend giggles about – what else can he do? – is the main event, the Big Kahuna, the top of the bill, the show-stopping grand finale starring the one and only Louis van Gaal. Following the final award, the gong for the fans' Player of the Year, which he presents to David de Gea, saying to the want-away goalkeeper in heartfelt tone, 'I'm very proud of you', the Dutchman goes to work. The performance is dazzling and masterly and like the movie star he could have been – could still be, there is so much life still fizzing through this sixty-three-year-old – he holds the room rapt as he sets off on a speech that is a rousing call to arms and a cleverly instinctive pushing of buttons, of the players, the staff, the fans seated before him. This is the essence of the man who followed the man who followed The Great Man. David Moyes could never do this and neither could Sir Alex Ferguson. Shadows falling? Pah! Ferguson could boss an audience like he could boss the training ground and dressing room and English football, but not like this. This is the night when Louis van Gaal shows exactly how it is going to be from here on in under him.

After making his bones on the fields of the Premier League by returning Manchester United to the Champions League, he can grab the microphone and roar, 'We were very close' about the gap to Chelsea, despite it being a fifteen-point chasm ahead of Sunday's final round of matches. The manager may have taken a few wines – who knows? – he may be lubricated and the margin to the champions of England may indeed be a light-year of a distance. Yet Louis van Gaal is somehow just making sense up there as he floats between the two dais, starting his routine with the words: 'I came in the stadium of Old Trafford, ten matches, thirteen points. And I came in and I saw by myself how I have to

for it!'" Van Gaal yells these last five words which are delivered in an animalistic cry that offers an oddly intimate moment, like the fetishistic moment in a film when the fourth wall of the movie star's on-screen persona is broken and for a moment a glimpse of the real human behind the act is offered. But Van Gaal does not care and after the claim about being close to Chelsea comes the denouement, the colour climax. 'Believe me, the players but also the staff but also the organisation like Manchester United shall do their utmost best and why? Because we have the best fans of the world. Thank you for that and I will see you next season again.'

Except he will see them again in a few seconds. Because as the camera pans to Jim Rosenthal and Hayley McQueen, the presenters who are innocently continuing the evening, back into shot bounds the Dutchman taking the microphone off McQueen. 'I want to say something,' he begins, but the raucous sound at his comeback is too loud. 'Pay attention to the manager!' Attention is paid. 'Ryan Giggs said to me, and he is always right, but in this case particularly right. I have said to you, you are the best fans in the world, but tonight I was a little bit disappointed and I shall say why.' Genuine fear courses through the room. Everyone is suddenly terrified. Everyone is looking at each other. Here it comes.

A pause.

Then: 'I have seen a lady who plays the saxophone fantastically. Give her big applause!'

What the?

After a split-second to contemplate what the manager has just done on this evening of 19 May 2015, big applause is indeed given, along with infinite belly laughs as off bounds the charming madness of King Louis. And after it becomes clear there will be no encore to the encore, the whirlwind that is the manager of Manchester United in situ continues to be reaped by the audience, by the television watchers and the media who go doolally for a vignette that will be consecrated in football folklore for a wee while. This has been beyond sterilisation and commodity, gleaming packaged product and veneer and puffed-up PR. This has been off-the-cuff disco with only one man on the dance floor. And he has funked it up big-style.

Chelsea are the champions, the best team by the span of a small nation. Yet Jose Mourinho is two years into his second stint at the club he managed successfully before and who came close to winning the title last year. He had the backstory, familiarity and foundation to succeed. Mourinho is the main rival, probably the only one to Louis van Gaal. And he knows that Louis van Gaal is a real and present threat to him and Chelsea. Last summer, as Van Gaal was starting to grapple with the gargantuan, continually transfiguring octopus that is Manchester United, Mourinho required only two players to make Chelsea the complete deal. And he acquired them: Cesc Fabregas and Diego Costa, both going on to be pivotal in the west London club's championship triumph. As Fabregas and Costa slipped seamlessly into a Chelsea squad who now had no weaknesses, Van Gaal was bringing in the new gang of six in Radamel Falcao, Ángel Di María, Ander Herrera, Luke Shaw, Daley Blind and Marcos Rojo. He had to shoe-horn all of them in while integrating himself, his methods and his philosophy at Manchester United.

As his former pupil, Mourinho knows what Van Gaal can be next season. In tactical acumen there is not much between them. What this year has shown is what the view was before it began: that the Dutchman and the Portuguese are the two best managers in the league. Comfortably. The games and results against United's rivals illustrate what Van Gaal has achieved this term. The scores against Chelsea were a 1–1 draw at home and the 1–0 loss at Stamford Bridge. And United did not look a class below in either game. Arsenal were beaten 2–1 at their place, drawn 1–1 at Old Trafford, but they turned the tables in the FA Cup, winning 2–1 in Manchester. Arsène Wenger is similar to the Manchester City manager, Manuel Pellegrini, in his almost stubborn refusal to tinker with tactics and approach, to try and ensure a result on any given match-day. Van Gaal does not suffer from this kind of blindness and the results against City suggest United were the superior of the two Mancunian clubs this term. The overall score of the matches between them shows this. November's derby at the Etihad was a close 1–0 defeat, a match in which Chris Smalling was sent off, forcing United to play with ten men for more than a half. The return fixture in April was the 4–2 hiding of Pellegrini's men, an afternoon during which United stunned City with how they rebounded from Sergio Agüero's early opener to blitz the visitors. So, 4–3 to United gives LvG's band bragging rights and confidence for next season. Liverpool, United's fiercest rivals, were beaten home and away – 3–0 at Old Trafford and 2–1 at Anfield, Van Gaal giving Brendan Rodgers some unwanted tuition in two ninety-minute lessons. This will always goes down well with the United enthusiast.

Considering David Moyes only managed to beat one of these direct rivals in the league – Arsenal, 1–0 at home in November 2013 – Van Gaal has illustrated how much more wised-up he is to follow Sir Alex Ferguson as the leader of the club. He may have been handed £150 million to spend on the six new players, but the lack of rebuilding done by Ferguson and Moyes, particularly in central defence and central midfield, meant he has had to be a juggler playing catch-up, while performing brain surgery to ensure his players could be retrained.

Now it is all about assessing the squad and deciding who is up to it next year. In this Van Gaal will be ruthless. If a player is over, he is out. The biggest let-down for the Dutchman may be Robin van Persie. Less than twelve months ago he was the captain of Van Gaal's Holland side at the World Cup. When David Moyes was the manager he was viewed at the club as only one of six genuine world superstars of the game, alongside Lionel Messi, Cristiano Ronaldo, Neymar, Gareth Bale and Wayne Rooney. Now, Van Persie finishes the season struggling to get into the Manchester United team. The fall has been so steep Van Gaal will listen to offers for his sale. Van Persie's chances of clinging on for another season may be dependent on whether United are able to bring in a replacement. There is no silver screen ending for the Galactico's Galactico, either. The Radamel Falcao Incident ends as a B-movie that will go straight to video as Van Gaal informs the striker he is not wanted next season. Jose Mourinho believes he knows better so how Falcao fares at Chelsea next year – should his expected move go through – will intrigue. This means that if Van Persie departs, too, the manager will need to buy two new strikers. And in the high-end of the football transfer market, this is not easy. Real Madrid's Karim Benzema and Tottenham Hotspur's Harry Kane would fit the bill.

David de Gea has still not signed on again and he appears certain to join Real Madrid. If he does this is searing headache time for the manager who will need to replace a goalkeeper who has won invaluable points over the last two seasons. It is a massive ask, especially as it is pretty darn hard to be the Manchester United number one because of the glare from the spotlight marked Every Mistake Will Be Magnified And Dissected And Not Forgotten.

Luke Shaw has had an injury-disrupted season, though he has convinced Van Gaal of his worth and he can look forward to next year if the left-back stays healthy. Despite the disappointing campaign Shaw has the manager onside, which is a comfort. Van Gaal indicates his value by stating he does not want the youngster to play for England Under-21s at the European Championship in June. And gets his way, the coach Gareth Southgate not selecting Shaw because of injury.

Wayne Rooney has been a success as captain, but his twelve Premier League goals are a paltry return for a player of his class. This shows how uninspiring the team have been – this low return still makes Rooney the top scorer. More chances must be created is the stark message. Also required is a gun central midfielder, a centre-back, and a right-back. Juventus's Paul Pogba and Arturo Vidal, Bayern Munich's Bastian Schweinsteiger, Southampton's Morgan Schneiderlin plus Borussia Dortmund's İlkay Gündoğan would be ideal for the first position. Dortmund's Mats Hummels is the preferred choice for the second; for the last one, Barcelona's Dani Alves was the number one choice, but after publicly criticising the club he performed a U-turn to re-sign for the European champions.

All of this is going to be another K2 to climb. Ed Woodward is about to earn his money, not least because this close season is of more import to the club, and thus Louis van Gaal, than last year. Once the campaign starts on 8 August, the manager will have the first ten matches to show who the genuine Manchester United are. He dare not mess them up. But he needs new players, he requires reinforcements. Without them United can kiss goodbye to success for another twelve months. And it could be a farewell to Louis van Gaal, though not with many embraces, if he is walked to the door due to failure. This is part of the fascination, of course. How it will end, whenever it does. Because while, at the moment, he is the big man of Sir Matt Busby Way, one day Louis van Gaal will be out. Only Sir Alex Ferguson gets to choose how he departs this club.

Epilogue

Louis van Gaal is alone. He started alone and he will finish alone. The first season at the first club, the last season with the last club, and this season with Manchester United. Solo. Solitary. A one-man act. Alone. A manager is always alone.

When the final reckoning comes, there is only one man whose thoughts and ideas and decisions are played out in public, on the field, and in the media. Who lives and dies by these. Whose family has to watch and cheer and comfort and support. Louis van Gaal has just done another year of this. Twelve months. From the fields of Brazil with Holland at the World Cup to the last field on the final day of the 2014–15 Premier League season at Hull's KC Stadium, and the goalless draw in match number thirty-eight. It is over and Louis van Gaal is weary.

Relief. This is what Louis van Gaal can feel. There is always relief. The cheeks puff out, the breath can be exhaled, the heartbeat slowed. Survival. This has been the priority of a first season in charge of Manchester United. He made it to 24 May, the final match and beyond, and he is still intact. The Iron Tulip is no David Moyes. He is Louis van Gaal. Mission accomplished. For now. He has Manchester United where he wants Manchester United. The club is hardwired into him. The players are his willing robots now. Their brains are reconfigured. The grey matter aligned. Remade. Retrained. They are ghosts in the Louis van Gaal machine. They play subconsciously as eleven Louis van Gaals. They have to because it is them or him. The truth that has been faced each and every year of his twenty-four as a manager: *them or him.*

He is in Portugal. In the Algarve. In the villa he calls his 'paradise'. Rest and Relaxation. The sun is blazing, the beaches are amber, the sea is azure and Louis van Gaal is at ease. But he is also plotting. In this game there is always plotting to be done. He is in southern Portugal and he can take his mind off the job, but the job always returns. Managing Manchester United. The manager of Manchester United. There is no real holiday here when there are deals to be done – always deals to be done or tried to be done. And the mind wanders. Back to the training pitches of Carrington which have fallen silent and the players who are on holiday, scattered across the world on beaches and in resorts. The mind wanders through thoughts of the return to pre-season and the tour of America and the psychogeography of the summer laid out before Louis van Gaal. Waiting. Waiting to happen.

It has been a struggle. But wait until next season. Wait until this close season is over. If Ed Woodward can corral the players Louis van Gaal wants, see how Manchester United will burn at the sun next year. This is what he wants. This is what is expected. This is what he has to do. This transfer window is crucial. Come the new campaign and the judgments will begin instantly about his 2015–16 Manchester United team. From the opening kick on the opening day against Tottenham Hotspur. The fixture is at Old Trafford. The same fixture as that Sunday afternoon in March when Wayne Rooney and his red men tyrannised Spurs and announced Sir Alex Ferguson was behind them and Louis van Gaal was before them. What is required is a repeat. In thirty-eight Premier League matches. In the Champions League. In the FA Cup. In the League Cup.

There is £150 million to spend again before 1 September, if Louis van Gaal should want. That would make a cool £300 million in twelve months given by the Glazers, signed off by Ed Woodward, and splashed out by the manager. He dare not mess this up. Any new buys must be the right ones because no one around here is going to accept the club finishing fourth again. Starting with Louis van Gaal.

Frustration. There is frustration at failing to win anything in his inaugural term. He is a winner. The FA Cup was the one. The best hope. A quarter-final at home to Arsenal and failure. A 2–1 loss and end of story, knocked out. A trophy in the first year would have bought more time and helped the players more. Currently, there is a weakness. The thought process is not yet wholly calibrated to how Louis van Gaal wants it. There has not been enough ruthlessness. Enough kills of foes on the football field. He continues to tell them to be savvy and cute and ruthless. He pointed to Chelsea and how they did it this season to become champions. Because Jose Mourinho has it right. Guard the ball so the opponent cannot score. Then score yourself and tighten up and continue to guard the ball. But this has not happened at United. Not enough. Despite his continual exhortations.

There will be more exhortations. There has to be. The players think he is tough. They talk among themselves about his scientific approach, how Louis van Gaal desires everything to be accurate and pin-point and meticulous. Sir Alex Ferguson was never like that. His were artistic and imaginative and evocative teams and he was the poet-in-chief. This United are precise, methodical and militaristic. They are soon to be heading through the months of summer, taking in the truncated two-week tour of the United States of America, towards the 2015–16 campaign.

They are Louis van Gaal's New Model Army. They are ready. They can never be totally ready. They will be kicking a ball soon, somewhere, and their commander-in-chief will be kicking every ball with them.

Sources

This book is based on my personal experiences while working on the Manchester football beat for the *Guardian* and *Observer*. The majority of the stories, quotes and anecdotes were gathered during the course of that work; some even made it into the newspapers and online (theguardian.com). Additional research material came from:

Daily Mail
Telegraph
Sunday Times
The People
Mirror
Independent
Daily Star
Manchester Evening News
Sydney Telegraph

MUTV
Sky Sports
Chelsea FC
BT Sports
ESPN
talkSPORT

Manutd.com
BBC.co.uk
ITV.com

OfficialWayneRooney.com
juanmata8.com

United We Stand fanzine

Borst, Hugo – O *Louis, In Search of Louis van Gaal,* Yellow
    Jersey, 2014.
Ferguson, Sir Alex – *My Autobiography,* Hodder & Stoughton,
    2013.

Acknowledgements

My thanks to Lucy Warburton and all at Aurum Press. To David Riding at MBA Literary Agents. The same to Marcus Christenson and Ian Prior of *Guardian Sport*, for their support. To Brian Oliver and Matthew Brook: two dear friends.

And to Diane and Derek Brereton, for all your support.

Finally, to my mother, who taught me to read before I started school – thank you, Mum x

Index